MW00999948

"This account of a famil, , , among the Kham community of northwestern Nepal is riveting and honest. Imagine living in a remote Himalayan village accessible only by a long mountain trek, where there is beauty barely touched by man. There you find a pre-literate people, shepherds who love to laugh but are well-acquainted with the cold terror of the shamanic world. Your house is regularly overrun by rats, and you endure the 'town crier' who announces when you sit down to eat. Your task is to make the gospel known among a people who believe you are sub-human visitors from the netherworld. You will appreciate the depth of insight, linguistic skill, and fearless commitment of David Watters and his family. This story not only inspires, it illustrates the use of missiological wisdom for international development."

—Bruce Graham

Associate Editor, *Perspectives Reader*; Director of Training, US Center for World Mission

"You have never read a book like this one. David Watters was the best storyteller I ever knew, partly because he had the best stories. He wrote his stories eloquently here with brutal—sometimes shocking—honesty, earthy humor, and self-deprecating humility. He faced challenges as tall as the Himalayas, and persevered. He faced grave personal danger on mountain treks, as well as from people who opposed his life mission for political or religious reasons. That mission was to translate God's Word and introduce it for the very first time to the Kham people: a lofty goal, accomplished only through God's providence and intervention. The book will inspire you. It will likely change you."

—Michael R. Walrod, PhD, DrCM

Former Ga'dang language Bible translator; Philippines President, Canada Institute of Linguistics, Trinity Western University

"Grab this opportunity to get a glimpse into the heroism of the cross."

—Vishal Mangalwadi

Author, The Book That Made Your World: How the Bible Created the Soul of Western Civilization

"David Watters pursued the call of his faith to cross over into a radically different culture. Hasta Ram followed his religious curiosity to cross over into a radically different faith. Their individual journeys brought them together into a relationship of deep respect and trust. This is the compelling story of this extraordinary shared journey and its impact on their lives and the lives around them, played out in the context of Kham culture and the national culture of Nepal in the 1970s and 1980s. In a brilliant way, the story ranges over a variety of issues related to a lesser known culture like that of the Kham."

—John Watters, PhD

David's first cousin, who, inspired by him, shared his love for languages, cultures, and Bible translation; International Executive Director (2000-2007), Wycliffe Bible Translators International

"David Watters tells the story of a double agent: an adventurer/ anthropologist/linguist more real than Indiana Jones and a Christian missionary... The book deserves a wider audience than the missionary narrative genre. This book reveals an exotic culture to be appraised by specialists and humanists and lets you sense the Christian depth of this remarkable man."

—Dr. Stephen Bezruchka

Department of Global Health, UW School of Public Health; Author of multiple books, including Trekking Nepal, now in its 8th edition

"Rarely have I read a missionary narrative so riveting—an account of two great men from radically different cultures, drawn together in deep friendship by a love of truth and the power of the gospel. The fine intellect of David Watters; his erudition, cultural breadth, and formal linguistic excellence; his disciplined literacy in many languages; and above all, his self-effacing intellectual honesty are here beautifully deployed in an unsanitized account of front-line apostolic faithfulness. Courageous obedience to the Great Commandment shines through these pages. This is a book that will inspire anyone who loves exemplary witness to Christ, especially in a time and place of adversity."

—Dr. David L. Jeffrey

Distinguished Senior Fellow and Director of Manuscript Research in Scripture and Tradition, Institute for Studies in Religion, Baylor University; Guest Professor, Faculty of Foreign Language and Literature, Peking University

At the Foot of the Snows

At the Foot of the Snows

BY DAVID WATTERS

WITH STEVE & DANIEL WATTERS

ENGAGE
FAITH

ENGAGE FAITH PRESS • SEATTLE, WA

Published 2011

Printed in the United States of America

15 14 13 12 11   1 2 3 4

ISBN 978-1-936672-12-7

Library of Congress Control Number: 2011940991

For information, address Engage Faith Press, PO Box 2222, Poulsbo WA 98370.

Scripture quotations marked (NASB) are taken from the NEW AMERICAN STANDARD BIBLE, Copyright © 1960, 1962, 1963, 1968, 1971, 1972, 1973, 1975, 1977, 1995 by The Lockman Foundation. Used by permission.

Scripture quotations marked (NIV) are taken from THE HOLY BIBLE, NEW INTERNATIONAL VERSION, NIV Copyright © 1973, 1978, 1984, 2011 by Biblica, Inc. Used by permission. All rights reserved worldwide.

Scripture quotations marked (NEB) are from The New English Bible, copyright © 1970 by Oxford University Press and Cambridge University Press.

List of David Watters' works courtesy of Himalayan Linguistics, Vol 10(1)

With deep gratitude
to the men, women, and children
who took part in this journey with us,
Kham and otherwise.

Dad passed away before being able to give any thought to the dedication of this book. There is no doubt in our minds, though, that he would have dedicated it to his wife and lifelong companion, Nancy Watters. On his behalf, we, his sons, Daniel and Steve, dedicate this book to our mom. Her support of Dad and commitment to the task was steadfast and strong. Her love for Dad and commitment to God made him a better man, and it was her devotion that many times kept him pressing on to stay the course. This is to a remarkable wife and mother.

Contents

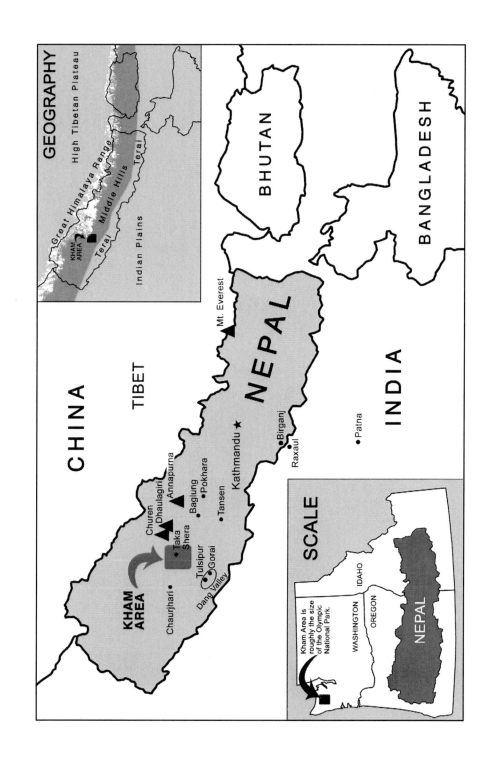

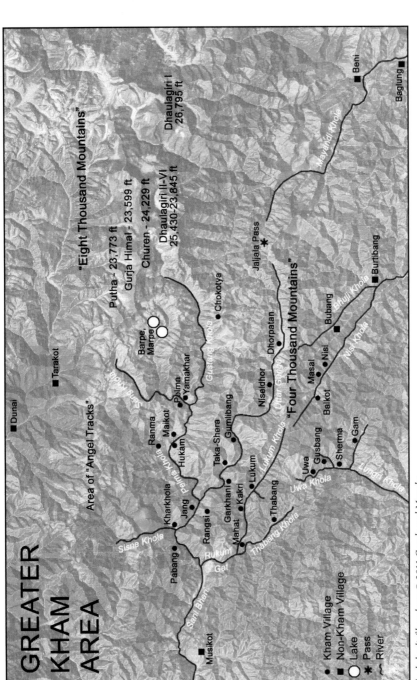

GREATER KHAM AREA

Area of "Angel Tracks"

"Eight Thousand Mountains"

Putha - 23,773 ft
Gurja Himal - 23,599 ft
Churen - 24,229 ft
Dhaulagiri II-VI
25,430-23,845 ft

Dhaulagiri I
26,795 ft

Jaljala Pass ✱

"Four Thousand Mountains"

Dunai ■

Tarakot ■

Musikot ■

Beni ■

Baglung ■

Burtibang ■

Bubang ■

Dhorpatan

Chokotya

Niseldhor

Masal ● Nisi ●
Balkot ●

Gam ●
Sherma ●
Gysbang ●
Uwa ●

Barpe,
Marpe ○○

Pelma ●
Yamakhar ●

Gumibang ●

Ranma ●
Maikot ●
Hukam ●

Taka-Shera ●

Lukum ●

Thabang ●

Kharkhola ●
Jang-Pelma ●
Rangsi ●
Garkhani ●
Kakri ●
Mahat ●

Pabang ●

Rukum
Gat

Sani Bheri
Sisne Khola
Sani Khola
Kyalkhola
Thabang Khola
Uwa Khola
Lukum Khola
Uttar Ganga
Gustang Khola
Bhuji Khola
Nisi Khola
Tungri Khola
Myagdi Khola

Kham Village ●
Non-Kham Village ■
Lake ○
Pass ✱
River ～

Shaded-relief base layer © 2011 Google and Mapabc

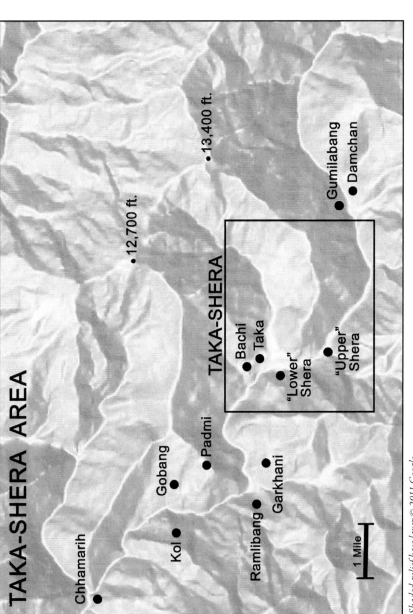

TAKA-SHERA AREA

- Chhamarih
- Kol
- Gobang
- Padmi
- Ramlibang
- Garkhani
- •12,700 ft.
- •13,400 ft.

TAKA-SHERA
- Bachi
- Taka
- "Lower" Shera
- "Upper" Shera
- Gumilabang
- Damchan

1 Mile

Shaded-relief base layer © 2011 Google

Foreword

Rarely does it happen, but when it does, you know that God has smiled on you: you are allowed by God to become part of another man's narrative. The walk is vicarious at first, but as you watch and listen, the journey quickly becomes your own. My introduction to this narrative occurred nearly a quarter-century ago in Port Angeles, Washington, when I invited a missionary couple to our home after church. We shared a delightful meal together, engaging in rich conversation. This was the first of many conversations around our dining room table with David and Nancy Watters regarding their adventure with God and the Kham people of Nepal.

The stories David shared were always rich with exciting adventures and filled with spiritual perception. My fear in reading his book, *At the Foot of the Snows*, was that David might not be able to capture in writing the same enthusiastic spirit and the same deep insights that came so easily around the dinner table. I quickly lost that fear as I read the first chapter. It was as if I were hearing the adventure of his faith journey for the first time. Every chapter's ending drove me on with anticipation to the next!

As you read this amazing account, you will find four recurring themes. David weaves these four themes into the fabric of his story much like the master composer of a fine classical piece of music (which David loved). The first is the growth of faith. As you read, you will find David's faith challenged. But through that crucible of life's testing, you will see spiritual maturity developing in his life. At the same time, you witness Hasta Ram's faith being born, which brings us to the second theme: friendship. Hasta Ram became David's trusted friend, traveling companion, and gifted language assistant, and he grew to be the spiritual leader of the powerful Kham church. As you read of David and Hasta Ram's friendship, your heart will long for such a gift from God. Thirdly, you will discover the fulfillment of God's promises, especially the promise to build His church. If God can bring forth a church in the heart of Kham country (and you will be amazed at how unlikely that seemed at first), it can happen anywhere. Finally, the theme of God's sovereignty is expressed repeatedly. It was God showing up in the timeliest ways that gave undeniable proof that it was God's will governing every step of this amazing journey. The four themes coalesce and reach their climax as David presents the Kham people with the Bible in their own language.

* * *

David was always ready for an adventure, especially if it held the possibility of danger and the unknown. He developed this love of adventure as a small boy. He was allowed by his parents to roam the desert in a small town in southern California. In the rich imagination of a child, he became a conquering crusader and an invincible destroyer of wicked villains. Living a carefree life as a child, he had no idea how much his imagination would be used by God in preparing him for a real battle against man's greatest enemy. His childlike dreams would become reality on a stage in the remotest parts of the world, the rugged mountains of Nepal. This book gives you a front row seat for that amazing adventure.

David's faith was always developing as he encountered the circumstances of life and reflected upon deep theological issues. As you read you will discover a man who was unafraid to ask God hard questions, a man unafraid to express his frustration. Life became so discouraging at times that he questioned the character of God and even his own faith. One can only imagine the pain and desperation of a father and mother in a remote village trying to hold off the spiritual forces of evil seeking to take control of their youngest son. Of course one asks, "Why, God?"

Many people, in writing a book, could easily hide the real struggles of walking with God in difficult places, but David invites us in to learn with him. If you are willing to walk with this family on their journey, you will walk paths through deep and treacherous waters, but you must also be prepared to stand on the mountaintops of joy and praise as God makes a way and gives the victory.

In *At the Foot of the Snows*, David also draws back the curtain on the difficult work of a linguist. You will be captured in his battle, as he seeks to hear the nuances of a language and then record it. To understand an unwritten language is one thing, but to capture the perfect expression of that language to fit into the spiritual book that would become the foundation of life transformation, is another thing entirely. Weeks of a painstaking search for the right words would pass before suddenly ending as he heard around a campfire an unexpected expression, finding it to be a perfect match! Patience, diligent labor, frustration, discouragement, and hard living conditions in an isolated village were all companions of a dedicated linguist.

David Watters was the man for the job, although he often questioned that very truth. He was one of the most gifted men I have ever known, yet he often pondered how all that fit into real life. He was brilliant, yet he was reluctant to accept the invitation from Oregon University to participate in their Ph.D. program in linguistics. He did not know how incredibly talented he was in the field of language. He never assumed he belonged, but that doubt manifested itself in gracious humility. This attitude gave confidence to humble porters, simple herdsmen, brilliant scholars, and even nobility, granting them permission to engage in a dialogue that was shaping his life and assisting him in his calling. His life is a composite of many who were free to write upon his heart. And he grew in faith!

* * *

You will likewise be blessed as you get to know another choice servant of God, Hasta Ram. This unique man was a mighty warrior of faith. I met him on his first trip to the United States. He struck me as a man of steel character, bold courage, and uncompromising conviction. Something inside me told me that no one would want to cross this man, yet his gentle spirit made him readily approachable. *At the Foot of the Snows* invites you into the center of this man's life and soul. You will discover as you read that every chapter of his life was written in preparation for a holy mission. His years as a simple herdsman, the world experience of serving in the elite British forces as a Nepali Gurkha soldier, and the curious mind that made him search for the meaning of a Christian booklet pushed into his hand by a total stranger while on a trip to India were all parts of an unsolved puzzle in his journey. The mystery and purpose for each chapter of his life would be revealed in his encounter with David Watters in Kham country. Their lives became welded together in a mission for God.

No difficult journey should be taken without the confidence that God is with you. God's presence in the most unlikely places became the catalyst for David and Nancy to press on to finish the job given to them. Throughout their story, God intervened at the right time to affirm this couple who had sacrificed everything, assuring them that they were in the right place, serving the right cause, at the right time. A miraculous path through a trial of certain death, the provision of a much needed language helper, a plane provided during a critical medical need, protection in the hut of a demon-possessed shaman, discernment in a life-and-death situation, and many other "God moments" encouraged this young couple that God was with them. Many years prior to this adventure, God had exhorted His servants to go out into the world with His message, and He promised to be with them. They found that God *was* with them! His promise was true!

* * *

One of my last conversations with David was again around our dining room table in Port Angeles. I asked him what chapter of life he was currently walking through. He said, "You know, Mike, I have walked with God in many places and in many amazing circumstances. I knew God could and often did intervene in desperate moments in my life. I knew Him as a great power and provider, but now I'm learning that He is also a great lover. I'm learning to love Him for who He is, not for what He does. It is a sweet time of life, just to be still and know He is God and that He loves me and I can love Him." Soon after that, David Watters died, and a new adventure began for him. I suppose he knows more about God's love now than he ever imagined.

His life reminds me that the faith expressed in Hebrews 11 still exists in this world. The stories of real faith adventures for the glory of God still happen. Hebrews 11 records just a few testimonies of many. The faith testimonies of Abraham, Moses, Noah, Sarah, and many others resulted in encouraging others to join the walk of faith. You are about to read one of those amazing faith testimonies. The account of David and Nancy's walk of faith encouraged me to embrace the story God is seeking to write in and through my life. I hope that as you read, it does the same for you. Learning to embrace the story God is writing in you may prove to be your greatest adventure. David and Nancy will be for you, as for me, an example of what it means to seek to live in desperate dependence upon the God who cares, the author and perfecter of our faith, the One writing each person's story.

Maybe one day David and I will sit around another dining room table in another place to exchange stories, but for now I will read and remember my dear friend in *At the Foot of the Snows*. As you read, I hope you realize God is smiling on you!

—Mike Jones, Sr. Pastor,
Independent Bible Church,
Port Angeles, Washington

Acknowledgments

The story told in this book would not have been possible without our many friends who have supported and prayed for us over the years. In a very real sense, this is your story, for without you, these pages would be empty. We, the Watters family, express our deepest gratitude to you for carrying us each step of the way.

Many of you have read through various draft forms of this book and given valuable input that has contributed to its final form. You are too many to thank individually, but your contribution is greatly appreciated and it has truly improved the book.

In particular, however, we would like to thank:

• Pastor Mike and Jan Jones. More than anyone, you have joined in our lives as close friends to laugh when we laughed and cry when we cried. We love you.

• Winnie Greenaway Palm, for your gift of encouragement and enthusiastic support as we committed this story to paper. Your help was more than you know.

• Anne Swenson. Your keen eye and insight made many improvements. But more than that, you were a listening friend who had endless patience for all the tears.

• Katherine Jeffry, for your generous gift of encouragement, time, and professional advice in the editing of this book.

Finally, all thanks goes to God, who led us down the valley to

Taka-Shera. It has been our greatest honor and privilege in life to serve Him in the journey He set out for us.

    Nancy Watters
    Steve Watters
    Daniel Watters

    Port Angeles, June 2011

At the Foot of the Snows

Prologue

For a brief time—from 1966 to 1976—the Summer Institute of Linguistics (SIL) had the unique privilege of pursuing linguistic field-work in the Himalayan kingdom of Nepal. Never before had that country been open to such a venture, and we all knew that the door could close as quickly and as unexpectedly as it had opened. But we had been caught up in a vision, the vision of introducing the Word of God to a people for the first time in their history.

We were convinced that this was God's timing. However short the time might be, we knew that our most enduring and valuable contribution to them would not be anything *we* could do or say but a written record of what God had done and said.

G. Campbell Morgan, one of the great preachers and expositors of the twentieth century, once wrote, "The story of missions the whole world over shows that the success or failure of missions has always been dependent on whether those brought to Christ had the Scriptures in their own language or not."

We had no guarantee that anything would come of our efforts. In fact, it was predicted that they would end in failure. The tolerant, all-embracing disposition of the Hindus might incline them to accept another deity into their pantheon of countless gods, but how would they welcome one who claimed to be the only God? Toni Hagen, the first explorer from the West to travel extensively in Nepal, wrote at the end of the 1950s that "such a tolerant nation is, of course, a bad field for missionary work; for they just cannot see why they should leave off venerating the old gods and start worshipping a new one."

Estimates were that there were less than a hundred Christians in the entire nation of some thirteen million people—adequate proof that our primary motivation for doing linguistic work in this nation did not represent much of a threat to the prevailing culture. But we were linguists too, committed to the pursuit of language for its own sake. As in any scientific pursuit, there is a beauty in language unique to itself, and the discovery of that beauty is motivation enough to make the pursuit worthwhile.

For Nancy and me, the risk was hardly worth considering. We preferred to work on these terms. If the message didn't speak for itself, and the people for whom it was intended would not accept it for what it was, the choice would at least be genuine, because it would be their own. But if they did accept it, we wanted it to happen not because it depended upon our presence and witness but upon the written Word and the witness of the Spirit of God.

As it turned out, Nancy and I had just seven years in this full-time, pioneering stage of our connection with Nepal; we didn't arrive on the scene until February 1969, the third year of the SIL contract. With us was our two-and-a-half-year-old son, Steve; two months after our arrival in the capital city of Kathmandu, our second son, Daniel, was born. We knew then that our time would likely be short, but we also expected these to be the best years of our lives.

SIL was there under the auspices of Nepal's Tribhuvan University, and our contract was to seek out and live with remote, tribal groups of the mountainous hinterlands—some as yet undiscovered. We were to document their exotic languages: devising alphabets, writing diction- aries, and making grammatical descriptions available for the use of future historians of language. The widespread belief of the intelligen- tsia of those days was remarkably prescient; they were concerned that the indigenous languages were rapidly being replaced by Nepali, the national language, and that unless they were recorded and sealed away in the university archives, they would be lost forever.

The "primitive" languages of the country had no writing systems and were spoken only in isolated pockets of the Himalayas. Knowledge about folk religions and cultural traditions in these areas was scarce as well; indeed, apart from what was contained in a few short reference works, it was almost nonexistent. The few accounts that did exist were sketchy, for the most part containing no more than a paraphrase of facts discovered by the British during their years of colonial rule in the Indian subcontinent.

The British had never actually colonized Nepal. In a few border skirmishes with the Nepalese from 1768 to 1816, they conquered some of the north Indian plains belonging to Nepal but were no match for the inhabitants of the mountains. They gained such an admiration for the intrepid Mongolian tribesmen they made a deal with the Nepalese government. In exchange for the privilege of hiring their soldiers, known as Gurkhas, as mercenaries for their worldwide campaigns they promised to recognize and honor Nepal's status as a free and independent kingdom.

Tiny Nepal, perched in the foothills of the Himalayas just off the plains of northern India, literally had its back against the wall. With little choice but to comply, it agreed to the deal, and the land itself was insulated from the ravages of the outside world. In the ensuing years, thousands of Nepalese Gurkhas enlisted as special commandos in the British army. They fought with the British on every front in every military theater around the globe and gained for themselves the reputation of being some the toughest, most loyal fighting men in the world.

Landlocked in the security of its mountain fastness and protected along its southern border by a superpower, Nepal was in a unique position to maintain its security, and for a century and a half pursued a foreign policy based on isolationism. The real beneficiaries, however, were the Ranas, an excessive and hedonistic regime jealously guarding their realm for their own advantage.

Watching the colonialists at close range, they gained a mistrust of foreigners, and loathing the possibility of a restraint on their abuses of power, they coined the phrase: "With the missionary comes the musket, and with the Bible comes the bayonet."

Education was forbidden, and conversion to any religion outside of Hinduism was made a serious crime. Apart from the presence of a "British Resident" whose job was similar to that of an ambassador, no foreigners were granted entry into the country, and even the capital city could not be reached by road until the late 1950s. There was no firsthand knowledge of the interior of the country; everything that was known was gleaned from the tales and descriptions of the Gurkhas themselves.

Through Britain's military alliance with Nepal, the British had collected information on the so-called "military tribes" living in the mountains—some general cultural notes, a few word lists, and even some rudimentary grammatical descriptions. For the benefit and orientation of British officers in charge of Gurkha regiments, what was deemed the most useful information was published in the form of military handbooks.

Apart from one or two exceptions, very little new research had been conducted on the people of Nepal. The British military handbooks, along with George Grierson's monumental, early twentieth-century *Linguistic Survey of India*, which included a volume on the known languages of Nepal, were still the most reliable sources of information.

When India gained its independence from the British Empire shortly after World War II, Nepal began emerging from its isolationism. Casting off the yoke of the Ranas with the help of the Indian government, the Shah kings were restored to power, and in 1951 King Tribhuvan, in an attempt to modernize and to reverse the ravages of the former government, threw open the doors of his country to the outside world.

Within a few years, the little-known kingdom was gaining a certain notoriety in the West, mostly through the exploits of mountaineers who came to conquer the world's highest peaks. Sir Edmund Hillary, along with Tenzing Sherpa, was the first to reach the summit of Mt. Everest in 1953. The feat was repeated in 1956 by a team of Swiss mountaineers. Americans made it to the top for the first time in 1963, along with a support team of over nine hundred Sherpas and other porters carrying twenty-nine tons of goods.

Before long, all the major peaks had been conquered, and the name of the Sherpas had become indelibly etched on the consciousness of the world as a word synonymous with "mountain guide" or "porter." But to most people, Nepal in the mid-sixties was still a country shrouded in mystery, and the name "Kathmandu," immortalized in Kipling's poetry, still evoked images of barbaric splendor.

Nancy and I arrived in Nepal on February 6, 1969. Our first assignment, for the next seven months, was to gain a working knowledge of Nepali, the language of commerce, government, and basic communication throughout the kingdom. When we were not immersed in our studies, we scoured the libraries of Kathmandu and every conceivable book shop for information on indigenous peoples and languages. Not a lot was available.

One notable exception of general usefulness was a new book by Nepalese anthropologist Dor Bahadur Bista, *People of Nepal* (1967). It was the most complete work yet available. In addition to the usual military tribes, Bista, who taught at Tribhuvan University, discussed a number of heretofore unmentioned groups. By his own admission, the book was not intended to be exhaustive, nor did he attempt to give much indication as to the linguistic affiliation of the peoples discussed. Nonetheless, it was a step in the right direction, and we gained from it some new leads on possible sites for linguistic research.

In a British government publication, *Nepal and the Gurkhas*, I came across a tantalizing statement that was to change our lives forever. A chapter on one of the primary military tribes of the Gurkha regiments, the Magars, stated that the Magar language "is never spoken by the real Puns," one of the seven traditional Magar clans. The Puns, it went on to say, "speak a language of their own known as Kamkura" ("kura" means "talk").

I made an appointment with Mr. Bista, who in his book had made no allusions to such a distinction, and asked for his opinion on the accuracy of the statement. A very humble and gracious man, Mr. Bista told me that he had never been to the northern part of the Magar homeland, the residence of the Puns and three other Magar clans—the Budhas, the Ghartis, and the Rokhas. "Much speculation," he added, "has gone into many statements about the tribal groups of Nepal, but not much of it can be corroborated. That's why the SIL proposal was approved at the university: to settle some of the ambiguities and give a clearer picture of what the situation really is."

When I indicated my eagerness to explore the homeland of the four northern Magar clans and find out for myself the true linguistic situation, he was delighted to support me. He arranged an appointment for me the following week with Balaram Gharti, a northern Magar who was a member of the National Parliament in Kathmandu. The meeting was cordial and pleasant, but, to my disappointment, Gharti had grown up outside his ancestral homeland.

He spoke Nepali as his mother tongue and had no first-hand knowledge of Magar dialects. Furthermore, he shared the conventional, bourgeois view on tribal languages, reckoning that from one extreme of the Magar homeland to the other, only one language existed. "Even though slight regional variations might be discovered," he stated, "intelligibility would certainly be universal."

Mr. Bista, like me, was not convinced and arranged a meeting for me with a young Magar of one of the southern clans who spoke the language as his mother tongue. He was currently enrolled as a student at Tribhuvan University. To my surprise, he supported the claim that there was only one Magar language, a language intelligible to any of the clans, north or south.

I might have been dissuaded from pursuing the question any further at that point had it not been for another brief reference I had recently come across. Professor John Hitchcock, an American anthropologist at the University of Wisconsin, had approached the edges of the territory in question on a month's trek sometime in the early 1960s. Writing in 1966 in the introduction to his book entitled *The Magars of Banyan Hill*, he stated that the "Northern Magars... speak a Tibeto-Burman dialect called Kamkura. It resembles Magarkura but the two languages are not mutually intelligible."

Based on that lead, I elicited a vocabulary list of one hundred words in Magar from the university student I had met—a list commonly used by linguists the world over as a first, rough gauge of possible dialect differences. It was my intention to make a comparative list of the same vocabulary items in the northern Magar homeland. I quickly sent off a letter to Professor Hitchcock informing him of my interest and asking for advice on where I would be most likely to find speakers of the language.

Professor Hitchcock sent a prompt and cordial reply. Although he had never been beyond the fringes of Magar territory, he could apprise me of the names of some of their major villages. He was, furthermore, convinced by what he had seen and heard on his field trips that Kham (referred to by him by its local Nepali name, Kamkura) was indeed a language distinct from Magar. That was all the encouragement I needed, and with Mr. Bista's recommendation to the university that the Watters take up studies in Kham, we were ready to begin.

Armed with linguistic tools no more sophisticated than a scant hundred-word list in Magar and Nepali, I set off with a companion and fellow linguist, Gary Shepherd, on our first "linguistic survey." The two of us, along with our wives, had just completed our initial study of Nepali, and now it was our task, on this first foray into the mountains, to make contact with the people whose languages we hoped to study. It had been Gary's intention all along, with Barbara, his wife, to do linguistic studies in southern Magar. Nancy and I intended to settle down among the northern Magars and study Kham, the language of the Puns, if indeed such a thing even existed.

Chapter 1: First Encounters

Every place that the sole of your foot shall tread upon, that have I given unto you... Only be thou strong and very courageous.
—Joshua 1:3,7, KJV

It was the end of September 1969, and the monsoon rains had come to an end. The earth was awash with green, the skies were bright and clear, and the feeling of autumn was in the air. Wayne Aeschliman, our veteran SIL pilot from the Philippines, had flown us to the remote STOL (Short Take-Off and Landing) airstrip built by the Swiss at Dhorpatan on the south side of the Himalayas. Its original purpose was for carrying out humanitarian efforts—providing food, medicine, and some shelter—amongst Tibetan refugees who had fled over the mountains from the Chinese onslaught. It was from here that we began our journey, hoping to find southern Magars within a few days to the south and northern Magars within a few days to the north. Our plan was to be back at the airstrip in a month for pickup.

We hired two Tibetan porters, eager for employment, to carry our bulging backpacks containing food, clothing, and basic trail necessities. The lighter loads, we carried ourselves. The younger man, Angdrak, was

Securing porters in Dhorpatan

a Khampa from faraway eastern Tibet and had already been living in Nepal for several years. He was fairly conversant in the Nepali language—better than we were—and turned out to be an invaluable help to us. Though he didn't understand any English, he was smart enough to figure out what we were trying to communicate, and he became a good interpreter. Tsetu, the older man, was a refugee from Amdo Province in Tibet.

Traveling south for only two days along the Bhuji Khola river, it became quickly apparent that the two branches of the Magar nation were cut off from each other by at least two week's walk over rugged, mountainous terrain. Gary's southern Magar survey would have to wait for a later date. We encountered our first Kham speakers—people of the Pun, Gharti, and Budha clans—along the Bhuji Khola, one of the southern-most extremes of their traditional homeland. Their numbers here were sparse, with a large admixture of Nepali population; it was clearly a less than ideal place for carrying out long-term studies. The people here seemed unanimous in declaring a place called Taka-Shera as the unofficial capital of Kham country, a place just two days' hike west of Dhorpatan.

Our very first word list, elicited from a man of the Pun clan, confirmed even more forcibly what we had already suspected: apart from the most basic vocabulary, vocabulary which Kham also shares with other Central Himalayish languages, Magar and Kham show little affinity to one another and are hardly even related. Compared with the word list I had elicited from the Magar student in Kathmandu, no more than 13 percent of the words were even cognate, and only three out of the hundred happened to be the same.

It wasn't until many years later, in the archives of London's School of

Oriental and African Studies, that I came across a statement in a 1927 government publication, *Hand Books for the Indian Army: Gorkhas*: "It is probably no exaggeration to state that only the first three named castes [Rana, Thapa, and Ale] are pure Magars, for the latter three do not speak the Magar language and are somewhat different in appearance. The Puns and Burathokis [i.e., Budhas], who live in the high isolated parts of the Magar country, have languages of their own, which differ slightly from valley to valley. These languages have no affinity with Magarkura, and this fact alone is sufficient evidence to prove that they originally came of different stock."

I discovered, to my surprise, that the British, though making no mention of the Kham language in their early association with the Gurkhas, had, in fact, recorded observations related to the recruitment of various Kham-speaking clans. Arising from elitist colonial attitudes, many of the comments concern impressions of the relative quality and intelligence of various castes and potential recruits––statements that would now be considered racist and derisive. The Puns, for example, are described as "wild, quarrelsome, and of inferior intelligence." In reference to the Ghartis of the Bhuji Khola valley we had just descended, one recruiting officer writing in 1819 made the observation that "the Ghartis are of two kinds, Khas and Bhujial. The former are admitted to the military dignity; but the latter wallow in all the abominations of the impure Gurungs and do not speak the Khas [Nepali] language."

Three quarters of a century later, apparently the "abominable" class of Gharti was also accepted into the Gurkha regiments after careful screening. Writing in 1890, another officer observed that "by careful selection, however, excellent Ghartis can be obtained. The Bhujial Gharti lives in the valleys and high mountains to the north of Gulmi, above the Puns... Their tract of country runs along both sides of the Bhuji Khola (river), from which they probably derive their name. The Bhujial Gharti is generally a shepherd. He lives principally on the milk of sheep, and is almost invariably a man of very good physique and heavy limbs. He is remarkably dirty when first enlisted."

We were soon to discover that little had changed in the subsequent eighty years; most Kham speakers were still shepherds, not just the Ghartis of Bhuji Khola. Furthermore, they were of good physique and still remarkably dirty! As to their character, we found them to be hospitable and friendly in their villages. On the trail they made wonderful companions, trustworthy and hardworking, who endured hardship with little or no complaint. They were a cheerful and fun-loving people with a natural penchant for boisterous slapstick humor.

After our short excursion down the Bhuji Khola valley, we returned to Dhorpatan. From there we intended to head north into the high, rugged terrain of "Aath Hajaar Parbat," or "Eight Thousand Mountains," the northern end of Kham country. Though we had already heard in Bhuji Khola that Taka-Shera was the heartland of Kham, we wanted to delineate in some way the geographical boundaries of the language.

In Dhorpatan we met a young Thakuri official from Nepal's Dolpa District named Ashok, who was planning to travel by horseback the next day with his personal servant and porter to the north side of the Himalayas. He agreed to guide us for the first leg of our journey, "all the way to Tibet" if we wanted.

"The original homeland of the Khams," Ashok informed us, "was north of the Himalayas in the province of Dolpo, once a part of Tibet but subjugated by Nepal in some ancient war—a place where the language was still spoken in its purest form, having been handed down by the gods beside a magnificent, blue lake." Our two porters, learning that we might be crossing the mountains, spent the rest of the day making new pairs of snow boots for themselves.

The Tibetan monastery

We left at eight thirty the next morning, a company of seven men. After passing a small Tibetan monastery at the edge of the valley, we crossed over a low pass and lost all sight of human habitation. We were traveling across a part of Nepal few westerners had ever been privileged to see. For me it was the fulfillment of a lifelong dream.

Though beautiful beyond description with towering mountain walls, deep gorges, and raging rivers, the land itself seemed inhospitable except to mountain goats and snow leopards.

We kept to a small trail that clung stubbornly to the mountain walls, sometimes dropping steeply to cross some nameless gorge on a narrow log bridge. From one of these crossings, we began climbing sharply for the next pass and were suddenly overtaken by a cold, driving rain that turned quickly to snow. At the pass we came upon a small shed, almost collapsed, where we took shelter and built a fire until the squall passed.

As suddenly as it had started, the storm was over. The surrounding slopes were whitewashed in a coat of fresh snow. The skies cleared and the snow on the lower slopes began to melt in the brilliant light of the late afternoon sun. It was too late to go on, but Gary and I, delighted at the scene, headed up the alpine slopes with Ashok's rifle. We hoped, with a bit of luck, to bag a pheasant for supper. We took our time and finally relaxed on the hillside to soak some of the quiet and tranquility into our souls.

As we sat in silence, we spotted a flock of sheep ambling down the hillside grazing its way back to a camp somewhere below. They were followed by a shepherd who soon joined us. Tossing his heavy woolen blanket on the ground beside us, he leaned on one elbow and grinned in pleasure as the silence and the beauty of the scene formed a bond between us.

The man turned out to be a Kham of the Budha clan, and sitting on the hillside, we engaged in a short but pleasant chat, all of it in broken Nepali. I knew then that I would love these people; he was simple and genuine, and just as serene as the countryside he lived in. He looked as if he belonged there, an integral part of the good earth. I was grateful for the privilege of meeting him.

* * *

David soaking up the tranquility

The next morning we were up before daylight. Ashok informed us that it was still a long way to the closest village and if we didn't start early, we wouldn't make it that day. We first had to work our way upward to a 13,000-foot pass to cross the ridge ahead of us. Beyond, a mere fifteen miles by air to the northeast, rising out of the deep green of virgin forests far below, was the entire range of the mighty Dhaulagiri Himal, a subrange of the Himalayas. Her highest crown, Dhaulagiri I, thrust 26,795 feet into the cold, thin air, making it the seventh highest mountain in the world.

I have never ceased to be awed in the presence of such monarchs. Even the Khams who have grown up in their shadow, and who might be expected to take them for granted, tread before them in reverence like intruders into a silent, forbidden realm. Those who travel through these regions erect shrines at every high pass; it feels like the abode of the gods. Ashok, before going on, made an offering of flowers at the cairn of the mountain god.

Though in the Christian sense, Ashok was a pagan, I understood his instinct. It was a human one—the searching instinct of the poet, lost perhaps only to western, rationalistic man. G.K. Chesterton aptly wrote in *The Everlasting Man*: "The posture of the idol might be stiff and strange; but the gesture of the worshipper was generous and beautiful. He not only felt freer when he bent; he actually felt taller when he bowed... If a man cannot pray he is gagged; if he cannot bow he is in irons."

I was to learn in my years of association with these people that they had many dreams of the Reality that at first they could only imagine. Ashok's offering was but one manifestation of their searching instinct. When they actually encountered the Reality, they rejoiced in giving up the shadow for the substance. I was to struggle long to come to this realization. But when it happened, I understood as never before.

The apostle Paul speaks of the futility of human imagination devoid of God because it "worships the creature instead of the Creator." Job was the first to allude to it: "If I ever looked on the sun in splendor or the moon moving in her glory, and was led astray in my secret heart and raised my hand in homage, this would have been an offence before the law, for I should have been unfaithful to God on high" (Job 31:26–28). I, in my secret heart, was as guilty before God as those I had come to serve.

David pauses at a cairn in a high pass

From the pass we descended to the river below. Alpine meadows gave way to rhododendron forests, which in turn gave way to stands of Himalayan spruce, fir, and hemlock. In various places, benches of land opened before us, and small streams flowed down, meandering across the lazy meadows before leaping off the far edge in a roaring lather.

We reached the valley floor at about 8,000 feet, crossed on a solid wooden bridge, and headed up the steep other side till we reached the jagged spine of a rocky ridge at 10,000 feet. From there we traveled a punishing trail along the jagged knife-edge without water and without reprieve, undulating between 9,000 and 11,000 feet for one tiring mile after another. Khams of past generations in an ill-humored mood named it Dog Trail Ridge.

Dusk began to fall as we reached the end of the ridge, and in the murky darkness we could make out a raging river coming out of the glaciers to the north. Far below, at 7,000 feet, the fires of the village of Pelma flickered. The deep, throbbing beat of a single large drum started from somewhere in the depths of the gorge and was answered by a cascade of echoes off the stone walls. The drumbeat was joined by the eerie strains of what sounded like a snake charmer's oboe.

I stopped for a moment and shivered in the darkness. We were in the heart of "Eight Thousand Mountains," soon to experience our first encounter with the real Khams.

The rooftops of Pelma

We stopped for the night in Pelma, eating and sleeping in the house of a Tibetan family. The hearth was warm, and the food was good—mutton, rice, gravy, and squash. All the Khams, we were told, were in the village of Yamakhar on the other side of the gorge, engaged in a ceremony for ridding the village of the spirits of the dead. It was from there that we had heard the sound of the drum and oboe.

It wasn't until the next morning that we saw the raw and terrify-ing beauty of the land we had entered. The gorge was narrow, running north and south, lined on both sides by dizzying heights and stone cliffs. Waterfalls cascaded from the walls into the river below. A mile or two north, closer to its source, the gorge ran dead into a wall and careened sharply off to the west. I could hardly imagine that any trail continued on beyond this place.

The two Kham villages, built vertically on the steep mountainside, one row of houses on top of the next, faced each other like fortresses on opposite sides of the gorge. The river raged between them eight hundred feet below. On the other side, rising above the village of Yamakhar, Ashok pointed out the trail we were to follow. Etched into the rocky terrain, it rose and disappeared at the top of the gorge.

We crossed the river and started up the steep slope to the now-hidden village of Yamakhar. Sacred spots and altar stones along the trail were still sticky with the fresh blood of an animal sacrifice. Rounding a bend, we found the village suddenly before us. Dozens of people, some in wild costumes and grotesque masks, let out a tumultuous shout and bounded out of the village towards us.

We were immediately surrounded by a crushing crowd; drummers pounded out a thunderous din, and oboes joined in with an eerie, hair-raising strain. Gary, right behind me, shouted in my ear, "I think they're calling up the demons."

I stepped towards the drummers, and they turned as if to indicate we were to follow. As we made our way slowly towards the village in the midst of the noisy, reeling mob, I tried to explain our presence to one of the more influential-looking men, "We're here on business, and we'd like to get a word list of your language. Do you think that would be possible?"

He waved his arms, quieting the mob, and motioned for us to sit on the porch of a nearby house. As we attempted to settle in our assigned spot, the people pressed around, eager to see what we would do. Most were drunk, and the smell of liquor wafted by in waves. Wondering if I would make any progress at all, I started at the top of my list, speaking in Nepali. "In Kham what is your word for 'I'?"

In one voice the entire crowd shouted, "*Ngaa!*" I repeated the word, and they all laughed in delight. I continued on right through all hundred words. If I made a mistake, they would laugh and quickly correct me. It was the fastest word list I had ever taken and certainly the most entertaining. It also bore close similarity to the list we had taken in Bhuji Khola several days before. We were obviously still within the same language area.

We remained another half-hour, asking questions about neighboring villages and the dialects spoken there. They all agreed that every village in the valley for two days to the west spoke and understood the same dialect. They also agreed with the people of Bhuji Khola in saying that Taka-Shera was the linguistic center of the Khams. Based on that information, I felt sure that Taka-Shera was where we would probably end up living.

When we got up to leave, the raucous musicians gave us a noisy honorary escort up the first few hundred yards of the steep trail. They turned out to be friendly after all, something we weren't quite sure of when we first saw them clamoring towards us.

* * *

The next village we entered was a full three days away. Between lay the icy finger of the western edge of the Dhaulagiri Himal, an inhospitable region of the high Himalayas. The upper limits of the tree line reached as high as 11,000 feet. Above that was a belt of grassland reaching up to 15,000 feet. This high tract of land, gnarled and twisted, was formed into bowls and alpine amphitheaters separated from one another by broken cliffs and jagged spires.

This was the summer grazing land of the flocks of the Kham shepherds. It was also the world's prime habitat for the Himalayan blue sheep. Where blue sheep dwell, snow leopards also lurk in the silence of the rocks, beyond the gaze of man. Perhaps they watched us as we passed. A band of black crags and shale rose a thousand feet above the grassline up to the beginnings of permanent glacier. From there to the sky, the peaks thrust their snowy heads another 8,000 feet.

According to geologists, the Himalayas began their formation millions of years ago when the Indian subcontinent, once a large island, moved northward and collided with the Eurasian landmass. Eurasia, on the northern side of the collision, crumpled and buckled upward, rising in some places to a height of over five and a half miles. Remarkably, these mountains, the highest in the world, don't form a watershed. Rivers that form in Tibet on the slopes of *lesser* mountain ranges actually flow south *through* the Himalayas, forming the deepest gorges in the world. The peaks of Dhaulagiri and Annapurna, both over twenty-six thousand feet high, are only nineteen miles apart with a river flowing between them at less than eight thousand feet in elevation. Tibet was once an ocean floor, and almost all Tibetans carry a testament of this on their persons—red coral beads. The stones, formed in oceans, are found today on the world's highest plateau.

Himalaya is actually a Sanskrit word: *him* being the word for "snow" and *alaya*, "the place of"—hence, "the place of snow." *Alaya* occurs in many other Nepali compounds too: *bhojan-alaya*, restaurant ("place of feasting"); *ausadh-alaya*, pharmacy ("place of medicine"); *postok-alaya*, library ("place of books"); and *biswa-bidh-alaya*, university ("place of universal knowledge").

The western edge of the Dhaulagiri Himal

Dhaulagiri Himal, the range that we were traversing, is different from the other geological formations in Nepal. Annapurna, Everest, and most of the other ranges farther east are narrow upthrusts of rock with the highest elevations like a knife-edge. Dhaulagiri Himal, on the other hand, is a massive knot of elevated peaks and valleys covering an area of some six hundred square miles of nearly uninhabited land.

The fortress of Maikot

For three days we traveled in a silent world across the gnarled highlands of the Dhaulagiri massif, sleeping at night under rock overhangs. On the first day out of Yamakhar, in the red glow of the late afternoon sun, we could see far below us the ancient Kham fortress of Maikot, "The Fortress of Death." It sat perched upon the knife-edge of a steep ridge, approachable only by a single narrow trail. Across from Maikot, on a ridge on the other side of the deep river gorge, stood the village of Hukam, like a city upon a hill.

Gazing through the mists, I felt like a visitor to a bygone era, a bit like what I always imagined Joshua must have felt when he first set eyes on the walled cities of Canaan. But I also felt an unusual sense of the presence of God, as if every place the sole of my foot was treading was being claimed for him. I dropped behind the rest of the party so I could be alone as I walked the ridge; I was compelled to prayer.

On the morning of the third day, after sleeping the night in the bitter cold of 15,000 feet, we reached the main pass to the north at 15,500 feet. While still over forty air miles south of the Nepal–Tibet border, we were crossing into the cultural and geographical threshold of Tibet. From the pass down to the village of Tarakot was a single, steep path, dropping 6,500 feet. Since we had plenty of time to reach the village before nightfall, we walked with caution to prevent any kind of knee injury.

We started in frozen tundra, which soon changed to green alpine meadows, then to scrub coniferous forest. From there we marched into stately fir and cedar groves and finally into the red and yellow of deciduous forest in October.

Approaching the village, we could certainly see the Tibetan influence. Buddhist *gompas* and *chortens* dotted the hillside in a monastic array, and prayer flags fluttered from every rooftop.

The dense, beehive-like villages we found here are similar to the Kham villages we had just left behind on the southern slopes, both fashioned after the fortress-like cities of Tibet. Log ladders link the various levels of the stair-step complex to each other in a complicated maze. A network of winding passages cuts through the village levels, so narrow that in some places, the passages are better described as tunnels.

The inhabitants of Tarakot wear Tibetan dress, though they claim to be northern Magars of the Budha clan. Their language is even referred to by outsiders as Kham. They themselves refer to their language as Kaike, however, and after closer investigation, it is easy to see that it bears little resemblance to the Kham spoken on the south side of the Himalayas. In fact, it belongs to a totally different genetic sub-grouping of the Tibeto-Burman family. So much for Ashok's "pure Kham handed down by the gods"!

The number of westerners who had entered this forbidding world before 1969 could probably be counted on one hand. We suspected that we might never get the chance again ourselves and decided to make the best of the opportunity. It turned out that we were right. In the following year, Tibetan warlords, who intimated that they were commissioned by the Dalai Lama himself, organized a resistance movement in Dolpo, running terrorist attacks across the border against Chinese road builders who were pushing a highway westward across Tibet.

The conflict was known as the "Khampa Uprising." In fact, it had been going on inside Tibet since 1956. Even the CIA got involved and began making secret air drops of arms and ammunition to the Khampas; we all saw the blinking lights on the parachutes at night. Once, in Dhorpatan, in a case of mistaken identity, my family and I were invited to dinner with General Gyatso Wangdu, the commander-in-chief of the resistance movement. We were entertained in his spacious tent made from an American parachute. During the course of dinner, when he realized that I wasn't who he thought I was, he good-naturedly handed me fifty rounds of ammunition for my hunting rifle. "You're supplying it anyway," he said with a grin on his face. Two years later, before sitting down to a meal of roasted blue sheep, I thought of General Wangdu and raised a toast to him.

In about 1970, the whole area north of the Himalayas was designated a "restricted area" to foreigners for the next twenty years. In 1974, Nepal was pressured by the Chinese government to "do something about the Khampa problem," and the Royal Nepal Army was sent in to quell the uprising. The Khampas were vastly outnumbered, and in August General Wangdu was killed in an ambush on Tinker's Pass in far western Nepal. His body was put on public display in the Tundikhel Fairgrounds at the center of Kathmandu along with rows and rows of captured American arms. The Khampa resistance was over.

We stayed on the north side of the Dhaulagiri Himal in southern Dolpa for close to a week, collecting word lists of the languages spoken in that area. We moved slowly westward, staying as guests part of our time at Ashok's home in Dunai, the administrative center for the district. Since we were getting low on food supplies, we bought rice and flour and slaughtered a sheep that we cut into strips, smoking the meat and making the rest into sausages. Most of it we ate in the next few days.

The whole time we were in Dolpa, the clouds gathered every afternoon on the Himalayas to the south, dumping snow on the passes and coming lower every day. Looking at our maps we decided that the best thing to do was to get back to the southern side as soon as possible, rather than retrace our steps back to the pass we had come over nearly a week before. If we went back that way, we might not be able to cross over at all.

In the villages along the river, the people assured us that there was a pass directly to the south. But it wasn't until several days later that we learned from villagers living closer to the pass that the mountains would be impassable after the recent snows. Furthermore, it was obvi-ous to all of us that the snow was continuing to fall. It was from here that we decided to go as far as we could and make a firsthand assess-ment of the situation ourselves.

Frozen tundra gives way to alpine meadow

Chapter 2: Angel Tracks

Behold, I send an Angel before thee, to keep thee in the way,
and to bring thee into the place which I have prepared.
—Exodus 23:20, KJV

The morning was exceptionally beautiful, with little to indicate that every step was bringing us closer to danger. The air was cool and fresh with the sweet fragrance of pine, hemlock, and fir drifting up to us on the sighing breeze from the valley below. The trail we were following meandered along the edge of a ridge at about 9,000 feet, dipping in and out of tiny groves of alpine fir and cool, lush ferns. Rivulets of water splashed off the mountain slopes from above. Down below us, they gained in strength until they were lost in the roar of the river at the bottom of the gorge.

The songs of birds filled the air, and tiny minivets, some bright red, some bright yellow, flitted ahead of us from one bush to the next. Still ahead of us, off to the south, the western end of the Dhaulagiri Himal lay covered in snow, shimmering white in the morning sun. I was glad to be alive.

By early afternoon, Gary and I, along with our two Tibetan porters, descended to the edge of the ridge and came to Durgaon, the last little settlement perched on the northern side of the mountains at 9,600 feet.

The entire village was a hive of industry, as everyone participated in the joys of harvest. Children climbed in the branches of walnut trees, shaking the clusters loose, beating them with sticks. Smaller children laughed and scurried about on the ground to pick the nuts up. Some of the old folks sat in the warmth of the sun spinning wool while others busied themselves at their looms, weaving blankets for the coming of winter.

Pumpkins, squash, corn, wheat, millet, buckwheat, and potatoes lay on the flat rooftops in neat, plentiful piles. Teenage girls carried baskets of fertilizer to the fields as teams of oxen pulled and heaved in every acre in response to the cheering and cajoling of the sweating plowmen. Children on the hillsides sang and whistled in a happy and carefree manner as they watched their wooly flocks of sheep and goats. The feel of autumn was in the air, and it was a good year.

We stopped for about an hour in Durgaon, both to eat and to replenish our food supplies. All we had left were the last bits of smoked mutton and a little wheat. Food was plentiful here and easy to buy. Some villagers even gave us gifts of small bamboo purses lined with birch-bark, filled with tasty walnut meats.

But foremost on our minds was a question we had been asking for several days. "Is there a trail over this stretch of the Himalayas from here, and if so, is it still possible to cross over to the south side at this time of the year?"

Their response was what we feared. They turned and looked to the towering mountains, by now covered again in a thick shroud of white clouds. We knew as well as they did what that meant. We had seen the same cloud cover for several afternoons now, and each morning as we rose, we knew that the snow was a bit deeper than the day before.

The villagers did confirm for us that there was a trail cutting over a pass directly to the south. The mountains here, the tail end of the Dhaulagiri Himal, rose to 17,500 feet, and the pass was marked on our map at something over 15,500 feet. They also confirmed what our rough maps only hinted at—that the south side was perilously steep, a maze of cliffs stacked one on top of the other.

The mountain formations along this part of the Himalayan chain resemble a giant ocean breaker, swelling up on the northern side and crashing down on the southern side. "Without a guide," the villagers warned us, "it's impossible to find your way through the maze—even in the summertime when there is no snow!" But they were resolute in their refusal to show us the way, and no amount of pay would induce them to change their minds.

In their hospitality, they did offer to let us stay the winter in their village and then show us the way over the next summer, a possibility we didn't even want to think about. We had already been tramping through the mountains for three weeks, and our wives were undoubtedly expecting us back any day. Perhaps they were already concerned, but there was no way to get word to them.

Our two Tibetan porters didn't help matters when they sided with the villagers. They found little amusement in the descriptions of "snow up to a man's neck" and the all-too-graphic tales of the gruesome deaths of other travelers who had perished in foolish attempts to cross the mountains along this way. This was new country for them as well.

When the porters began to realize we were seriously thinking about trying to make it on our own, and that we expected them to follow us, they began nervously fingering their Buddhist prayer beads, muttering repeatedly in an agitated crescendo the sacred Tibetan mantra "*Om mani padmi hum.*" We reasoned with them that at least we could go up and have a look. If the villagers' reports turned out to be true, we could always turn around and come back.

So with few directions to go on, apart from the assurance that we could probably reach a cluster of abandoned herders' sheds before nightfall, we somewhat reluctantly left the peaceful little village behind and headed off

One of the herders' sheds

into the tumbled expanse of wild mountains before us.

As predicted, we came to the cluster of sheds less than an hour before nightfall. They lay at about 11,000 feet, nestled picturesquely in the last growth of timber rising up from one of the gorges below. Beyond was the high alpine country leading to the white peaks. Banks of snow lay piled in the ravines.

We hastily gathered firewood and water and in a few minutes had a cheerful fire blazing in the firepit. From the center of our shed, a row of stalls stretched to either end, sheaves of grass still in the mangers. Surrounding the firepit, rough planks covered the bare earth, affording the herders their only luxury—a place where they could stay dry and sleep out of the mud. We cushioned the planks with hay and stacked our backpacks against the far stone wall as a protection from the chilling breeze beginning to stir off the open highlands.

We hung our food supplies from the rafters to protect them from rodents, and soon the cooking pot was boiling with a savory mutton stew. With a fire before us and a roof over our heads, we soon forgot our problems.

After eating, we stooped through the low entrance and stepped outside for a brief look around. The clouds that had been clinging to the mountains all afternoon had dissipated, and the stars shone brightly overhead like gas lanterns in the dark night sky. A deep mantle of snow lay over the high, alpine country, and the mountains beyond took on a disturbingly sinister appearance. Shivering, we returned to the shed and the comfort of the red, glowing coals of the firepit.

The porters had no interest in venturing outside. They stubbornly remained seated on the far side of the fire with mirthless faces, fingering their prayer beads and chanting their endless mantras. Gary and I, too, were feeling a bit more unnerved than usual.

As our practice had been since the beginning of the trip, we took our Bibles from our packs and began to read to one another. But on this night more than any other, regardless of where we turned, comforting passages leaped from the pages—promises that God would never leave us nor forsake us, promises that even should our feet slip, we would not be utterly cast down. Filled with confidence and a sense of God's presence, we committed our night and the following day into his care. Settling into our sleeping bags, we both fell into a deep and untroubled sleep.

* * *

My first sensation the next morning was of a distant sound—*whoosh, whoosh, whoosh*—like a steam locomotive rounding the bend and making its way ever-so-slowly towards me. I was back on the Santa Fe Railway, lantern in hand, walking down a long row of freight cars. It was a cold night. The vision vanished as I heard the sound of snapping twigs and a deep-chested cough right beside me.

Floating along in that halfway-world between sleep and consciousness, I lay a few seconds longer trying to drift back into the pleasantness of my dream. But a nagging discomfort in the middle of my back made me twist in my sleeping bag, and I suddenly remembered where I was.

Poking my head out of the warm folds of my bag, I could see the first traces of dawn beginning to streak the eastern sky. The air in the herders' shed was filling with the sweet, pungent smell of juniper smoke. I could make out the figures of our two Tibetan porters in the half-light of early morning. Huddled over the firepit, wrapped in heavy woolen robes, they were trying to coax the few remaining embers of the previous night's fire back into flame. One carefully added dry twigs and juniper sprigs to the smoldering pile, trying not to smother it. The other, his back toward me, rocked slowly back and forth, pressing his weight against a sheepskin bellows—*whoosh, whoosh*—forcing drafts into the glowing coals.

A little flicker of flame worked its way upward through the dry twigs as the juniper needles began to catch the flames, hissing and crackling in tiny explosions of fire. In the dancing light I could make out the features of the two men intent on their work. The older man, whose back was toward me, had red ribbons braided into his long, black hair. The younger man, his face red in the flickering firelight, rubbed his hands near the flame. As he opened the front of his coat as if to wrap it around the fire and gather its warmth to himself, I could see a turquoise amulet hanging from his neck.

Today we would know whether the pass was crossable or not. We ate hurriedly and were on the trail before the sun made its first peek over the horizon.

We made our way across treeless grasslands broken up by rough terrain and rocky crags. We started on a trail, but soon all traces of it were gone. Patches of snow streaked the landscape where the wind had blown unchecked across the open highlands. As we worked our way to the top of a ridge in search of clues, the snow became deeper, and even the rocks were obliterated. The patches had turned to drifts. But right at the top of the ridge where the wind had blown the earth bare of snow, we could make out the faint traces of a trail. Beyond that, high above us on a distant, snowy ridge, there was a saddle between two peaks, and we assumed that we had found our pass.

Struggling steeply upward for at least another thousand feet, we could finally make out a rock cairn at the top of the ridge still a few miles short of the pass. With fresh enthusiasm we surged ahead, our lungs nearly bursting from the exertion. Up at the top, though, the gravity of our situation suddenly came crashing upon us: we weren't going to make it!

We stood at the edge of a great chasm separating us from the pass that was now hidden by gathering, swirling snow-clouds. The chasm was about five hundred feet deep, and the narrow ledges of the near-vertical precipice wall were piled deep with ice and snow. As we peered over the edge, afraid of getting too close, we noticed on a narrow ledge straight below us faint foot-tracks, almost covered over by drifting snow. From there they disappeared.

Stunned by the improbable discovery that someone else was trekking this wilderness, we were almost afraid to avert our attention lest the tracks should go away. Where had they come from? How did they get there?

We could retreat, or we could follow. The thought of going on made us tremble, and our porters flatly refused anything so stupid. How did we know that this stranger wasn't lost? After further reflection, Gary and I remembered the promises of the previous evening and the assurance that "though our feet should slip, we would not be utterly cast down." How else could we account for the sudden appearance of foot-tracks?

We concluded that the tracks were God-sent, and without further hesitation, Gary tied a hundred feet of nylon rope around my waist and lowered me over the edge. I cut steps in the ice and snow till I came to the first tiny ledge below. Then, wedging myself between some rocks, I took up the slack in the rope while Gary descended to join me. With two of us having gone ahead, the steps we left were deep and solid, and the porters gingerly worked their way down to us. We repeated the process, skirting one ledge after another, carefully zigzagging back and forth. The strange footprints silently forged ahead, sometimes almost obliterated by blowing snow.

An hour and a half later, we were at the foot of the precipice. The clouds had rolled in, and we were swallowed up in dense cloud. We were in a total whiteout; our visibility was reduced to zero. The sky was white, the air around us was white, and the earth we walked on was white. We stumbled blindly into drifts of snow, unable even to see them.

But just out ahead, fifty feet away, we could make out the faint indentations of the foot-tracks. Any closer, we couldn't distinguish them, and any farther away, they were hidden by cloud. On they went without the slightest deviation, straight towards the pass 1,500 feet above us.

Suddenly the cloud began to thin, and looming off to the right and left were great mountain spires. Directly ahead of us, between the two spires, the summit cairn stood silent vigil over the pass.

It appeared we had come to the very edge of the world. For the first time, I began to wonder if we would come out of this adventure alive. Cliffs swept off for hundreds of feet, even thousands. Their magnitude was intensified by the swirling clouds, which sometimes opened up and allowed us to see a bit farther but never allowed us to see the bottom—if indeed there was one.

We lost all sense of distance, and even of time. The earth seemed to extend downward forever and then curve beneath us into nothingness. We could do nothing but stand there in utter silence, totally mesmerized by the frightfulness of the scene.

It's hard to know how long we stood there. But we were suddenly snapped back to reality by a sense of what we had to do next. It was growing late, and to turn back was out of the question. To do so would probably trap us in darkness on the face of the treacherous precipice we had just descended. Nor could we stay the night at 14,000 feet without shelter. We had to go on. The tracks had gone over the edge down to a

We had to go on

ledge just below us. We did the only thing we could do: we followed.

The strange footprints forged ahead, skillfully showing the way through the most formidable-looking country I have ever seen. One cliff was stacked on top of another, forming something like a giant staircase. To figure out how to circumnavigate just one level without being hopelessly blocked by the next one down would be an impossible task, especially in the swirling cloud. To us, one rock looked the same as another, one direction as good as the other.

Once, when the tracks began a steep ascent, we foolishly ignored them and followed our own instincts, only to be trapped at the lower end by a straight drop-off. We returned to the tracks and followed them across a narrow ledge on a high, vertical precipice. We couldn't see the bottom because of the fog, but whether it was a hundred feet down or a thousand feet down made little difference. If we slipped, we would plunge to our death. There was only one route through the maze; everything else was a dead end. The tracks led the only way.

We quickly dropped in elevation and just before dark began coming out of the snow. Remarkably, the footprints brought us out onto a mountain trail. There was still no place to stay, so we continued on into the night with our flashlights. At about ten thousand feet, we came to a glacial stream at the bottom of a deep gorge. We were exhausted, but grateful to God to be alive.

In a single day, we had ascended five thousand feet and then descended another six thousand—a total of eleven thousand feet, some of it at altitudes three miles high! We ate the remainder of our food and fell into an exhausted sleep on the stony ground.

The tracks led the only way

* * *

The next day we continued down the steep trail until we came to the village of Sisne at about mid-morning. The village was built like a fortress on the side of a cliff; the only way through it was across a row of flat rooftops. Demon temples and shrines guarded the entrance.

As we entered the village, a man on the rooftops above us began to scream and howl. His hair was scraggly and matted, his clothing shredded. Leaping down to our level, he rushed past us, shrieking as he went. Hiding in a corner, he began to moo like a cow and bray like a jackass. I could feel the hair on the back of my neck standing up. As we started down a ladder to the next level, I kept my eye on him, afraid he might rush us like a mad dog. The rest of the villagers stood around passively, doing nothing. They were obviously used to him and his behavior.

We stopped to buy food, but the villagers were most inhospitable and showed no interest in being helpful. Only after much coaxing did one man finally sell us some potatoes and corn. With some more persuading, he produced some firewood, and we were able to cook our food. The people here were Thakuris, and their language was a strange western dialect of Nepali.

We asked about the stranger whose tracks we had been following. No response. Didn't they hear us? We asked again. They answered impatiently, almost angrily, "Nobody! Nobody crosses the mountains now." When we insisted that we had, they dismissed our claims with laughter. Apparently, they thought we were hunters, skirting along the lower ridges from farther east. From that moment on, we began to refer to the strange footprints as "angel tracks."

We learned also that this was the first valley to the west of Kham country. At least now we had a rough idea of its outside boundaries. Bhuji Khola lay at the southeastern extreme, and this valley was just off the northwestern corner. By the next day, they assured us, we would be coming to the western edges of Kham country, and Taka-Shera would be found a day's walk to the east up the next major tributary.

For two days, we stumbled around in the deep gorge of the Sisne Khola valley. The trails were poorly maintained and often dead-ended in some nameless forest. No one would give us directions. Every village we passed through was protected by the same demon shrines and altars. No one would give us food. We tried to buy chickens but to no avail; all had been dedicated to sacrifice. They wouldn't give us lodging in their villages, and they drove us from their cattle sheds. They were as mean as the demons they worshipped. We had to spend the night in the open without food. If we hadn't been so weak from hunger, we probably could have made it to the major tributary in a day. But in our weakened condition, we could barely go on.

Late in the afternoon of the second day, we spotted a village below us at the junction of two rivers—the beginning of Kham country. Our spirits lifted, and we felt a new burst of energy. By early evening, we arrived in the village, but the place was deserted. Grass grew deep around the doorsteps, and all that could be heard was the sighing of breeze in the treetops and the rustling of swirling leaves in the empty lanes. It felt strange, like ghosts were lurking in the shadows. But the breeze kept her secret, and the mystery of the abandoned village remained. Vertical cliffs at the river's edge prevented us from going any further upriver, and the only way out was to backtrack and struggle up the side of a steep hill, clinging to the grass and bushes as we went.

Just before darkness, we leveled out a thousand feet above the river and heard the sweet sound of dogs barking. Human habitation? Coming around a bend, we saw before us a small cluster of houses. A man was running out of one of the houses to see what the commotion was all about. He must have been shocked to see our strange party straggling in. When he heard our story, he was moved to pity and asked us to stay the night with him and have some food.

Our host, though not a Kham himself, had had most of his dealings with Kham people and had apparently learned his hospitality from them. He prepared a feast of chicken, cornbread, buffalo yogurt, eggs, and tea! The next morning, fearing we might get lost again and miss the critical spot to ford the river, he volunteered to take us to the point himself and help us across.

* * *

We could have reached Taka-Shera that evening, but the two days of heavy exertion without food was beginning to take its toll. The offers of hospitality in the Kham village of Garkhani were too good to pass by, even if it was only three thirty in the afternoon. One of the Khams, a Pun by clan, met us at the entrance to the village and welcomed us with no small greeting. "The sahibs have come, the sahibs have come," he shouted to all.

He ushered us to his house, called for his wife, swept off the veranda, rolled out a mat, and spread rugs for us to sit on. In a short while, he offered us cups of hot tea and asked if there were anything we wanted. "Well," we answered a bit hesitantly, "would it be possible to buy a chicken?"

"Of course it's possible," he replied. "How about two!" In a flash, he was off and returned with a big rooster tucked under each arm. Then, he was off again to fetch some *ghee* (clarified butter) and wheat flour. He killed the first rooster and tossed it into the fire to burn its feathers off. We were soon coughing and gasping, our eyes burning and noses running, as we pressed ourselves closely to the floor to get some air.

"You must not do your chickens this way," he observed in amusement as he continued working, a grin on his face. He took the chicken from the fire, ripped it in half with his strong bare hands, and began pulling out the innards. He laid them in the coals to roast, sizzle, and pop while he proceeded to hack the rest of the chicken, bones and all, into splintered little bits of meat with his long, curved *kukri* knife. He set a wok on the fire, and tossed in a lump of *ghee*. As the *ghee* began to sputter, he tossed in the meat along with a few crushed chili peppers.

He plucked the innards from the coals and passed the choice pieces to us. As we chewed, smacking our lips politely, he would reach over occasionally and stir the wok.

"So what brings you to these parts?" he asked.

"We've come to learn Kham," we replied.

He laughed with delight. As he busied himself with the meal, he offered a suggestion.

"I'll tell you what," he said, "I'll tell you some of our words, and you write them down! How would that be?"

"That's a great idea," I said, surprised at his eagerness. I reached for my notebook with the list of one hundred words. "I have a list here," I said. "I'll ask you for a word, and you give me the answer. Would that be okay?"

"I'm ready," he said, bursting with eagerness like a kid playing a game.

The second word on the list was the word "you." "How do you say 'you'?" I asked.

"Well," he replied, "if it's one person, we say it like this, if it's two people, we say it like this, and if it's three people, we say it like this."

I was amazed. I didn't even know that Kham had a special dual form in addition to the singular and plural forms. When I asked the word for "big," he gave me in addition the words for "small," "long," and "short." When I asked for "man," he also gave me "woman," "boy," and "girl."

At the end of the list he said, "Now you read back what you've written, and we'll check it." As I went back over the list, he would interrupt me on occasion and say, "No, you've written that one wrong," and we'd work on it till I had it right.

I had almost forgotten I was hungry. Suddenly the food was ready, and he placed before us a delightful meal of stir-fried chicken, wheat cakes, and gravy. As we shoveled the food down, he kept reaching into the pot with his ladle and slopping more food onto our plates. Towards the end of the meal, he reached across the fire to put more food onto my plate. Stopping briefly, his face close to mine, he looked into my eyes and said, "About our language, Sir."

"Yes?" I replied, returning the gaze and pausing to let him continue.

"Well," he said, "after you learn it, maybe you could write some books in Kham so we could read in our own language!"

Something jolted inside me. Could it be that this man had already been prepared by God for the coming of his Word? I replied with all the solemnity I could, "That's just what I hope to do."

I never saw that man again, and he never saw the Book we translated into his language. Some years later, the next time I was in his village, I asked about him and learned he had taken ill and died. I have often wondered about that man and how he figures in the kingdom of God. Did he somehow know who we were?

Jesus said in the Gospels, "He who receives a prophet in the name of a prophet shall receive a prophet's reward" (Matthew 10:41). For me, this man was something of a forerunner for the coming of the gospel to the Khams—their Melchizedek, welcoming us with bread and wine. Today his children, all believers, tell me they still remember the day I came to their village and was greeted by their father. It was the first time they had seen a white man.

First would come the big rams

The next morning, our friend gave us another meal like the one we had the night before—chicken, wheat cakes, and gravy. He then bid us farewell, informing us that the Taka-Shera dialect, though slightly different from his own, was considered by all as the most prestigious form of the Kham language. He reckoned that Taka-Shera would be the best place for me to pursue my studies. We would be there, he assured us, in just a few hours.

This recognition of Taka-Shera as their unofficial capital kept coming up again and again. I expected tribal people to be a bit more ethnocentric, to consider their own dialect as the central one, with all the others sounding a bit strange or funny. But that wasn't the case for Kham. They seemed to be unanimous in their assessment of which dialect was the most central and prestigious.

As we proceeded up-country, the surrounding mountains began to grow to fantastic proportions, and the valley began to narrow. The slope on the south side of the river with the cool, northern exposure was covered with beautiful spruce and fir forests, coming almost down to village level. The slope on the north side was almost bare of trees as high as one could see. Flocks of sheep, some as large as five or six hundred animals, grazed on the steep, green slopes.

As we continued along the way, we encountered frequent flocks of several hundred sheep being driven along the trail. Their numbers kept increasing, until their passing was almost continuous. First would come the big rams, thick in body and proudly carrying their heavy, curling horns. Then would come the ewes with their skipping, frolicking lambs. It was clear that the Taka-Shera Khams were a prosperous people. I was to learn later that they owned about twenty thousand sheep.

Taka-Shera turned out to be a cluster of four villages with a total population of some five thousand

Taka (foreground) and Bachi (background)

Taka, a giant beehive

people. On the south side of the river, the side we were traveling, the valley floor suddenly opened up to a narrow strip of land no more than two hundred yards wide, extending about two miles upriver. There, just off the bench at the foot of the slope, lay the twin villages of Upper and Lower Shera. They were separated by about a mile of barley fields that occupied the only arable land—the narrow bench along the river.

On the north side, built on a shelf several hundred feet above the river, was the village of Bachi. Farther upriver, in a side valley coming out of the northern mountains, was the village of Taka, situated on the rim of what appeared to be an ancient lakebed. Taka was the largest and most impressive of the four villages, with about three hundred houses stacked one on top of the other in a single cluster. It gave the appearance of a giant beehive clinging to a wall.

I was filled with excitement, thinking that one of these villages would very likely be the future home of my family. But my excitement was tempered with a feeling of fear and apprehension.

Could we really accomplish what we hoped to do? Were we just throwing our lives away for an idealistic dream? But more than that, what about the isolation? It seemed almost the height of folly to expose my family to the possible dangers of such a place.

I knew I could count on Nancy; she wouldn't be afraid. But what about our kids? Steve was three years old, and Daniel only seven months. If anything should happen to them, we wouldn't stand a chance of getting them out. The nearest road was in the Terai, the geographical extension of the plains of India into Nepal, 150 miles away over several ranges of mountains. The STOL airstrip in Dhorpatan was only two days away. But the Tibetan refugee project located there shut down every winter, and with it went the two-way radio. During the winter months, we would have to live beyond the reach of anyone's help, totally isolated from the outside world.

But one thought kept intruding upon my consciousness: surely God was in this place! When there was no possible way out of the mountains, I had followed the footprints of his angel through the snow. And just as he had promised Moses, his angel had brought me, too, to the place he had prepared. Having come this far, would I turn back now in fear?

Shera's rooftops

* * *

Gary continued on that day with Tsetu, the older porter, in the hopes of reaching Dhorpatan in two days and making contact with Kathmandu on the Swiss radio. Tsetu was like a horse heading for the barn. I remained in Shera to make living arrangements for the family. Angdrak, my porter, had a bond-friend in Lower Shera.

Bond-friend relationships (similar to other cultures' "blood brother" relationships) across tribal boundaries are common in Nepal. People of the Himalayas spend much time in travel, and to have a bond-friend in an adjoining tribal area is an advantage to both parties. They are bound by oath to help each other when one travels in the other's territory, giving food and shelter like they would to a member of their own families.

Angdrak's bond-friend, Krishna, lived right in the center of Lower Shera. He was out on the hills with his sheep when we arrived, but his widowed mother cordially invited us in to enjoy the warmth of the fire. She sent one of the children in search of Krishna while she prepared a snack of boiled potatoes for us. Krishna's younger brother, a lad of seventeen or eighteen years, arrived within the hour, explaining that Krishna would not be able to come before dusk. Then, after giving us the ritual greetings required for bond-friends, Krishna's brother sat with us to enjoy the potatoes.

Angdrak began to explain who I was and that I wanted to live in his village with my family. I had come, he said, not for my own interests, but for the good of the people themselves. The boy listened quietly and, after eating, took us into the village to look at two possible living places. The one was an old, run-down, abandoned house; living there was out of the question. The other was a large, well-built house, its only disadvantage being that it was occupied by a large extended family. Our family would be restricted to one tiny room in that house.

Later in the evening, Krishna himself returned home from the flocks along with the rest of his brothers. They were all handsome specimens of manhood, large and strong, with an air of quiet confidence and serenity. They were shepherds, barefoot and simple, clothed in homespun garments with large, woolen coats. But they were men worthy of respect. I was impressed by their kindness and generosity towards me, though I had done nothing to earn it. While they ate cornmeal mush that evening, they served Angdrak and me a meal of honor—fried chicken, rice, and gravy. The rice, they had obtained on their latest trading excursion to the south. They refused to accept any pay for it; we were guests of the family.

That evening as we sat on the floor around an open fire, engaged in friendly conversation, I reveled in the richness of the experience. Amongst themselves they chatted in Kham, and I was captivated by the sound of it. It sounded melodious and free, rich in flavor and laced with humor. They were quick to burst into full-hearted laughter as their mirthful eyes danced in the firelight. I couldn't wait to begin learning this language myself.

Finally Krishna turned to me and offered the family house to me if the one room I had seen in the village was not adequate for us. In a couple of weeks, he explained to me, the whole family would be going south for the winter with the sheep, and the house would be vacant until springtime. "If you want it, you can have it," he said. I thanked him and accepted his offer.

Before sleeping, I opened my Bible and read: "Every place on which the sole of your foot treads, I have given it to you... Just as I have been with Moses, I will be with you; I will not fail you or forsake you... Do not tremble or be dismayed, for the LORD your God is with you wherever you go" (Joshua 1:3, 5, 9). I knew now that God was in this place. All I needed to do now was bring my family back and get started with the real adventure.

Chapter 3: Taka-Shera

The path meets the sun at a small hamlet, one of the very primitive communities still to be found in these deep inner canyons of the Himalaya. If [the other villages] had a medieval air, one enters the Dark Ages [here]. [They] heap up offerings of goat heads in their primitive temple. Brutal human effigies in wood protect the low stone huts, and half-wild curs rage at strangers from the roof-tops. The women wear black cloth, the men soot-colored clothes of other cultures, the children rags; every face is masked in black, where ceaseless exposure to manure dust, pine smoke, and soot makes filth endemic.
—Peter Matthiessen (on a Kham village), The Snow Leopard

Nancy was the brains and inspiration behind the next stage in our lives. I returned home to Kathmandu on October 19, 1969, eager to share my adventures with the woman who shared my life. I had missed her immensely, this being the first separation of our married lives. She had experienced the loneliness, too, but hers was the more intense loneliness of the one left behind. Now we were a family again, and our lives were richer even than before. We had taken the first step; we sensed the presence of God, and we were filled with anticipation for what lay ahead.

Nancy wanted to hear it all: what I'd seen, what I'd experienced, what I'd felt. I tried my best to describe it. But how could I adequately portray the majesty of the mountains, the beauty of the people, the strangeness of the villages? No matter—she would soon see it for herself. But the haunting thought that kept nagging me was that in spite of all its beauty, we were headed into a land of cold austerity; isolated from the rest of the world, without communication, and with little to offer in the way of creature comforts.

Nancy listened to my stories with as much eagerness as I experienced in telling them. But she wasn't naive; she understood the dangers and difficult odds as well as anyone could at the beginning of such a venture. She was as convinced as I was, though, that this was the place God had for us, and she began to prepare, over the course of the next couple of weeks, to organize the needed supplies. We didn't know yet how much we could depend on village food supplies, so she had to plan, as well as she could, against every contingency to carry us through the next three months. We knew we could probably count on cornmeal, barley flour, and potatoes. Anything else, we would have to carry in.

While I made another short trip with Gary to help him find a suitable location for his family among the southern Magars, Nancy made repeated trips to the bazaar, laying up stocks of rice, flour, oatmeal, sugar, milk powder, tea, and coffee. She purchased a few delicacies, too—a limited supply of noodles, tomato paste, cans of tuna, and cheese. She canned jars of meat, vegetables, and fruit, just enough that we could indulge ourselves once a week. The dry goods, she packed into plastic bags and then stuffed into sturdy cloth bags. The canned goods, she put into metal trunks and small wooden chests. They were nailed shut and bound securely with leather straps for later transport on the backs of mules and horses. In addition, we had pots, pans, enamel cups and plates.

We also carried basic medical supplies, enough for ourselves and a little extra to help the villagers. And, of course, what would a research expedition be without books, paper, notebooks, and a portable typewriter?

Since I had already seen how smoky Kham houses could be, I went to the trouble of converting one of our thirty-gallon shipping drums into a small heating stove, complete with hinged lid, ash grate, damper, and chimney. The stove, along with three canvas army cots, was the sum total of our furnishings. Nancy and I would each have a cot, and the boys were still small enough that they could sleep at opposite ends of the same one and still have room at their feet for their puppy to lie between them. The wooden chests and metal trunks could be converted later to chairs and tables as we needed them.

We flew to the Tibetan refugee camp of Dhorpatan on November 14, 1969. The aircraft was a Cessna 206 with a special Robertson STOL conversion kit, but our load limit was only 800 pounds (about 360 kilograms). Included in that limit was our own personal weight—a little over 300 pounds (about 140 kilograms) for the whole family back in those days, when we were still trim and the kids were small—but it also included an official government observer, a requirement on all flights to make sure we weren't using our aircraft for covert operations. The weight remaining for supplies was something under 400 pounds (about 180 kilograms). Because of that limitation, we scheduled another supply flight for November 27. Our original plan was to stay out till February 10, but with a flight coming out just two weeks later, we had a second chance to revise the schedule if needed.

The day of the fourteenth was filled with the excitement of adventure, not only for us but for the Tibetans as well. Angdrak was in Dhorpatan to greet us, and everyone else crowded curiously around as we began to unload the plane. Able-bodied men and women shouldered boxes, duffel bags, and trunks and helped us store them away in a little house nearby, where we would spend the night. Angdrak quickly made arrangements with his older brother to transport our goods to the village by horse train.

This would be one of the few times we would use horses to haul our goods. Hiring Khams to carry loads on their backs is much more reliable, much quicker, and far less expensive. But we didn't know that yet. From Dhorpatan to Taka-Shera is a distance of about twenty-five miles, with only a few hamlets between. Kham porters, even with eighty-pound loads, never take more than two days to reach the village. But a horse train takes three. The drivers have to stop mid-afternoon to allow their horses grazing time, and then they're slow at getting started in the morning.

Nancy astride the horse, with Daniel on her back

The same day, an older Tibetan gentleman, a former official of some importance in one of the eastern Tibetan provinces, offered to sell me one of his riding horses. The horse was a real beauty, a six-year-old chestnut gelding; strong and stout, he walked with a smooth, rapid pace. I spent a couple of hours in the afternoon racing him against other Tibetan riding horses, and he was beaten by only one.

After some haggling, I finally bought him for seventeen hundred rupees, equivalent then to $170 in U.S. currency. Nancy and I felt he was a good investment, especially knowing how beneficial he would be in traveling back and forth with a family. We were not disappointed. Over the next four years, we made the trip often. Alone, I could ride at a steady canter between the village and airstrip in just six hours.

We pressed our horse into service the next day. Angdrak and his brother arrived in the morning with seven pack-horses. Some were carrying salt for trade in Taka-Shera, and the rest would carry our supplies. Most of the Tibetans in Dhorpatan made their living plying the salt trade—an important niche in the local economy. Sheep need salt. Without it, they lose their appetite, fall prey to sickness, and die.

Before the Chinese takeover of Tibet, the people of Dolpo transported salt by yak caravan from the salt lakes of the Tibetan plateau, bringing it as far as the Kham village of Maikot. From there, the Maikoti Khams supplied it to the other Kham villages, including Taka-Shera. But now that the northern trade routes had been sealed off by the Chinese, all salt coming into Nepal had to come from India.

In the Kham villages, one measure of salt would fetch three measures of maize or barley. The same grain in India would fetch three measures of salt for each measure of grain. And so everyone benefited. The Tibetan refugees had grain to eat, and the Khams had a ready supply of salt for their twenty thousand sheep, something they would have had great difficulty supplying on their own all the way from India.

We left Dhorpatan at nine in the morning on the fifteenth, with Angdrak and his brother driving the horse train. Nancy rode our horse, with Steve seated in the saddle in front of her and Daniel in a baby-carrier on her back. I had planned originally on carrying Daniel myself, but I ended up carrying the thirty-gallon heating stove instead.

Tibetans, I discovered, hate carrying loads on their backs if they can avoid it, especially awkward loads. They're used to the luxury of horse and yak caravans. There's no easy way to balance a drum on a horse's back—not even as a counterbalance for an equivalent weight on the opposite side. So the Tibetans refused to touch it, and I ended up carrying it on my own back the thirty miles. I grew to loathe that thing and didn't regain my fondness for it until it was installed in the house, stoked up with a warm fire.

The valley between Dhorpatan and Taka-Shera lies on a high bench of land extending as an outgrowth off a spur of the Dhaulagiri massif. Here the river runs straight west, blocked on the south side by a high ridge. As a result, this valley lies in a partial rain shadow and is much drier than many Himalayan valleys. It's much colder, too, and though the valley begins at about 10,000 feet in altitude, it traps the cold from the high mountains. It is not suitable for crops until it drops to about 8,000 feet, near Taka-Shera. From the upper end of the valley to the first permanent habitation (excluding Dhorpatan, which is by and large only a summer residence) is a distance of some thirty-five miles—a rare bare expanse on the heavily-populated south side of the Himalayas.

But this valley is one of the most beautiful regions in all of Nepal; it has been only lightly touched by man. The ridge on the south side is relatively gentle, the lower slopes heavily forested with giant hemlock and fir, with trunks five and six feet in diameter. The higher slopes, rising to over 13,000 feet, are velveted with green alpine meadows. The north side is much more rugged and high, with snowy mountains visible above the

The rushing Uttar Ganga

lofty, barren crags. Wild Himalayan goats live in the towering crags along the edges of the rugged cliffs just above timberline.

As the trail wound its way in and out of the side valleys, the view was ever changing. The forests were deep and dark, with an ocean of ferns and delicate plants growing beneath the spreading branches of the great trees. From vantage points, we could look across the forested slopes, sprinkled here and there with the flaming red of maples and the shimmering yellow of birch trees. On occasion, the trail would drop to the level of the river, which grew in size and strength as we moved westward. It tumbled and rolled around great boulders, the water itself a light glacial-green and infinitely clear. Deep emerald pools formed behind natural dams and burst out in a thunderous rage.

White-capped redstarts, a type of bird also known as a river chat, skimmed the surface of the water, darting from rock to rock. Brown dippers, their tails bobbing up and down, would plunge into the water and emerge in a green pool further down the rapids.

We all came to love this valley. Nancy loved it as a place for solitude and prayer. She often walked alone, sometimes ahead of the rest and sometimes behind, as she poured out her soul in praise to her Creator. She prayed for the Khams, too. An entry from her diary on our first trip reads: "Oh, may these beautiful people, living in this beautiful land, come to know You as their own and rejoice in You as their Redeemer."

Both nights on the trail, we pitched a tent for sleeping. The Tibetans slept under a tarp canopy stretched from the piles of gear and saddle-bags to pegs driven into the ground. Frost was heavy on the ground both mornings. We cooked our food on an open fire, and we carried our food supplies with us. Steve was old enough to know that life was at its best. Even Daniel, sitting in his mother's lap, wrapped in heavy blankets, seemed to revel in the firelit company under the cold stars. Watching the dancing fire, he was soon overcome by drowsiness and drifted into a sound sleep.

The horses grazed most of the night, the tinkling of their bells and the sound of munching grass in the small meadow a constant reminder of their presence. The Tibetans drifted in and out of sleep throughout the night, occasionally jumping to their feet to stand at the edge of the clearing and shout high-pitched calls into the forest. The horses were in constant danger of falling prey to leopards that lurked in the shadows at the edge of forest clearings.

At three thirty in the afternoon on the third day, two hours after the sun had already set behind the towering ridge that marched up from the south, we rounded the last bend in the gorge and there before us, in the valley opening, lay the cluster of villages known collectively as Taka-Shera. The villages of Upper and Lower Shera were already deep in shadow, giving the false impression that night was close at hand.

Nancy was riding on horseback with the two boys a full quarter of a mile ahead of me. As I watched them ford a small stream passing along the edges of Upper Shera, an inexplicable, cold terror thrust its icy fingers deep into my heart. It was a terror all of us were to feel in the months to come, and it always seemed to strike first as we rounded the last bend in the trail: we felt like intruders into a sinister, forbidden realm.

A half hour later, we arrived in Lower Shera and made our way to Krishna's house at the far end of the village. Dozens of children, some jumping from behind stone walls and others darting out of narrow alleyways, began a noisy procession behind us. As we proceeded, they shouted out to their friends on the rooftops above, who in turn shouted into the doorways of the houses on the upper levels. Within minutes, hundreds of curious people surrounded our doorway.

The pack-horses were already feeling sore and cantankerous after carrying their cumbersome loads the whole day; with the added agitation of being rushed upon by hundreds of people, they kicked several people to the ground and bit at others. Trying to get the loads off the animals and to the doorway of the house, I was feeling as disgruntled as the horses, but I had to act with a bit more civility.

The door of the house was secured by a chain and padlock, and Nancy and the boys, unable to get into the house, were crushed into a corner of the porch. Those lucky enough to get to the head of the crowd were pulling on their clothing, pinching their white skin, and stroking their blond hair. As we piled our gear beside the door, everyone was tugging at the loads, demanding that the boxes be opened so they could inspect our treasures.

To our great relief, Krishna finally arrived. Irritated at the unruly behavior of the villagers, he shouted a few angry words at them, forcing them to make a bit more room. He unchained the door and helped us get our goods inside. But with everything heaped inside, there was precious little room for any of us even to move around. As darkness began to settle, the crowd slowly dissipated.

We stabled the horses in the cattle byre below the house with a few bundles of straw, and then Krishna built a fire for us in the firepit on the porch. There we cooked a simple meal, and after eating, Krishna, with the two Tibetans, went off to find lodging elsewhere in the village. With the light of our flashlights, we opened some of our boxes, located our kerosene lamps, and then cleared a space inside the house around the firepit just big enough for the four of us to sleep.

The boys, tucked into their sleeping bags, were soon fast asleep, and Nancy and I slipped out through a private side door leading onto the terraced rooftop of the house below us. The night air was cold, and we stood in silence, shivering at the scene before us. The moon had not yet crested above the ridge, but its glow was already beginning to light the sky. In its eerie light the mountains seemed to tower higher than they did in the light of day. Our minds raced with strange imaginations, and everything took on an exaggerated appearance. We both knew all too well that the closest semblance of civilization was at least a week's hike away over several ranges of mountains; we felt better not talking about it.

Across the river, a mile away, the great village of Taka, a single structure of three hundred tightly connected houses, rose in black shadows on the sides of the mountain like a mighty fortress. Tiny red lights, the fires of pitch-pine torches, flickered occasionally in the murky darkness as people moved silently through the labyrinth of the village's dark passages. Then the torches would sputter out, casting all in darkness again.

The distant sound of a shaman's drum broke the silence, and Nancy slipped her hand into mine. Grasping it firmly, I tucked it into the warmth of my coat pocket. "I'm scared," she whispered quietly as she shivered next to me. I was, too, but I couldn't admit it. At least one of us, I thought, had to pretend everything would be all right.

We slipped back into the tiny room. The boys were asleep on the dirt floor, oblivious to the strange world we had entered. Boxes were stacked against one wall, and against another, saddlebags and stocks of supplies were heaped in piles: medicines, canned goods, and sacks of rice and beans.

Slowly, the irony of the situation began to dawn upon us. We had labored years for this—studying, training, planning, and preparing—and now this was it. The sum total of our belongings was stacked into a small heap of wooden boxes and smelly leather saddlebags. Home was a tiny, dirt-floored hovel with a ceiling so low we weren't even able to stand upright. We were living with wild, unrestrained people, whose language we couldn't understand. Worst of all, we couldn't guarantee our own safety, and in the case of a real emergency, we could do nothing for our children.

The first seeds of doubt were beginning to make their way into our consciousness. Were we really following God's calling, or were we recklessly pursuing our own foolish romanticism? Our confidence died a bit that night.

Chapter 4: Learning to Cope in Bumbleville

The rough buildings have wood doors and arches, and filthy Mongol faces, snot-nosed, wild, laugh at the strangers from the crooked windows. Among the raffish folk [of this place], dirt is worn like skin, and the children's faces are round crusts of sores and grime. They give off an earthy smell of sweat and fire smoke and the oil of human leather.
—*Peter Matthiessen,* The Snow Leopard

Angdrak stayed on with us as a hired hand for our first stay in the village. He seemed to have a good understanding of the kinds of things we needed and knew how to go about obtaining them for us. He had engaged in numerous salt trading trips to this very village, and he knew a lot of people. Now he acted as our go-between. He bought potatoes and eggs for us, did most of our cooking, ran errands, and negotiated deals. His presence made our adjustment a whole lot easier.

His one irritating vice was a penchant for liquor, and he often came back from the village late in the night, almost too drunk to stumble up the stairs and crawl into his sleeping bag. On the mornings following, it was too much for him to get the fire started and dump a little oatmeal into the cooking pot. At times he was useless until midday, suffering from a hangover and a throbbing headache.

We did our best at making our little hovel as livable as possible. Kham houses usually consist of three rooms. On the ground level is a cattle byre, the back half of which is dug into the mountainside. This forms a foundation for the upper levels of the house. At night, the cattle are bedded inside on a layer of clean corn stalks with a few bundles of

Villagers occupy the floor above the cattle

The cattle yard and "private corner"

straw and fodder for feed. Twice a year, once in the spring and again in the fall, the byre floors are cleaned and the compost plowed into the fields. In front of the byre is a small, walled-in cattle yard where the cattle congregate each morning for milking and sunning before being taken to pasture. From the cattle yard, stone steps lead to the second level of the house, the level occupied by people.

In a semi-private corner under the stairway, partially protected from the pathway, the occupants of the house defecate on the floor. Scavenger dogs and pot-bellied swine keep those corners clean, but they mess up the rest of the village with their own excrement. Adults clean themselves with water, but for babies and small children, the wet, warm tongue of a dog is readily available. When they're finished relieving themselves, they bend forward, feet spread apart, and invitingly call, "Cho cho." The dogs come to lick their bottoms clean. The worst part, though, was watching the same dogs lick the platters clean at the end of a meal.

An outer room or veranda, open on the front and facing south if possible, to secure what little warmth there is from the winter sun, is the place for carrying out domestic daytime activities—spinning wool, weaving, sewing, stilling liquor, grinding grain on querns (hand mills), and daytime cooking. The outer edges of the veranda extend a few feet over the cattle yard, forming a roof beyond the outer wall of the cattle byre. Here, protected from the elements, a supply of firewood is stacked to the ceiling.

The veranda, used for daytime activities

From the veranda, a narrow doorway no more than four feet high leads into the inner room of the house. There are no windows, only a small smoke-hole less than a foot square for ventilation. The room is as dark as an unlit coal cellar, even in the daytime, and one can't find one's way around without a light. A firepit occupies the central part of the room. The ceiling is no more than five feet high, and soot from the fires of countless generations hangs in beehive-like clusters from the slats and beams of the low ceiling. Until we cultivated the habit of moving around indoors in a perpetual back-aching stoop, our hair and clothes were filled with soot and grime.

We never used the fire inside the house but did all of our cooking at the outer firepit during the daylight hours. The intense smoke inside the house was too much for our sensitive eyes, noses, and lungs. For warmth, we installed the thirty-gallon stove I had built in Kathmandu. We thrust a chimney, complete with all the necessary bends and elbows, out through the small ventilation hole. The area in the center of the room, which had been occupied by the firepit, gave us a few extra feet of precious living space. Sitting inside at night with the outer door locked and the kerosene lamps lit, we were snug, warm, and comfortable and enjoyed a few hours of respite from the ever-pressing crowds.

We had been in our house less than two weeks when we were awakened one night by the noise of rattling, crashing, and banging everywhere in the room at once. While Nancy and I groped for our flashlights, a copper pot crashed to the floor from a wooden shelf. Then came a shrill squeak, and I knew.

"Rats!" I croaked to Nancy in a stage whisper. "It's a horde of rats."

The rats were entering along the support beams connecting the long rows of houses. They were running across the floor, wriggling into cracks and crevices, and poking their noses into everything. Nancy's first panicked reaction was to grab Daniel and shove him into a large, empty suitcase that had small holes in the lid. The rest of us shrank into our bags, pulling the covers over our faces as the creepy little monsters noisily scampered through the house and all over us for the next fifteen minutes. Rats landed across the room as we kicked and flailed from inside our bags.

This became a regular occurrence; every three or four weeks we would have another rodent invasion. Because the whole village is inter-connected, the rats have access from one house to the next. They travel in troops, completing their full circuit in a month or less.

The dark inner room

* * *

As unpleasant as being overrun by rats might sound, it wasn't as difficult as the almost total disregard for privacy we had to endure from the people. You could kick rats, people you had to relate to with a certain amount of civility. Privacy may well be the most highly prized commodity in our Western societies, at least it seemed so to us; it was certainly one of the most difficult to give up. In Shera, we were never beyond the reach of prying eyes.

After we had been in the village about two weeks, the people discovered that we made a habit of eating early in the evening around the outside firepit. They decided to place a sentry, the town crier, on a boulder above the house. As soon as we would pull the pot from the fire, the crier would climb a ladder to a vantage point further up and cry into the village, "They've started eating!"

Before the food was in our plates, the nearer ones were already arriving. As the porch filled, we would sometimes be almost pushed into the fire. Those directly behind us would press against our backs and peer over our shoulders. Hacking and coughing, they would call out detailed descriptions to the less fortunate ones at the back of the crowd. Describing everything on our plates and how we went about eating, their comments were often punctuated with roars of laughter.

Among themselves, it was considered rude to watch someone eat. It was at mealtimes that unwanted and lurking spirits could be passed on to others, and great care always had to be exercised. Even in the absence of malicious intent, a person's safety could not be guaranteed. Such was common knowledge. If a visitor arrived at another's house at mealtime, the caller would politely wait outside smoking his pipe until given the assurance that he was welcome to venture inside to the sanctity of the family hearth.

But things were different for us, primarily because we were outside the rules that govern close-knit, communal societies. We couldn't even speak their language. We conversed with them in broken Nepali, and the gibberish we used among ourselves made no sense to them at all.

This alone was enough to establish us as sub-human, on par with dogs and idiots.

There was another behavioral principle at work, too, something we didn't even suspect. When you begin life in such a village, your first encounters are very likely to be with the less desirable members of the community—the fringe elements, the busybodies and gadabouts. The honest, hardworking citizens—the core of the society—are often the quiet ones, busy with their own lives and minding their own business. It was some time before we had significant dealings with any of those citizens, and it was also a good while before we realized we were being treated with less respect than they demanded of each other.

We just thought these were crude, offensive people—but that wasn't entirely so. They had never seen the likes of us before, and adjustments were being made in both directions. On the one hand, they were testing our limitations, and we, ignorant of the rules and careful not to offend anyone, were accepting everything they dealt.

* * *

One of the great strengths of most tribal people is that they know better than to take themselves too seriously. The flip side, of course, is that they don't take anyone else seriously either. The instinct is to see life in a comic light, and in the end, self-aggrandizement is the biggest joke of all. Village elders, chieftains, and headmen come from common village stock, and no one, regardless of status, rises far above his humble beginnings. There are no titles or uniforms to distinguish the great from the humble.

Living together in close proximity, everyone is everyone else's intimate, and nowhere is this more apparent than in their frequent travels across vast reaches of alpine wilderness. Thrown together into tiny stone huts for shelter, there is no one who doesn't know the sound of the king's or the headman's flatulence; though perhaps this is not as bad as the alternative—discovering that the emperor has no clothes. Jokes about such matters abound.

What sets the truly great man or woman apart from the rest is not birth but something else: wisdom, good judgment, a deeper humanity, or sometimes just plain cunning (which is brought down quickly). The Khams' closest neighbors to the west are high-caste Hindus—the Brahmins and Chetris (including the Thakuri Shahs) of Rukum—who, like the children of Abraham, claim elevated status and privilege based upon their birth. Positions of power, too, are passed on as birthrights, a laughable idea that, according to Khams, inevitably puts idiots in charge. "A Hindu prince," the Khams like to remind their children, "is the object of constant pampering and, unattended, doesn't know not to wipe his arse with nettles."

When such people venture into Kham country, they are treated with feigned deference, but all the while, the Khams look for opportunities to make them the butt of some joke. Brahmins, for example, like to claim that cornmeal, the staple diet of the Khams, is unacceptable to Brahmins because of their high birth. They demand rice of their hosts, but with the reminder that even rice, prepared by a lesser people, can be made *chokho* ("holy") only by adding generous allotments of *ghee*. The Khams oblige them by adding beef or pork fat—an anathema to the Hindus. Usually, no one is the wiser, but the Khams feel a whole lot better, having put their smug and self-imposed rulers in their place.

Teenage girls are the most uncouth. They get great amusement out

of speaking to an outsider in Kham with feigned sincerity, using speech so vulgar that anyone would be shocked. Their girl-friends are always close at hand, rolling on the ground in fits of laughter. When a group of girls meets a lone stranger on the trail, one of their most common forms of greeting is, "How is your erection today?"

I never knew how to respond to that one. Was I supposed to say "It's doing great" or "Not so good today as yesterday"?

One day an old man working in his fields overheard what was going on, and after the girls passed he called me to his field. "They'll always treat you like an outsider until you respond with the right answer," he said.

"You mean there's a right answer?" I asked in disbelief.

"Just say," he instructed me, "if I used it on you, it would kill you!"

The next time I was greeted with the usual greeting, I gave the instructed response. The girls rushed into the field below, hid behind some boulders, and laughed uncontrollably. Word spread quickly that "Sahib knows the answer," and I was bothered no more.

I have watched teenage girls sit across the fire from some unsuspecting Nepali official as he eats rice as a guest in their homes. When their parents' backs are turned, they lift their skirts and expose their genitals. To the prudish Hindus, it is more than they can bear. We, of course, were not exempt from any of this and were exposed to the full range of Kham initiation rites. Even Angdrak, the Tibetan Khampa, was astounded by the crudeness of the villagers' behavior, especially that of the women and girls. Although he had a bond-friend in Shera, he had never been exposed to this behavior over such a long time. After his initial stay with us, he refused to return ever again. He had had enough.

But the most disturbing thing was our own response. We had come halfway around the world with idealistic visions of what it would be like to serve these people, and now that we were here, we found ourselves secretly hating them more every day. *What's the matter with these idiots,* we thought. *Can't they see that we're doing this for them?* The British, writing a hundred and fifty years earlier in their military handbooks for the Gurkhas, had it right after all: recruits from these parts weren't to be trusted. They were "wild, quarrelsome, and of inferior intelligence."

At first we refused to admit our feelings even to ourselves, but we couldn't avoid them forever. At night, together, Nancy and I began to cry out to God to help us love these horrid people. Was it even possible?

Then, gradually, another problem began to emerge. It had to do with the Khams' questioning of our intentions. We kept staying on. Whatever for? We were becoming suspect. We had arrived, of course, bearing official letters from the university and other government agencies. But this only corroborated our collusion with officialdom, a source of much of the Khams' grief and pain for generations. These people knew about exploitation.

Early in the 1900s, a time some of the old men still remembered, the ruling Ranas had discovered that the people of these northern valleys were engaged in a lucrative copper mining industry. People like the Khams tunneled into the mountains with crude hammers and chisels, following the hidden veins, dragging out to the surface the precious, green ore. They smelted it in their own smithies and fashioned ornate water jugs, drinking bowls, and other beautiful vessels.

There was no need, even, to search for export markets. The goods sold themselves. Tibetans brought them coral, turquoise, salt, and other commodities in trade for the copper. Tribes to the south brought rice, grain, and colorful fabric. Then the Ranas levied an annual tax of nine dharni (about forty-five pounds, or twenty kilograms) of pure, smelted copper per household on each of the villages. There was nothing left for trade, and the mines were shut down. Today, there is as much copper as before, but no one knows how to mine it anymore.

It was assumed, at first, that we had come from Nepal—a faraway country that most knew of only as a name. They lived in their own land of "Tunam" on the borders of "Four Thousand Mountains" to the south and "Eight Thousand Mountains" to the north. As they observed us strolling up and down the river, or clambering about the hillsides with cameras in hand, the rumor began to spread that we were the advance front of an invasion army.

They were convinced that we had discovered gold and precious gems in their valley and would soon be taking over. We became vaguely aware of these sentiments when old ladies would appear at our doorway and ask for protection when the invading armies arrived. Who knows what may have happened if the rumor had persisted. We doubt if the rumor had much credence with the younger people, but it was confirmed to us on more than one occasion that, yes, this was a topic often discussed around Kham hearths at night. But through a strange set of circumstances, the rumor changed to something even more bizarre.

As we began to learn bits and pieces of their language, the people questioned us more and more about who we were and where we had come from. One afternoon, an old man, after watching us closely and quietly for a long time held out his closed fist. Pointing to the top of his hand said, "We live here." Then, pointing to the underside of his fist, he asked, "Did you come from here?"

"Yes," I replied, astounded that an old man from the mountains would know something about the roundness of the earth.

He eyed me closely for a long time while those around him sat in shocked silence. Then, slowly he asked the clinching question, "When it's daytime here, is it nighttime there?"

"Yes," I assured him with enthusiasm.

"And so when it's nighttime here, it's daytime there," he added with finality. When I assured him that this was also true, everyone cast knowing glances at each other and, shaking their heads, they quietly left.

Over the next few weeks, the question of our origin was the one most asked. It wasn't until much later that we learned the unintended significance of what we were saying.

In Kham cosmology, the universe is composed of three layers: the overworld inhabited by gods and divine beings, this world inhabited by humans, and the underworld inhabited by demons and the dead. The underworld is the exact inverse of this world. What is dark-skinned here is light-skinned there, and when it's daytime here, it's nighttime there. Even offerings made to deceased ancestors have to be given in an inverse fashion. They are placed in a broken vessel and presented upside down to ensure that they will arrive whole and right-side-up in the underworld. If cloth is part of the offering, even the thread in the fabric has to be spun counter-clockwise.

Unwittingly, we had confirmed that we came from the land of the dead. Because we were visitors from the netherworld, it was clear to them that we were lost spirits, having come back to the wrong world. The normal rules of common courtesy could be suspended in our case without shame.

Several years later, after I had learned to speak Kham fluently, I watched the tables turn, quite comically and unexpectedly, to my own advantage. I was passing through a remote Kham village in a valley I had never visited before. I propped my load on a stone wall in the center of the village and asked, in perfect Kham, for a drink of water. Suddenly leopard-skin rugs were spread on the terraced rooftop, and I was politely asked to be seated.

The women of the village quickly scurried to their cooking fires and began preparing food. I found myself alone with an ancient, wrinkled man with a few strands of white whiskers hanging from his chin. He sat directly in front of me, no more than two feet away, gazing at me unblinkingly as his hands continued automatically to turn yarn on a small spindle. "Where's everyone gone, and what's all the commotion about?" I asked.

Holding the spindle between the palms of his hands and setting it in motion with a swift spinning action, he replied, "It's not often that the gods come to visit us!"

* * *

Every village has its know-it-all, someone eager to demonstrate to those around him his superior grasp of things too profound for the simple minds of the average villager. In Shera this person was Hakalya, and he was a constant source of irritation to Angdrak. He hung around from morning to night with apparently nothing better to do than impress other passersby with his detailed explanations of how our gadgets worked.

One afternoon when no one else was around, Hakalya demanded of Angdrak a description of the contents of one kitchen box he had not yet seen opened. Angdrak pulled out a cardboard box of laundry detergent. "This," he said, "is a special spice the sahibs put into their food for flavoring."

"Give me a taste," Hakalya demanded.

"Oh, I couldn't do that," Angdrak replied, "the sahibs would be angry."

"Just a bit in the palm of my hand," he pleaded. "They'll never know."

"Well, all right," Angdrak agreed, feigning reluctance, "but pop it into your mouth quickly, and then suck on it slowly to get the full taste."

With the soap powder in his mouth, Hakalya realized he had been made the butt of a joke, but he pretended as long as possible not to notice. Finally he leaped from the porch and disappeared into the village. We didn't see him again for several hours, and when he did return, the topic never came up again.

Each of us developed our own methods for stealing a few moments of privacy. None of them are what I would recommend as models of behavior, but we were desperate. Nancy, one afternoon, was inundated by a houseful of wenches and hags who began pestering her incessantly. They demanded empty tin cans and other items. When she couldn't produce what they wanted, they continued with persistence and eventually began pulling her hair and twisting her breasts.

After Nancy had had all she could stand, she poured a small bottle of kerosene (which they could identify only as water) into the all-but-dead firepit. She added a few sticks, and as the coals began to produce a misty gas, she pretended to chant a few magic charms over the firepit. Waving her arms about, she tossed in a match, and the firepit burst into flame. The women nearly trampled each other getting out of the house, and she had a couple hours of peace.

* * *

In spite of that single act of desperation, Nancy did much to alleviate suspicions during those early months. Though it was inconvenient and attracted even greater numbers of visitors, Nancy set up a small clinic on the veranda of our house to help lighten the obvious burden of suffering to which these people were constant victims. Not being a trained nurse, and lacking proper facilities or supplies, she was limited in what she could do. Many diseases were in their advanced stages, and

Nancy treats patients

she could do little but give them medications to alleviate some of their pain. But in many cases, especially when dealing with cuts, abrasions, burns, ear and eye infections, broken bones, and parasites, there was a lot she could accomplish.

There was one factor working in Nancy's favor: it was obvious that everyone was suffering from intestinal parasites, especially tapeworms and roundworms. If a case baffled her or she knew there was no permanent solution with her limited resources, she could always give her patients a dose of worm medicine. The results were always impressive and immediate.

People boasted with each other about how many worms they had dropped, or the length of tapeworms they had produced. Harka Bahadur, the village headman, returned one morning, a triumphant grin on his face, to brag of forty-one large, white ascarides from a single stool. Another was proud of a single tapeworm more than thirty feet long.

The villagers were quick to recognize Nancy's obvious compassion and were eager to repay her kindness with eggs, potatoes, grain, and other foodstuffs, their only means of exchange. Things were beginning to change. Thankfully, we were, too.

Steve with his catch

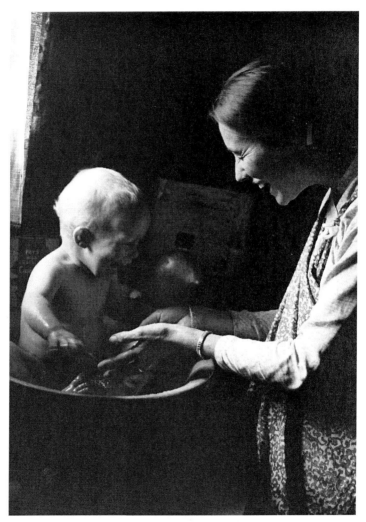

Nancy gives baby Daniel a bath

Chapter 5: Hasta Ram Budha

O good old man! how well in thee appears
The constant service of the antique world,
When service sweat for duty, not for mead!
Thou art not for the fashion of these times,
Where none will sweat but for promotion.
—William Shakespeare, As You Like It

As scheduled, I returned to the airstrip in Dhorpatan on November 27, 1969, to meet the next plane and collect the remainder of our goods. Nancy and the boys remained in the village alone, a gutsy thing to do this early in our tenure. We were scheduled to leave as a family on February 10 for Kathmandu, but while in Dhorpatan, I learned of the strong possibility that Dhorpatan might be snowed in by that time. So I arranged for an earlier pickup, on January 19, and returned to the village as quickly as possible with our supplies.

As it turned out, heavy snows fell on the very night of the nineteenth, and the airstrip remained snowbound for at least a month afterward. Furthermore, we had at that point just finished the last of our food supplies and had only seven rupees (seventy cents) left to our name. A long trek over the snowy mountains without money would have been impossible; we made our exit just in time.

I had been trying, persistently, to find someone in Shera willing to accompany us to Kathmandu and to help me learn Kham. Some expressed a mild interest, but all made excuses in the end, turning down their chance to fly off in the "great iron eagle" from Dhorpatan to the legendary land of "Nepal." In so doing, they turned down the tempting offer of an easy salary as well.

In desperation, on the afternoon of January 14, I decided to cross the river to the village of Taka to seek the counsel of the village headman there. I had met him once before, and he seemed a reasonable man. Could he recommend a suitable language helper? I hoped so.

Though less than a mile away as the crow flies, it takes some effort to get there. The bridge is a mile upriver, where it spans the cascading waterway in three dizzying stages. The logs cling to the tops of boulders. From there, the trail turns downriver for a mile and a half, then climbs steadily for about two hundred feet until it enters the ancient dry lakebed on the slopes of which the village rises steeply.

Practicing for Magh Sangrat

When I arrived at the village entrance, I saw a dozen men in a nearby field pulling arrows from a target. It was *Magh Sangrat*, the big day for archery contests and bouts of drinking. The headman was with the archers, and I began making my way towards him. My attention was arrested, though, by a man standing at the edge of the group. He was a well-built, handsome man with an engaging smile and intelligent face. Something about him stopped me in my tracks. A voice inside me kept saying, "That's the man. Take him!" I stopped for a moment, regained my composure, and stepped up to him.

"You come with me," I said in Nepali, without hesitation.

He looked startled. "Who, me? Why? Where are we going?"

Realizing then that I hadn't even introduced myself, I said, "Don't worry, I'm the sahib from across the river. My family and I are leaving for Kathmandu the day after tomorrow, and I want you to come with us. I need someone to teach me Kham."

Still surprised, he replied, "Well, if you're looking for a teacher, I'm sure you could find someone in a village this size."

"I'm not looking for just anyone," I answered with conviction. "I've come for you!"

He paused for a few seconds, not sure what to do. He could see that I was serious, and after some talk with his friends, he invited me to his house. "Come, meet my family," he said. "Besides, I need to talk with my wife about this. I'm not sure she'll agree."

When we arrived at his house, he spread a rug on the floor and asked me to sit. He called out to his wife, and she emerged from the inner room. "We have a guest," he said, "the sahib from across the river. Put on the teapot." That was my introduction to his wife.

As the two of them busied themselves preparing tea, they began discussing my proposal in the secrecy of their own language. Their looks were stoic, and I couldn't tell how the conversation was going. Then suddenly, without explanation, he turned to me and said, "Okay, I'll go with you. When do we leave?"

I didn't attempt to hide my delight. "We'll leave the day after tomorrow as soon as it begins to dawn," I said excitedly. "I'll come by to see you again tomorrow afternoon to make the final arrangements."

I returned to Shera that evening, arriving just before dark. I told Nancy the good news. "Not only have I found someone willing to go with us," I told her, "but there's something strangely compelling about him that I can't explain."

The man's name was Hasta Ram.

The right man

* * *

"The night after our first meeting," Hasta Ram told me some months later, "was one of the most fitful, restless nights I have ever spent." Sleep eluded him. "Why did I agree to go with a man I don't even know?" he asked himself over and over again. "And why did he specifically want *me*?" It just didn't make sense.

He tried his best to come up with a reasonable excuse to stay home, but nothing seemed right. He had already given his word, and he had never gone back on his word.

Finally, in the early hours of the morning, he fell into a disturbed sleep. He dreamed that he was standing in a large meadow with a great throng of people around him. Suddenly, he saw me approach, walking rapidly on tall stilts with Nancy by my side. He watched me walk directly towards him, bypassing all others. "Come, it's time to go," he heard me say. Without hesitation, he picked up his rucksack and followed me down the trail.

A rooster crowed, and he woke from his sleep. He rubbed his eyes and wondered at the meaning of this strange dream. Suddenly, it was clear to him. There was no doubt that he had to go. Whether for good or ill, he didn't know, but this was his destiny.

When I arrived at Hasta Ram's house again on the following afternoon, he seemed absorbed—about what, I couldn't tell. He spread out a sheepskin rug on the veranda and asked me to sit. He wanted to "ask me a few questions," he said.

Oh no, I thought with disappointment. *He'll probably give me an excuse why he can't come.*

He struck up an amiable conversation, told me a bit about himself, and asked questions about my family. He said he had observed us at a distance from across the river as he sat on the hillside some afternoons with his cows.

Then, suddenly, he asked, "Is the ring on your finger a religious symbol?"

"Well, sort of," I replied. "It's a symbol of marriage."

"But you're a Christian, aren't you?" he asked.

"Yes I am," I replied, wondering at his curiosity.

Then, point-blank, right out of the blue came the question: "Do you know about one called Jesus Christ?"

I was astonished. Unable to find my voice, I nodded my head in the affirmative and stammered, "Where did you ever hear that name?"

Without answering, he got to his feet, took a small key from his pocket, and walked to a locked metal trunk in the corner of the room. He turned the key in the lock, opened the lid, and drew out a small Nepali booklet, dog-eared and worn, the pages brown with age, some falling loose from their staple binding.

"I read this book every day," he said, "as I sit with my cows on the hillside. I carry it everywhere I go. It tells about one called Jesus, but I have not till today found anyone who knows anything about him. If I go with you, will you promise me something?" he asked.

"What is that?" I asked.

"I'll teach you my language,"

Hasta Ram and David study together

he said. "But I'd really like it if you would teach me all you know about this man."

My heart beat wildly. "I can do that," I answered. "I'd be happy to teach you all I know about him."

"Then I'll go with you to Shera tonight," he replied. "I'll sleep on your porch, and we'll leave for Dhorpatan at the break of day."

The following morning, January 16, we left Shera before daybreak. The walk to Dhorpatan, twenty-five miles away, had no habitations along the way, and we needed to reach our destination before nightfall.

Since most of the Tibetans would already have left on trading trips to the south to escape the bitter cold, we knew it would be difficult to find accommodation. It's an unpleasant experience to arrive in a village after dark and stumble from house to house trying to find someone to take you in. It is worse yet when most of the village is empty and the houses are boarded up.

We met no one the entire way, and we seldom stopped. Though long and tiring, the trip was pleasant. Nancy rode much of the way, with Steve seated in the saddle in front of her and Daniel in a baby-carrier on her back. On occasion, she dismounted and walked a mile or two to exercise her legs and get her blood circulating. Only Daniel, riding in the pack, was unable to move much. But he complained little and somehow managed to keep warm in spite of the cold.

At various points along the trail, we encountered small streams that in the summer had tumbled noisily out of the forest. Now they were as silent as the land itself, frozen in their courses. One large stream was a frozen cascade, a thick layer of gnarled ice clinging to enormous boulders by its icy fingers. Below, deep beneath the ice, the faint sound of trickling water could still be heard. From one side to the other was fifteen or twenty feet, and the surface was too slippery for the horse to get a sound footing.

Hasta Ram went out onto the ice and chipped a pathway across its surface with a sharp stone, tossing gravel onto the surface as he went. Then, we carefully led the horse across to the other side. The ice easily supported his weight. It was bitterly cold.

Nancy and the boys in front of the frozen stream

Hasta Ram chips a path through the ice

* * *

Heavy darkness fell when we were still about two miles short of Dhorpatan. As we rounded the last bend, the village came into full view. The only light we could see emanated from a kerosene lamp in the Tibetan monastery a hundred feet above the trail. So that was where we headed.

We pounded on the door, and the monk who opened it was so astonished when he saw us that you would have thought he had seen a ghost. After the initial shock, he welcomed us in and introduced us to the chief lama. We were soon seated around the clay stove in the monastery kitchen, sipping yak-butter tea and enjoying a meal of noodles and mutton.

A few years later, the same chief lama was discovered to be a *tulku* (a high reincarnation of a prominent lama lineage). He is now the *rimpoche* (head abbot) at one of the great monasteries of Bodhnath in Kathmandu.

The lamas were especially interested in Steve, then just a little over three years old, though he was small for his age, which made him seem even younger. But his demeanor was serious, and he spoke with intelligent curiosity. He asked (in Nepali) about the things he observed around him, directing some of his comments to the monks themselves. They began treating him with unusual deference, apparently thinking that he, too, might be the reincarnation of some great soul.

Because of the monks' interest in Steve, they offered us, for the two nights we stayed there, the ornately decorated shrine room where the chief lama also had his sleeping chamber. In the shrine room, they kept their religious artifacts, butter lamps, incense, rows of Buddhist scriptures, and *tangka* paintings. In addition, three wooden beds richly laden with thick, ornate Tibetan carpets were pushed against the walls.

The chief lama gave Steve the grand central bed, and Nancy and I were given the two side beds. We put Daniel into an apple crate stuffed with rags and warm bedding. A thermometer hanging inside the room read ten degrees Fahrenheit (minus twelve degrees Centigrade). The floor was made of moist earth, now frozen hard and covered with white frost. Hasta Ram slept with the monks in the monastery kitchen. There, they kept the fires burning and passed the nights far more enjoyably than we did. Sometimes, high privilege has its drawbacks. Actually, I wondered if the lamas ever slept in the ice room at all.

The plane arrived from Kathmandu on January 19, as planned. Wayne Aeschliman, our pilot, told us later that he almost wept when he saw us. We were thin, and our skin was black from the soot and grime of two months of smoky fires and sooty houses. We had almost no way of keeping clean. But he sensed our exuberance, too, and he could see that in Hasta Ram we had found a prince of a man.

*"A good shepherd grazes his sheep on the
firstfruits of the alpine meadows."*

Chapter 6: From Shepherd to Soldier

Now therefore, thus you shall say to my servant David, "Thus says the LORD of hosts, 'I took you from the pasture, from follow-ing the sheep, that you should be ruler over my people Israel.'"
—2 Samuel 7:8, KJV

After arriving in Kathmandu, we began to learn more about Hasta Ram. From childhood, he had grown up as a shepherd, watching his father's sheep. In the summer, he lived in the high alpine country north of the village at altitudes between 12,000 and 15,000 feet. Living in black, goat-hair tents, he roamed from one mountain ridge to the next and from one alpine bowl to the next, always in search of fresh grass.

A Kham watchword says, "A good shepherd grazes his sheep on the firstfruits of the alpine meadows." He keeps his tent in one place no more than five or six days. Each morning, he leads his sheep in a differ-ent direction, working outward like the spokes of a wheel, until he has grazed an entire area. Then, he moves to a new location as fresh as the last.

Hasta Ram's father was a harsh and unforgiving man. He held his sons responsible for the loss of every sheep, whether by disease, acci-dent, or predators. Every loss was answered with a sound beating and the discipline of an unpleasant task—like going several thousand feet down to timberline to bring back a load of firewood.

One year, early in the summer, shortly after moving his sheep to the alpine meadows, a late snowstorm cut Hasta Ram off from village food supplies. He waited four days in vain for his supply man, and then, in a weakened state, he killed one of the sheep to keep himself alive. When his father learned of it, he punished him severely.

Hasta Ram began to despise his father and longed to get out from under his thumb. In the early 1940s, he started hearing rumors of a war in the outside world. He also heard that the British in India were eager to recruit "Mongolian" tribesmen from the highlands of Nepal to fight in their foreign campaigns. They were especially interested in men who were accustomed to harsh conditions and capable of carrying heavy loads for long distances. Better still if such men had no education: they would be less likely to question orders.

In 1943, when he was eighteen years old, Hasta Ram left his father's sheep in the care of a trusted friend and ran away from home to join the army. He traveled with another friend who was also eager to join. His friend had been to India once before and knew the way to the recruiting station. The two boys walked barefoot 150 miles over ranges and ranges of mountains until they came to the plains of India.

Hasta Ram recounted later that while living in the mountains, listening to rumors of war, he had also heard about great "flat places" on the earth. He imagined that they were nothing more than openings in the mountains, like the valley of Dhorpatan, a mile and a half wide.

"When I arrived in India, I was astounded," he said. "The flat land went on and on so far that eventually we even lost sight of the mountains."

The two young shepherds eventually arrived in Gorakhpur, one of the British recruiting stations in northern India. When the recruiting officer saw them, he was impressed: two sturdy, well-built lads, barefoot and dressed in coarse homespun garments. After a thorough physical, they were inducted into the army and issued military uniforms. On their first inspection, the officer stopped in front of Hasta Ram, looked him up and down, and began to laugh. "Son," he asked in amusement, "have you ever worn shoes?"

"No, sir, I haven't," Hasta Ram replied.

"I didn't think so," the officer said. "You have the left shoe on your right foot and the right shoe on your left foot!"

The entire regiment burst into laughter. Hasta Ram, his face burning red with embarrassment, vowed he never would made that mistake again.

All the new recruits were given a tour. They were shown their barracks, the officers' quarters, the mess hall, the latrines, the drill field, and all the rest. Then, each man was given a bit of pocket change to buy cigarettes and an occasional cup of tea, enough to last them until their first payday.

In the next two days, Hasta Ram went three times to the canteen for a cup of tea. On his third visit, he assaulted the soldier assigned to mess duty and gave him a good thrashing. The fight was broken up, and an officer came running to ask what the scuffle was about.

"I've come now three times for a cup of tea, and not once has this man given me a chunk of meat," Hasta Ram complained. "All I get is colored water." The Kham areas at that time served Tibetan-style tea, which was more like soup, with barley and bits of jerky in it.

The officer grinned and explained amicably, "This is tea, son. Nothing more than colored water."

After that, the British liked him even more. *With a bit of discipline,* they thought, *we've got a real soldier here.*

* * *

It was quickly apparent that Hasta Ram spoke little Nepali, so they held him in Gorakhpur and put him into Nepali classes, introducing him to the world of reading and writing. They also put him on a special high-calorie, high-protein diet, along with a rigorous body-building regimen.

From there, Hasta Ram was shipped to Hyderabad (now in Pakistan) for special commando training. He was one of the best and learned quickly. Hand-to-hand combat was the bread and butter of their courses. Their specialty was to penetrate enemy lines, *kukri* blades drawn, and dispose of the enemy quickly and silently before the victim could let out a cry.

He had finished his training and was ready to be sent to the European front when the Second World War ended. So he was sent instead to Japan with the British Occupation Forces to maintain peace and order until a new government was operational. In Tokyo, he participated in the great celebration parade of the Allied Powers under the supreme command of General MacArthur.

As part of the occupation, he was assigned to ten months' duty as a full-dress color guard at one of the eighteen gates of Emperor Hirohito's palace. There were three men at each gate: one was a Nepali Gurkha, and the other two were British, Australian, or American.

In August of 1947, India gained its independence from Great Britain. With the war over and the British Empire on the decline, the British retained only a fraction of their Gurkha regiments. The rest were turned over to the new Indian government. The Indians were eager to employ their services against the newly emerged and threatening nation of Pakistan.

The choice of who would remain with the British and who would be turned over to the Indians was purely random, decided by lot. Hasta Ram's regiment, the Fifth Royal Gurkhas, was turned over to the Indian government. For the next eighteen years, until 1965, his military career was spent in India.

Hasta Ram always regretted the loss of British command. "The British officers," he used to tell me, "always led their men into battle. We had great admiration for that."

* * *

Shortly after Indian partition, Hasta Ram was engaged in numerous battles against Pakistan over the sovereignty of Kashmir. A ceasefire was arranged by the United Nations in 1949, but the area is still in dispute. Border disputes between India and Communist China later erupted in both the high Himalayan regions of northwestern India and in the North East Frontier Agency (NEFA) lying between China and

Burma. Hasta Ram was engaged on both fronts during different parts of his career.

Hasta Ram recounted the story of one particular skirmish against the Chinese army in northeastern India in which the battle became heated. With sheer grit and outstanding courage, the Gurkhas managed to turn the tide and had the Chinese on the run. Suddenly, Hasta Ram realized that they were without a commanding officer. Running back to a grove of trees, he found the officer, "a coward of an Indian," trembling in fear behind a tree.

In a flash of rage and disgust, Hasta Ram lowered the point of his bayonet to within inches of the officer's chest. "Take your pick," he said, "lead us into battle, or die with a blade through your gut."

The officer, with his back against a tree, sucked in his stomach to avoid the bite of the cold steel. Hasta Ram shouted at him again.

Too frightened to cry out, the officer pleaded with his eyes. Hasta Ram backed off and motioned him forward with the point of his bayonet. Without a word, the officer jumped to his feet and marched into battle. He survived and never spoke a word of the incident to anyone.

I heard many such stories from Hasta Ram and knew from the start that if I wanted to keep his friendship and respect, I might be called upon some day to act with courage when flight would be a more natural choice. I hoped that I wouldn't disappoint him.

* * *

Hasta Ram knew how to fight, but he also knew how to serve. He drew a sharp line between servant and master, and an unusual relationship grew between us that persisted for many years. His military background was evident in nearly everything he did. In Kathmandu, we gave him a bed in my small study upstairs, which became his living quarters. When I went up the stairs in the morning, he would snap to attention and give a sharp salute.

This kind of relationship was disconcerting to me. All I wanted was to be his friend, not his commanding officer. But he would have nothing of it: I was the commander, and he was the soldier awaiting orders. Many times in the afternoons, I would tell him that he was free "to do anything he wanted for a couple of hours" while I did some typing. Instead, he would head for the garden to do some weeding because "if Sahib is working; how can I loaf?" If he did decide to go out, he would appear at my doorway, click his heels, and stand at attention until I acknowledged him.

"What is it?" I would ask.

"Sir," he would reply, "with your permission, I request thirty minutes' leave to make a trip to the bazaar."

"Go ahead," I would tell him, "take as long as you like; I'll be busy here for a couple of hours." He would return in exactly thirty minutes, never exceeding his original request.

Eventually, I convinced him that this was a civilian job and he didn't need to salute every time I entered his room. It took another five years for the rigidity to go out of his spine and still another five for him to grow into the God-given role he was meant to have.

Hasta Ram grew in confidence and learned over time how heavily I relied on his judgment. We developed a deep bond of mutual trust and respect. The time would come when Hasta Ram would be the irrefutable *hakim*, the man in charge, especially in the village. The villagers, in their struggle against a repressive government, would turn to him; they recognized his leadership as innate and incontrovertible. He drew the lines in the village and expected all of us to comply. Authority was natural to him, and he wore it well. But I'm getting ahead of my story.

Hasta Ram and Steve

Chapter 7: Believing God

*Do not be astonished to see simple people believing without
argument. God makes them love him and hate themselves. He
inclines their hearts to believe. We shall never believe, with an
effective belief and faith, unless God inclines our hearts, and we
shall believe as soon as he does so... It takes no more than this in
order to convince men whose hearts are thus disposed and who
have such an understanding of their duty and incapacity.*
—*Blaise Pascal,* Pensées

When we arrived in Kathmandu for the first time, I gave Hasta Ram
a Nepali New Testament. "This book," I told him, "tells more about
Jesus Christ, the one you've been inquiring about. Read it when you get
a chance, and if you have any questions, I'll try to help you."

From that day on, he spent all his spare time reading the Bible. Much
of it was extremely difficult for him to understand; it had been translated into a high, literary form. But he stuck with it anyway. Many of
the words were borrowed from Sanskrit and could be understood only
by an educated elite. The vocabulary was certainly beyond my ability,
and I was of little help to him.

Before long, I found something more suitable: a book of Bible stories
from both Testaments. At least he could begin to understand some of
the historical foundations of the Christian faith. But more than that,
they stirred within him deep longings after God. He read the stories
over and over again.

Fortunately for us, a small Christian fellowship had been meeting
weekly in Kathmandu for a couple of years by that time. It was led by a

gifted Nepali Christian from Darjeeling, India, Pastor Robert Kartak. The meetings were held in his own home. It was estimated in those years that there were less than a hundred Christians in the entire kingdom, a country of some 13 million people. About thirty or forty of these lived in Kathmandu, and some twenty or twenty-five attended the fellowship in Pastor Kartak's home.

I explained to Hasta Ram one day that there were a number of people in Kathmandu who followed in the ways of Jesus. They met together weekly in a Christian teacher's house. Nancy and I were going; would he like to come along?

"Sure, I guess so," he replied, a bit nonchalantly, not sure what to expect. So we took him to his first Christian meeting on January 26, 1970.

Hasta Ram was spellbound, his heart strangely moved. "It was like warm oil," he explained later, describing an enveloping feeling of comfort. He had no doubt that these were the very words of God—the God he had been seeking for years. He experienced his life's *Eureka*!

During the week, interspersed with our linguistic studies, I would have him read specific Scripture selections and then try my best to explain them to him in my rough Nepali. But his real stimulus came from the weekly meetings, and he could hardly wait for each one to arrive. It would be years before I could explain the Scriptures fluently in Kham, the language through which they would become permanently lodged in his soul.

* * *

We did a short family stint in the village from April to June 1970 and then returned to Kathmandu for the monsoon. Hasta Ram remained in the village, and we joined him again in the fall, this time for a longer stay.

After the fall harvest, Hasta Ram asked if I would like to join him on a blue sheep hunt in the mountains north of his village. He was aware that I had a good hunting rifle, and he was anxious to see how it

Hasta Ram views the high, tumbled country
Above: A hunter bags a Himalayan Thar

would perform. Like other Khams, he had nothing but an old muzzle-loading musket, hand-crafted in some remote village. Such weapons are largely ineffective unless the hunter can get within a few dozen yards of the quarry—a hard thing to do with mountain sheep in open alpine country. I was delighted at the prospect of such a hunt, having seen a number of these majestic animals from a distance when I crossed the Himalayas with Gary the year before.

We set out on a fine Saturday morning in November 1970, carrying a tent, a week's supply of food, and cold-weather gear. We crested the ridge above the village at 12,500 feet and began making our way across high, tumbled country towards the foot of the high glaciers. This was the country Hasta Ram had roamed as a boy, caring for his father's sheep. He knew every turn, every rock face, every alpine grazing bowl. We spent our first night in *Shedan Pup*, the "Abominable Snowman's Cave." Stories have it that only a generation ago, people used to put plates of food at the cave entrance and find the plates empty the next morning.

"Of course it was a *shedan*," they would tell me. "What else could it be?"

I could think of lots of things, especially after the snowman debacle in Taka early one morning. A group of villagers had come, banging excitedly on our door and saying that there was a baby *shedan* in one of the millhouses upstream. They could hear him crying. When I got there, people on their way to the potato fields were already making a high detour across the steep slope above the mill.

Their behavior even had me scared, but I really wanted to see one of those darned things, even if it grabbed me. I approached the mill cautiously and pushed the door open with my walking stick, ready to turn tail and run as soon as it said *Boo*! When my eyes grew accustomed to the darkness, all I could see was an empty room—no baby snowmen here. Then, I heard him cry. My eyes darted towards the mill shaft in its wooden bearing through the floor, and I saw the shaft rotate very, very slowly. At the nine o'clock position of each rotation, it let out a pitiful little squeaking cry. Somebody had failed to shut off the mill stream properly. So much for the *shedan*!

* * *

On the second day of the hunt, we spotted a band of twelve blue sheep making their way across the scree below us. They hadn't seen us yet, and I settled in behind a rock, waiting till they stopped. It would be a long shot, but if I didn't shoot now, they would soon pass out of sight. I squeezed the trigger, and the report echoed off the mountain walls. The sheep bolted and disappeared in a couple of seconds. I had missed; the shot went high. That was my first lesson in high-altitude marksmanship.

Anxious to vindicate myself for such a poor shot, I later shot the head off a snow partridge at a hundred yards. This time I aimed low.

That night, after embellishing our usual fare of roasted barley with a nice, plump partridge, we settled into our tent for the night. An icy wind swept off of the mighty Dhaulagiri range and, unabated across the high alpine slopes, tugged at the flaps of our tent. We lay quietly in our bags, drawing cheer from a small storm lantern flickering between us. Hasta Ram began to speak.

"I've been reading those story books you gave me," he began. "You know, the ones about God's dealings with his people."

"Yes?" I replied, encouraging him to go on.

"Well, I've been reading that much of their suffering came as a result of rejecting God and following after false gods. So I've made up my mind; I've decided to give up the old village gods and follow in the ways of Jesus. Already, last month, at one of our big festivals, I refused to put up the fetishes over my doorway. My friends tell me I'll die, but I don't think so."

The icy wind, in a sudden gust of fury, reached its angry fingers in through the tent flaps. The little flame faltered for a moment, almost

An icy hunting camp

dying. We paused, cupping our hands around the lantern, and then

Hasta Ram continued. It seemed he had hardly noticed. Only I had felt the sudden fear at being surrounded by the harsh, cold wilderness and protected by only a thin tent.

"What do you think," he asked, "will I die?"

I shivered for a moment and began to answer as best I could. "All I can tell you for sure," I replied, "is that you'll be blessed in ways you can't now imagine. But I can't say that you won't suffer. True, you won't need to worry about the old gods, but we still live in an imperfect world. You'll likely suffer from your friends, or even from the government, but you'll go through life with an inner peace and a joy that comes only from God. You've done the right thing, my friend."

Huddling together, we prayed aloud for a few minutes and then blew out the light. Hasta Ram settled into a deep sleep. But I continued to pray through much of the night. How would he fare? Could the tiny flame survive in the harsh climate of these inhospitable mountains and valleys? His expectations would certainly be dashed at some time or another. But with a heart of faith he could recover—couldn't he?—and begin to discover the true inner path, the journey that God had mapped out for his life.

Little did I know then that I had nothing to fear. My time would have been better spent praying for myself. In the years to come, Hasta Ram would teach me the ways of a Christian disciple.

David, with Putha in the background (23,773 ft.)

Chapter 8: A House of Our Own

The house was a perfect house, whether you like food or sleep or story-telling, or just sitting and thinking best, or a pleasant mixture of them all. Merely to be there was a cure for weariness, fear, and sadness.
—*J.R.R. Tolkien,* The Lord of the Rings

In December of 1969—almost a year earlier, on our first stay in the village as a family—we knew that with the coming of spring, Krishna's family and household would return, and we would no longer have a place to live. We would need a place of our own, and the sooner we got started, the better. Angdrak contacted some of the village leaders for me, and we began our negotiations. I was impressed. The whole process seemed highly efficient, and a consensus was reached promptly with hardly a hitch. In fact, it seemed almost too efficient; we were ready to begin construction in two days.

The only haggling, I noticed, was among the elders themselves, and though I understood no more than a bare minimum of the language, the discussion seemed to hinge on the issue of a building site. The dissenting voices were soon silenced, and the next day, we were assigned a beautiful site towards the eastern edge of the village, on the main pathway to the river. I suspected then that family alliances and clan politics had to do with the selection of the land; I wasn't wrong.

The next evening Angdrak and I were invited to a feast in the clan house of the man who was to be the chief beneficiary of our deal—the council chief. It was a sumptuous affair. We sat together in a large room, almost like a hall in comparison to the hovel we lived in. Flaming sticks of pitchpine on spiked metal lampstands gaily lit the room. A wild boar was roasting on the fire, and brass drinking bowls were kept filled with barley beer by quick-eyed, fleet-footed servant girls. *Hors d'oeuvres* were also plentiful: roasted potatoes plucked from the coals of the fire; chicken hearts, livers, and gizzards; and, of course, the choice parts from the innards of the boar. Sweating cooks labored over the fires, stirring the food to perfection.

There were eruptions of good-natured laughter as one joke rolled into the next, and lips smacked as one tasty morsel followed another. This was the Kham culture we would come to love, but as yet, we were still outsiders. This was one of my most memorable early introductions into their way of life.

Each village had its own council, its own style of administration, and its own ways of allocating village treasury funds. In due course, I was to learn that Lower Shera was recognized by all the other villages as being the most corrupt. In the better-managed villages, taxes and fines were allowed to accumulate and then applied to civil projects like trail main-

Lower Shera, looking east

tenance, bridge building, and water canals. Most fines were levied for fairly minor, but real, infractions, like allowing livestock to encroach in other people's corn and barley fields or cutting firewood in areas selected by the elders for reforestation.

In Lower Shera, the management style was more like a mafia operation. Council members spent a great deal of time plotting together and enacting bogus laws calculated to exploit the common villagers for petty cash to finance the council's daily drinking orgies. There was no village treasury; the council consumed it all. When they ran short of cash, they simply generated a new tax—dog tax, pig tax, or whatever—and then sent their henchmen around to collect. Anyone who refused might have a cow or a sheep seized.

The house we were building was to go eventually to the clan members on whose land we were building. As long as we lived there, we paid no lease, but when we left, the house would be theirs. In actual fact, when we did leave, the house went to the clan leader who was also the council chief. We, of course, were the only ones too naive to foresee that event from the first day of the contract.

When the dimensions for the house were being laid by driving stakes where the foundation was to be dug, the council chief kept protesting that a house of such modest dimensions was not fitting for persons of our importance and eminence. He kept pulling up the stakes and extending the boundaries. I would move them back to their original positions, and the debate would start all over again. Finally, we settled on a compromise, and the work began. I failed to realize that he was negotiating the size of what would be his own house, and his preference was for something a bit more grand.

Apart from two stonemasons and one skilled carpenter, all of the hard manual labor for building the house was assigned to the *kamis* and *damais* of the village, the occupational castes. They quarried stone from the mountainsides and carried it to the site on their backs. They carried water from the river and mixed the mortar. They cut the timber and dragged it down off the slopes using long bamboo ropes.

Every Kham village has its segregated community of such castes— the only real caste distinction in their otherwise classless society. The occupational castes are a people of Indic origin and belong to the lower echelons of Hindu society. It's difficult to surmise how many generations they may have lived in these communities. It must have been a long time; they speak a hybrid form of Nepali as their mother tongue, and a notable feature of their language is its inclusion of dozens of Kham verbs governed by Nepali affixes. To understand this creole, one needs not only a good command of both languages but also an innovative imagination.

The *kamis* and *damais* are the only vocational specialists of the village, and rather than farming like the rest (which they do on a limited scale), they make their livings as practitioners of specific occupations,

Damai musicians

the so-called menial tasks. The *kamis* are the blacksmiths, who forge implements of iron, copper, and other metals. The *damais* are the tailors and musicians. Their most important services are required at weddings, funerals, and other functions that necessitate the use of drums, oboes, and other instruments.

For a *kami* or *damai* to make a living in a Kham village, he must secure sufficient clients to patronize him, forging a lasting relationship, which continues unbroken from one generation to the next. Each Kham family is required to make annual payments of grain to the blacksmith or tailor they patronize and to make other small gifts throughout the year, especially at harvest time. In return, blacksmiths are required to forge and sharpen the tools of their clients and hammer out and shape their cooking vessels for free. At the time of death, the deceased's blacksmith is required to break the soil of his client's grave.

The occupational castes are kept at a level of poverty and bare subsistence, often reduced to begging and negotiating for higher commissions. If one accepts the general rule that people rarely rise above society's expectations of them, theirs is a case in point. They tend to be quarrelsome, unreliable, difficult to work with, and constantly threatening to strike for higher wages. The Khams, of course, regard this as proof that the workers are an inferior class of people and have to be treated with severity. *Those castes could certainly never be trusted with matters of consequence,* they think. The idea that the Khams might themselves be contributors to the problem has apparently never crossed their minds.

The contract for the construction of the house was made with the village council—the sum total of 2,500 rupees (the equivalent of $250 dollars). We learned that the laborers had been informed of a lesser figure, which, of course, only proved to them that they were indeed being exploited. The deadly cycle of mistrust was strengthened, and this infuriated Nancy and me. We assured the workers that at the completion of the construction, we would personally distribute the money ourselves based on prevailing pay scales for the various occupations. Skilled masons and carpenters were at the top of the scale, with stone carriers receiving slightly lower wages.

We weren't yet fully aware of the strict separation between the castes, and we probably committed numerous blunders that were disturbing to Kham sensitivities. The occupational castes are never permitted inside Kham homes, and Khams are not permitted to eat food or drink water from their hands. But because most of our laborers belonged to such castes, we had frequent and familiar dealings with them. The Khams were still too proud to work for us, and when anything needed doing, we had to depend on the lower castes. Anytime I needed to make the journey to Dhorpatan to pick up supplies that had been delivered to us by air, I had to depend on the lower castes for porters.

On our second village visit, in the spring of 1970, construction on our new house was completed, and we moved in. With Angdrak no longer with us, Nancy employed the services of a young sixteen-year-old *kami* girl named Rozan to help with cleaning, washing, and even some food preparation. She was a sweet girl, a good worker, and when she saw we treated her with dignity, she was entirely reliable and gave us her full loyalty. Though the arrangement did not quite gain the full approval of the Khams, they came to accept it. We were somehow different, and they realized that we operated under a different set of assumptions.

* * *

The walls of our new house were made of stone about eighteen inches thick, quarried half a mile away. The quarry site was full of numerous fracture lines and, using iron pry bars, the stone was removed in slabs about four to six inches thick. The stones came in irregular shapes, but with a sharp blow of a hammer along one of the fracture lines,

The house walls: a stone and mud sandwich

the leading edge would come out relatively straight. The straight, leading edges of the stone would form the inner and outer edges of the wall, while the rough, irregular edges of the stone overlapped in the center and were held together by mud mortar. That way, only the stone face of the wall was exposed to the elements, and the mud mortar was kept dry on the inside.

The inside walls of the house were plastered with a mixture of mud and cow dung. The naturally occurring straw in the dung kept the mud from cracking and formed excellent plaster. The smell was gone as soon as the mixture was dry—or so we thought. One eventually gets used to the smell of living in a barn.

The main room of the house was twelve feet deep by twenty feet long. This was the living area; there was a kitchen at one end, complete with a homemade counter, an eating table, and a mud cookstove with a steel plate for cooking. At the other end was our thirty-gallon heating stove, a small *saal*-wood desk, and two steel-framed canvas chairs, where we would spend the evenings reading. At either end were two, two- by three-foot, glassed window frames, constructed out of thick slabs of good, solid pinewood.

The floor of the main room was made of a collection of the larger unbroken slabs of stone from the quarry laid in concrete. Off the main room were two inner rooms, both for sleeping, each with its own window. One was the kids' room and the other was Nancy's and mine. Leading from one of the sleeping rooms was a wooden staircase ascending to two identically sized rooms upstairs. One was a study, and the other was a storeroom. Both were covered by a pine shingle roof.

At the front of the house, along its entire width, was an enclosed porch eight feet deep with a wood-storage room at one end. Except for the two stories at the back half of the house, the entire front part of the house was a single-storied structure with a flat terrace roof like those of other Kham houses.

When the house was completed, with all the glass installed and the stoves fully operational, it was nothing short of magical to some of the older Khams. In their world, darkness, smoke, and warmth all come together; one cannot be separated from any of the others. When they entered our house, they found the room well-lit by the light coming through the windows, the room toasty warm from the stove, and no smoke; it was expelled through the chimney.

One old man, whom we nicknamed Mr. McGoo because he could hardly see past his nose and was always losing his cows on the hillside, came to visit every afternoon. He would bang on the front door and call out, "God, are you home today?"

"Stop saying that, would you?" I would insist lamely as I opened the door. "What do you want?"

"Oh, only to sit beside your fire and chat," he would reply. Then, heading straight for the stove, he would sit on the floor, rubbing his hands in its warmth, and gaze around the room in awe.

"Mr McGoo"

* * *

Nancy expanded her medical work once we were established in the new house. The front door was a Dutch door so that the top half could be opened while the lower half remained closed. Patients could be dealt with as they waited on the outer porch without her having to admit them inside unless their condition called for it. The lower half of the Dutch door had a collapsible countertop, which could be lifted for counting out and dispensing medicines. A shelf hung from the ceiling just to the right of the door for easy access to medications and examining instruments.

As Nancy grew in experience, she gained familiarity with most of the common diseases in the village and could usually make a correct diagnosis based on a few prevalent symptoms and a little inquiry into the history of their malady. She was also called upon to treat dozens of serious illnesses for which nothing could be done—things like blindness, cancer, liver and kidney failure, and everything else imaginable. Even with her limited facilities and lack of training, she successfully managed some pretty amazing treatments. She delivered mothers from breach births, she set broken limbs, she cut away the rotting flesh from the feet of badly burned infants and stopped their spreading gangrene.

Once, she had to remove a man's finger. She had already tried less drastic measures, but the finger was only getting worse. Dry bone was now sticking through infected flesh, and it was beginning to look ugly. Realizing she was going to have to take it off, she psyched herself up by saying, "Don't worry, Nancy, don't worry. It's only a chicken bone; it's only a chicken bone." And then—pop!—she snapped it off between her thumb and forefingers. She trimmed away the bad flesh, covered the bone, and *voila!* it healed nicely (minus the upper joint, of course).

Kham villages are dangerous places for kids to grow up. They are built on steep mountainsides, and there are sharp, jagged rocks everywhere. And there is no end of things to fall from: rooftops, ladders, terraced pathways, and narrow log bridges spanning rows of rooftops. Nancy closed dozens of ugly gashes. One of the most memorable was when a shaman brought his eight-year-old son with several inches of his scalp torn open from front to back. His hair was matted, and it was clear that his scalp was filthy. Before getting to the job of patching the wound, Nancy realized that she had to shave the area and clean the scalp to prevent infection. She cut away the excess hair with scissors, and then using an aerosol can of shaving cream, she sprayed the scalp with foam and began to shave it clean.

When the shaman saw the foam emerge from the can, he became clearly upset and disappeared into the village. He returned shortly with a rooster under his arm, and then, taking off its head, he began to dance in a circle, chanting and spraying blood all over the kitchen walls. Nancy had already sterilized and cleaned up the wound and was getting the scalp back into place. Pushing Nancy aside, the shaman reopened the scalp to see what strange thing she might have implanted. The blood began to gush again, and Nancy grew furious at the unnecessary pain inflicted on the boy. Mustering all her strength, she shoved the father out the door and locked it behind him so that she could finish stitching the scalp in peace.

Shera, with the Watters' house farthest left

* * *

In spite of the progress we were making in developing trust with some members of the community, our patience was constantly tested. We were making very little progress in learning the language. Most of our dealings were still with the low castes of the village, and no Kham

*The kitchen side
of the main room*

*The living side
of the main room*

*An evening
by the drum stove*

*Daniel gets a
bath by the stove*

*David works
in his study*

The storeroom

expressed any interest in teaching us their language. We were still somehow sub-human.

We installed screens on the outside of the windows to protect them from stray stones, but the people ripped them off within a few weeks because it was too hard for them to watch us through screened windows. If someone needed a plank of wood, they would simply climb the terrace behind our house and steal one of the shingles off our roof.

Every morning, I would take the horse about a thousand feet above the village for grazing to a slightly indented area on the mountain slope. There, I would tether him to a stake with about a hundred feet of nylon line. In the late afternoon, before dark, I would climb the hill to fetch him. On repeated occasions, the line would be stolen and the horse would be missing, too. I would head off to the west, a full hour's walk away where he would be grazing untethered in a meadow more to his liking. Finally, I resigned myself to taking him to the far meadow where I didn't need to tether him any longer. I saved myself a lot of nylon line, but it cost me a couple of hours in riding and walking every day.

One evening after dark, when the kids were asleep and we were enjoying the quiet of the evening, torches appeared at the front door accompanied by the shouting of impatient voices and a loud banging of fists. "Open up," they demanded, "we want to see you."

"Come back in the morning," I shouted back, "we're getting ready for bed."

There was a brief interlude of silence, and then came the crashing noise of splintering wood as the door burst inwards against the force of a sharp kick. Three wild, muscular young men, all of them nomadic Kham shepherds from the high alpine meadows, came tumbling in through the opening with loud, boisterous laughs. They were dressed in homespun clothing with black skullcaps and dark wool blankets about their shoulders. Tucked into their waist bands were long-bladed *kukri* knives.

Their crazed, excited eyes took in the whole scene at single glance. One snatched up our radio, and the other two grabbed our kerosene lamps. Then, they headed back through the doorway and out into the barley fields as quickly as they had come.

We sat in stunned silence, wondering what to do next. There wasn't much we could do but grope around in the dark. Thirty minutes later, the men returned with the goods. The radio was damaged a bit—they had pried the cover loose with knives—but it still worked, and with a little effort, I was able to restore it to reasonable condition. They hadn't stolen anything. They just wanted to look at our stuff.

In those first months, as Nancy and I struggled with our attitudes towards those we had come to serve, we finally recognized that we couldn't go it alone. We began crying out to God every night before going to bed, begging that somehow he would give us a supernatural love for these people who seemed anything but lovable. Gradually, he began to bring about a change in our attitudes, and we were able to see the villagers more as he sees them. In a diary entry from April 1970, Nancy wrote:

> We are enjoying our work, but I must be honest and say that there are many problems, too. It's not a bed of roses; thorns are always present. People pull our screens off. They yell at us and bang at the door, even breaking it down because we don't give them what they want. These people are a tough lot. How do we love them? They steal our stuff, call us bad names; they are rude and disrespectful. Can we really help them? Are we wasting our lives for nothing? We fall on our knees each night and search our hearts, and see our inadequate ways. We know now we can't love them, but Christ can love them through us if we are completely willing to let his love flow through us. God is even now moving. It's hard and slow, but I can't think of a better way to use my life. The Cross of Christ cuts across every barrier of culture, time, and space.

Within a few days, something of considerable significance occurred. I had not taken my horse to pasture that morning but kept him tied at the side of the house, feeding him from a stock of fodder purchased in the village. Early in the afternoon, a young man cut the rope, tossed a halter over the horse's head, and went riding up the valley as fast as he could go. Nancy called upstairs to my study, "Someone has just stolen your horse!"

I leaped down the stairs and ran outside only to see him disappearing into the distance. I looked up into the village and could see dozens of people assembled on the rooftops, laughing. Going back inside, I said to Nancy, "I don't know what to do," and I began to pace the floor. Suddenly, everything came clear. "I know the answer," I said, and then I sat down to wait for his return.

Twenty minutes later, he came riding back with a triumphant grin on his face. As he pulled up the reins in front of the house, I stepped up to the horse and leaped at the man with all my force, hitting him on the chest with both fists in a single blow. He sailed off the horse, landing awkwardly on his back. In the background, I could vaguely hear a surprised murmur reverberate through the village. The young man looked shocked, and jumping to his feet, he quickly dusted himself off and darted into the village.

Going back into the house, I said to Nancy, "I don't know why I did that. I didn't do it in anger; I just felt that that's what needed doing." For the next two hours, I was in misery. "What have I done? What have I done?" I kept murmuring to myself. Our shaky acceptance in the village would certainly be ended, not to mention that we might be murdered in our beds tonight.

Two hours later, the young man returned, knocked at the door, and offered me a peace offering of some choice pieces of meat.

I invited him inside, glad for the chance to make amends. Nancy offered him some tea and biscuits, and the breach was mended. We became close friends. Stranger yet, our relations with the whole village suddenly began to improve. They had been testing us, and now they knew that we, too, had human feelings and demanded the same respect they demanded of each other. Who would have guessed that the answer lay in knocking somebody off my horse? That isn't what they taught me in Sunday School!

Nearly two years later, in February of 1972, on one of our typically three-month stays in the village, an entry from Nancy's diary reveals that God was indeed changing our attitudes toward the people:

> This time in the village is the best yet. The more we live with the Khams, the more we love and respect them. We're learning more of their language and more about their culture. At the same time, we're learning to drop more of our own. It doesn't happen overnight; it's a process. As we learn to grow and love Jesus our Lord more and more, so does our love for the people grow. At times it seems so slow, but at last we feel we have made it over the hump.

The Watters family on their roof

*"As we learn to grow and love Jesus our Lord more and more,
so does our love for the people grow."*

Steve shows off his model plane

Chapter 9: The Sitting of the Young Men

Quite a number of marriages are secured by capture. Capturing a girl is usually done at festivals and fairs amidst confusion and quarrelling, or sometimes quietly in the village when the girl comes out of her house to fetch water.
—*Dor Bahadur Bista,* People of Nepal

The topic of sex is treated with ambivalence in Kham culture. To speak of it seriously is taboo and a source of great embarrassment. Nothing, on the other hand, is quipped about more frequently. For us, hearing it constantly alluded to in vulgar terms or not-so-subtle jokes was tiresome and off-putting, and as a result, we missed out on learning a lot of their views regarding courtship and marriage.

The official story, promulgated by their elders, was that the Khams had a puritan society, free of adultery, incest, and even adolescent experimentation. It was impossible to get anyone to tell what really went on, and some even claimed that they followed the Hindu ideal of arranged marriages. But we were to learn that that wasn't usually the case.

Late one afternoon, just before the time when village girls go to the river to draw water, we heard shouting and arguing outside our house. A girl from Lukum, who was visiting friends in Shera, was coming up the river-trail carrying a jug of water. She and another girl were surrounded by a gang of teenage boys pushing and tugging at them. One boy had managed to grab hold of the girl from Lukum and was dragging her by the hair. The girls were putting up a good fight, screaming, biting, clawing, spitting, and even clobbering their assailants with sticks and stones.

We rushed out of the house and were immediately baffled to see the whole village assembled on the rooftops, cheering and laughing. But that didn't stop Nancy. She spun around and shouted at me, "Do something!"

"What am I supposed to do?" I replied lamely, looking up at the villagers and realizing that something was happening that I didn't understand. Things just weren't adding up.

But while I hesitated, Nancy lunged into the fight. She picked up a hefty chunk of firewood from the woodpile and began swinging wildly at the boys.

The assailants backed off, surprised and shocked to see an angry white woman throwing punches their way. I was dazed, too, and in the slow motion of the ensuing events, I began to realize that a ripple of laughter was erupting from the village. Suddenly, everything was in disarray, and one of the village men rushed to Nancy's side.

"This is a wedding," he explained, pulling her gently aside. "Just leave them alone, and everything will be all right."

Nancy, stunned with disbelief, stepped aside, and the "wedding" proceeded as planned. I couldn't believe it either. It was like Fred and Wilma Flintstone on a back lot in Hollywood.

Alas, though, this was the real world, and in this version, there would be no cozy, secluded cave for the sweating cave man to drag his woman to. Up in the village, the amorous couple was brusquely pushed into a room, and the door was shut behind them. A boy was hoisted to a vantage point on an abutting wall where he could see into the room through the cracks between the ceiling beams. The crowd retreated.

Before long, the boy turned to the crowd, tugging at his leggings in a game of charades. Everyone laughed. A short while later, he wrinkled up his face, squinting his eyes and wiggling his tongue. More howls of laughter. Finally, he turned with a triumphant grin on his face and thrust his index finger through a circle in his other hand. The crowd cheered. We had just witnessed a "kidnap marriage," perhaps the most common form of marriage in Kham society at that time.

In most cases, kidnap marriages are planned elopements and the whole drama is staged. The fight especially is acted out as a parody on a woman's lot in life. Marriage for a woman is viewed as a tragedy in the classical sense. She is expected to leave her own village and family and become a servant to her new mother-in-law. She bears her husband's children, in a tragic number of cases losing her own life in the process. Women who survive childbirth typically suffer the agonizing loss of about half their children. Some of a woman's screams at a kidnap marriage come with genuine feeling.

It turned out that the kidnapping we had just witnessed was fully staged, and the next morning, the new couple, smiles on their faces, appeared at our doorway, asking Nancy to patch up their cuts and bruises incurred in the "wedding march."

The wedding procession

* * *

Not every kidnapping is performed with the consent of the girl, however, and the so-called marriage is actually a dreadful rape. Once, after Steve and Daniel were grown, the three of us were traveling through a valley where they speak a dialect of Kham barely intelligible to the people of Taka-Shera. We stayed in one village for a week, the guests of a family with three grown sons—two married, and the middle one still single. He had been attacked by a leopard five years earlier, and his face was grossly disfigured. No girl would have him.

The middle son came home late one night, dragging with him a girl he had captured in the forest. She was from another village. The boys and I were sleeping on the porch, but it was impossible to sleep: we could hear the sounds of sobbing, slapping, and beating coming from the single inner room. They continued on through half the night. The girl was unwilling, and the whole extended family scolded and reviled her until the rape was finally consummated.

Minutes later, the elder brother appeared by my side, asking if I had any sleeping pills. Whether out of anger or embarrassment, I was unable to look at him. I turned my back as I dug into my satchel and handed him a couple of aspirin. I had no idea who they were for, but I hoped they were for the girl.

The next morning, after a sleepless night, the girl emerged from the house with the demeanor of a beaten dog, her face bruised and her eyes swollen. She was devoid of emotion; her will had been broken, and she was now the chattel of her captor family. We were sickened.

Two years later, I learned, the girl escaped. Many more years later, during the Maoist conflict, she became a Maoist commando, the head of a women's brigade. When she killed, it was reported, she liked to castrate her victims: "Take that, you bastard!"

Marriage can be hard in a Kham village, and this obvious fact is commemorated once a year in a midsummer festival known as *Chop Zhyas*, a kind of anti-Valentine's day. It is a comic enactment of the tragedy of marriage, with all its inequities and inescapable suffering, a time when the women can vent some of their pent-up anger. Young men and women assemble on a rooftop, each wearing the clothing of the opposite sex. The women, acting out male roles, attack the skirt-wearing men. Wrestling them to the ground, they smear them with mud, and perform acts of mock sexual intercourse. The acts are performed with as much vulgarity as possible, and some are blatant enactments of bestiality. The festival is highly popular and produces riots of laughter.

* * *

Our house was at the edge of the village, only two houses in from the entrance. It was a great vantage point, from which we could observe all kinds of comings and goings. Often, just after dark, a group of young men from Upper Shera came dancing into town to the beat of a drum. They were dressed in their finest, wearing new turbans on their heads and brass ringlets on their ankles.

When we inquired about what they were doing, they replied that they were going to *dhapa chusine*, "the sitting of the young men." It sounded kind of important, like a junior village council or something. When we inquired in the village for more explanation, we didn't get much clarification.

"Oh, they're just a bunch of guys getting together to sing and chat," they said. Well, they didn't strike me as a local garage band or anything, so I began to think of them as some kind of junior council or poetry club.

"Wow, what an opportunity," Nancy said to me one afternoon. "You haven't been able to get a reliable language teacher, so why don't you ask the guys about joining them tonight?"

"You think?" I asked stupidly.

"Sure, go for it," she replied, trying to be encouraging.

That night, when the turbaned drummers came by, I asked, "Would you mind if I go along with you one of these nights?"

"Of course we wouldn't mind," they replied, obviously delighted. "We'll stop by tomorrow evening."

Word spread quickly. Women filed past the door all day long, asking Nancy the same question, "Is it true that your husband is going to the sitting of the young men?"

"Yes," she replied. "He thought it might be fun."

"Fun? Good God, are you serious? You mean you don't mind if he goes out at night?" they asked.

"Of course not," she replied, with a confidence that amazed them all.

Shortly after dark, the young men arrived. I stepped behind them into the darkness, my notebook and pencil ready at hand. The drummers escorted us to a large house in the center of the village with a spacious front porch and firepits at either end.

My eyes took in everything in a sweep. I saw couples sitting beside the fires singing traditional love ballads—contests of wit, with the girl's line sung in answer to the boy's line. As my eyes darted across the room, I saw too that there were cozy huddles in some of the shadowy corners, moving bodies wrapped in woolen blankets.

I sat down, and immediately a pretty young girl vaulted across the room and threw herself into my lap. The surprised look on my face amused everyone. "What's happening?" I asked stupidly.

She brushed my questions aside and began nibbling on my ear with tender kisses. "This, Sahib, is *dhapa chusine*," she said with obvious merriment.

I returned home in a few minutes, stuttering and flushed. I blushed partly because of embarrassment; Nancy could see that the experience had made my blood race a bit. Clearing my throat repeatedly, I tried to explain to her what the "sitting of the young men" really was.

* * *

Meeting potential husbands

It was many months before we discovered anything resembling the truth about the "courtship houses." In a village the size of Shera, there might be several such houses. After puberty, the girls begin frequenting specific houses with their girlfriends. This is where they meet their potential husbands. The girls in a given sorority are related in such a way that all of them are potential marriage partners to the boys who visit the house. Rules prohibiting marriage across certain clan boundaries are strict, and suitors are often required to visit girls from adjoining villages.

According to the village elders, nothing sexual occurred in the courtship houses, but the young men, in private, refuted that claim. It was hard to know who was giving the accurate account. Were the old men telling the truth and the young boys only bragging about their sexual exploits, or was it the other way around? If the boys were telling the truth, how could one account for the surprisingly low number of unwanted pregnancies? Such pregnancies almost never happened, it seemed.

Out on the trail, away from the village, the men felt more free to talk openly; there was a kind of campfire camaraderie. So I broached the topic with some of my porters one evening. "Why," I asked, "do you really go to such houses?"

"For sex, of course," they replied, laughing. "Why else would we go?"

"But if that's true, why do none of the girls become pregnant?" I asked.

"You mean you don't know?" they asked, in a tone that meant "How stupid are you, anyway?"

A teenage girl with her heavy load

Then, they explained a time-honored "fact of life," proven through the generations. "If a girl changes partners regularly," they explained, "she doesn't get pregnant. That happens only when she settles down with one man for a long time."

This so-called fact seemed totally preposterous to me, but they swore by it. Some months later, Nancy and

I had opportunity to talk to a doctor friend who had worked in Nepal for several years about this seeming impossibility.

"To them, it would seem true," he explained, "but something more basic is the real explanation. Girls in their early teens are the work-horses of the village. They carry loads, they cultivate the gardens, they gather firewood, they grind the corn—a never-ending litany of tasks. Their ratio of body fat to muscle is so low, and their menses so light, that they simply cannot become impregnated. When they marry and settle down to a more sedentary lifestyle, they put on fat and are ready for conception."

* * *

Only in a single, rare virginity cult does sexual purity seem to be prized in Kham society. But it has nothing to do with morality, only with power. In exchange for her virginity and a host of dietary prohi-bitions, the gods bestow certain powers upon a "living goddess." She is given the ability to influence weather, heal disease, and predict the future.

We knew such a person, a teenage girl named Hitu who was our next-door neighbor. She and Nancy became good friends. She never visited the courtship houses, and Nancy was relieved to have someone to talk to without the constant banter about sex. We didn't know it then, but her aunt was a "living goddess" from the village of Thabang, two days walk to the southwest. Nancy's friend had apparently been singled out to be her successor in the virginity cult.

One day, Hitu became possessed, but the family pretended not to understand why. Hearing only that she was ill, Nancy and I went to visit her. When we entered the dark room, we were greeted by an unusual voice coming from the corner.

"Sit down, my friend," the voice said huskily in English. (A surprise to us! No one out here knew English.)

Nancy shone her light into the corner and was surprised to see Hitu, huddled there in blankets, her eyes glazed over. "What's the matter?" Nancy asked.

"The goddess has come," she replied in Kham, not speaking English again.

Not fully comprehending, Nancy took her pulse and found her heart rate down around fifty. Her hands were cold and icy. The girl laughed on occasion and made crazy, disconnected statements. Some of them were in Kham, some in Nepali, and some in a harsh tongue that she claimed was the voice of the goddess.

We could see that the girl was possessed by a spirit and asked the family for permission to pray over her. But they wouldn't hear of it. They were hoping to make a good deal of money from her.

In an hour, Hitu began to come out of her trance. Her pulse began to normalize and her body warmed.

"Come with me. I must purify myself at the river," she said as she took Nancy by the hand.

Nancy went along, but as the spirit began to release the girl, she became savage and violent. Guttural sounds came from her throat, and with superhuman strength, she began heaving river boulders, some toward Nancy.

I was unaware that this was happening. Since the girl had gone for purification, I stayed back behind the bank of the river to give her privacy. When the two of them finally emerged, the girl was normal again, but Nancy was visibly shaken.

* * *

Two days later, relatives from Thabang arrived at Hitu's house bearing gifts and the news that her aunt had died. The spirit had already moved to its new host.

The gods often disciplined Hitu for dietary infractions. She craved *ghee*, she told us, but she was physically unable to get her hand into the jug. A force beyond her own prevented her. Once she managed to sneak some salt, also prohibited, and the gods responded by forcing her to stand rigid for an hour, her hands held straight out in front of her.

Eventually a small temple was erected for Hitu, where she lived like a nun. People came to her from far and wide, and she became a source of regular income for the family. Finally, at the age of twenty-four, she died, thin and emaciated. Most blamed the gods for her death. Her temple and shrine began to deteriorate and eventually crumbled—a stark reminder of the cost of making deals with the gods.

Chapter 10: Terrors from the Other World

When I was traveling in the north, I came upon a heap of wood in the mountains, and as I just wanted to cook some dinner, I set this on fire. Now, under this heap was buried a well-known Tungus shaman, and so his amagyat leapt into me.
—*Czaplicka,* Aboriginal Siberia

We had been making periodic visits to Taka-Shera for about a year and a half before we had any real contact with shamans. They came with the shepherds in their annual migration from the south.

The shepherds' arrival in the villages was always timed to coincide with the barley harvest in late April or early May. As soon as the fields were cleared of straw, the sheep moved in. There, they would be bedded nightly for about a month, until the fields were ready for plowing and the planting of maize. The sheep provided nitrogen-rich fertilizer. By early June, the sheep would begin to move into the northern highlands, grazing higher and higher as the snows receded. Then, late in August, they would begin their descent from the highest ranges, and by October, shortly after the maize was harvested, they would again be back in the fields.

The arrival of the shepherds was nothing short of magical. Families were reunited, and with the harvest just in, there was plenty to eat and drink. Shepherd boys, fresh in from the crude sheep camps, chased after village girls with as much restraint and finesse as goats in rut. The girls feigned offense but without much success; they clearly enjoyed all the sudden attention.

Goat-hair tents appeared overnight

Almost overnight, the population of the villages doubled (nine months later, too), and every open space was filled with bleating sheep and the patter of thousands of tiny hooves. Like coursing water, they crashed through barriers, burst over terraces, and spilled through tiny openings. They never stopped. The shepherds, trying vainly to keep them in check, sprinted ahead, whistling, shouting, and throwing pebbles. There were hefty fines for letting your sheep into someone's garden.

Goat-hair tents and bamboo sheep pens appeared in the fields overnight, and soon, as more and more fields surrounding the village were occupied, the place took on the air of a city under siege. In the evenings, as the men readied their suppers, the tents emitted smoke, and soon a thin blanket of acrid, cow-dung smoke hung above the fields. Enormous, shaggy-haired sheep dogs—Tibetan Mastiffs—apportioned daily with generous allotments of sheep's milk and cornmeal mush, were chained at the tent flaps with heavy iron chains. The pet name for many of these creatures included some variant of the word for "bear." They weren't to be messed with. Their job was to guard the sheep from leopards and

The shepherds

wolves and the camps from marauders.

I visited the sheep camps when I could, often taking Nancy and the boys along. Once past the ferocious dogs and in the interior of a tent, I always felt like I had entered another world. Skins and furs were piled in the corners, meat was laid out on racks above the fire, wooden churns and jugs hung from pegs, and ancient muzzle-loading muskets were tucked into the tent rafters. In some of the tents, I noticed more mysterious artifacts— feather headdresses, bear-skin vests, drums, and "witch sticks." These, I learned, belonged to the shamans.

The shamans are practitioners of an ancient tradition that goes back in an unbroken chain to Siberia, Mongolia, and Central Asia. Within this vast ethno-geographical area, shamans are regarded as specialists in the human soul. Only the shaman is capable of entering into communication with the spirits and bartering with the capricious gods of the valley. Men need him, especially in times of crisis. Illness is such a crisis, thought to be caused by the loss or aggravation of one of a person's nine souls: only the shaman is capable of retrieving or calming it. At the time of death, the soul must be escorted safely to the underworld: only the shaman, a psychopomp [a spiritual guide for a living person's soul], knows the treacherous way through the dark underground labyrinth haunted by lurking demons.

* * *

Although the shamans were plentiful among the settled village populations, my impression of them would always be colored by the arrival of the shepherds. The heart of true shamanism seemed to reverberate with an awareness of the terrifying forces of nature; as long as its practitioners lived life out-of-doors, face-to-face with nature, the religion was in a constant state of renewal. If the shamans settled down to farm their own land in established communities, their shamanism seemed to lose part of its natural life force, and many of its themes became institutionalized. The shamans who moved with the shepherds seemed more virile, more in touch with the living religion.

The shaman's costume is a menagerie of natural history. Across his chest is a bearskin vest. Sewed onto it, covering his ribs, are the tusks of a wild boar, one on the left and one on the right. Adorning his head is a feather headdress, made of the red wing feathers of the female Himalayan Monal pheasant, the *danphe.* On his back are the skins of numerous animals—red pandas, monkeys, otters, martens, and squirrels. His drum is stretched with the skin of the fleet-footed goral antelope.

The shaman is first and foremost a hunter, and the skins adorning his costume are a testimony to his skill. But though these animals have been brought down by him in the chase, they are in a broader sense his friends, his helping spirits. When he kills them, he apologizes. He succeeds only because they understand.

The shaman's costume is a menagerie of natural history

In many of his songs, the shaman retells the story of the animals adorning his costume, as in the following chant for a drum skin:

All the wild animals, we tried their skins,
but the gods weren't happy, the spirits weren't pleased.
So we went on a hunt, we went on a search.
Down in the low country, down in the plains,
they tried the skin of the buck, they tried the skin of the doe,
and the gods were happy, the spirits were pleased.
But up in the mountains, high in the crags,

the buck won't do, the doe isn't right.
So we went on a hunt, we went on a search.
We tried the mountain ram, we tried the mountain ewe,
but the gods wouldn't come, the spirits wouldn't show.
We tried the mountain billy, we tried the mountain nanny,
but the gods wouldn't come, the spirits wouldn't show.
Then we tried the antelope buck, we tried the antelope doe.
You, oh antelope buckskin, you were the one,
you, oh antelope doeskin, you rose to the need.
When we beat on the drum, the drum is joyful.
The skin of the antelope resonates, the drumskin sings.
The gods are happy with you, the spirits are pleased.

The shaman's power in the supernatural realm comes from his animal spirits. Without them, he is helpless; with them, he is powerful. In trance, through the help of his serpent spirit, the shaman crawls into holes beneath rocks and boulders in search of a patient's missing soul. The serpent spirit is especially useful around marshes and water springs where the peevish water gods lurk.

The leopard spirit is the shaman's favorite mount. He rides him across *upalna nam*, the sky and the vast reaches of alpine country at the foot of the snows, and he rides him into *talna nam*, the dark and frightening underworld where he has to face Sepa Serong, the god of the underworld. Back in *ber nam*, the world of men, the shaman re-enacts his supernatural journey for all to see. This world becomes the mirror image of all that happens in the spiritual realm.

Calling spirits with his drum

Numerous times, I have watched shamans go into trance and begin their supernatural journey to retrieve a missing soul. It always happens at night, when most of the world slumbers. The host family sits up to watch, and on occasion, neighbors come to follow the proceedings.

The shaman sits in the place of honor, at the head of the firepit; his audience sits across from him. Dressed in full regalia and a feather headdress, he begins to call his spirits with the hypnotic beat of his drum: *tata taon, tata taon, tatata taon, tatata taon.*

The shaman's first challenge is to convince his audience that he has transcended the natural plane and has made the crossover to the supernatural. The gods arrive, his body shakes, and the shaman thrusts his hands into the fire. He washes his face in hot ash, and he eats live coals. He falls on his back, his body stiffens, and he begins to convulse. The *lama* spirit arrives, and the shaman begins to speak in an unknown tongue, the secret language of the gods. Animal calls pierce the darkness. It's a show intended to inspire awe, indicating that the shaman has transcended the natural world.

* * *

One night in the village of Taka, I watched chief shaman Bal Bahadur and his assistant in action. Bal Bahadur was one of the great masters, but I was never quite sure of his mental state. He was a nice enough person, but he always seemed on the verge of psychosis. Even in his "normal" state, he laughed with a strange laugh, his movements were jerky, and his eyes darted around like he saw things—things you'd better not ignore. Whenever I was with him, I kept glancing over my shoulder. Who was he looking at, anyway?

Bal Bahadur fit the shamanic prototype. In the Siberian tradition, a true shaman is one who narrowly recovers from a paranormal, hysteroid experience and manages to regulate it. Some would-be shamans are less fortunate. Their insanity drives them to suicide.

Bal Bahadur's assistant was a timid man named Tulba; the two made a good pair. Each knew the other's drumbeat well, and one drumbeat answered to the other. But as the night wore on, some of the onlookers began to grow weary, and several left. At about one o'clock in the morning, when there were just a handful of us left, a *lama* spirit from Mount Kailas came upon Bal Bahadur. He began to sing in a beautiful, lilting manner, dancing gracefully around the room. He moved back to the fire and began to speak in the secret language of the *lamas*.

I'm not sure what made me do what I did next. I was tired, I guess, and the drumbeat was making my head swim. Besides, how could I, a well-educated, twentieth-century man, be taken in by someone who claimed to be talking to the gods of Kailas? I couldn't just sit there. Like a man coming out of a stupor, I posed a challenge: pretending to understand Bal Bahadur's secret language, I replied to him in English.

Bal Bahadur whirled and stared at me in surprise. He quickly scanned my face and spoke again in his secret language. Again, I responded in English. The onlookers gasped. They begin whispering to one another. "Under the power of his spirits," they said, "Bal Bahadur can even speak in English." I kept responding, and Bal Bahadur smiled. He thought I was helping him.

The onlookers were amazed and asked, "Can he understand you? Are you really talking with him?" Then, I did something stupid.

"Ha!" I said scoffingly. "He's just pretending. I just accused him in English of being a charlatan, and he responded with an agreeable smile."

Everyone laughed.

Bal Bahadur descended on the fire. With both hands he scooped up the contents of the firepit and dumped it into my lap. I leapt to my feet, brushing off the hot, flaming coals. Now, in the dim glow of the remaining coals, I could see him swoop down on the iron cooking tripod. His arm went back in the darkness, and he slung it towards me with all his might. I ducked, and it narrowly missed my head and, with a thud, connected with the man behind me. Landing on his back, he groaned and held his head with both hands, blood flowing from an ugly gash.

Bal Bahadur grabbed me roughly by the wrist. "Come into the inner room," he said, speaking in Kham. "I want to talk with you."

"What's the matter with right here?" I responded warily. "Just say it, I'm listening."

"I want to talk with you inside."

Obediently, stupidly, I followed his leading. Bal Bahadur lit a lamp and chained the door behind us. He motioned for me to sit down. Unblinking, I watched every movement. He opened a wooden chest. At first, I thought he was going for a knife, but instead he pulled out a wooden jug, a clear glass bottle, and two brass drinking bowls. Dipping his finger into the jug, he scooped out a generous gob of honey and divided it into the two bowls. Then he poured in a clear, fiery, vodka-like liquid, stirred, and handed one bowl to me.

What color are my eyes?

"What color are my eyes?" Bal Bahadur asked me.

Not quite sure what to say, I looked at his bloodshot eyes and stammered, "Well, they're red, I guess."

"That's right," he said. "That's because they're full of lightning. I can see right through you."

"What do you see?" Probably not a smart question.

Bal Bahadur didn't answer. He lifted his bowl to his lips and motioned for me to do the same. "Aha," I suddenly realized, "Bal Bahadur is apologizing." Relieved, I accepted the drink; in so doing, I apologized for my own actions, too. That was the most threatening encounter I ever had with a shaman, but it ended well. Many shamans were subsequently to become my friends.

* * *

Two weeks later, I went back to watch Tulba and another shaman, Khadga, perform. This time, through various divinations, they determined that the patient's soul had slipped through the hole of a cavern at Jaljala Pass, thirty-five miles east of the village. To retrieve the missing soul, one of them would have to make the terrifying journey to the

Tulba beats his drum as he begins his journey

underworld. Neither wanted the assignment, so they drew lots. Tulba
lost the toss; he would have to go, and Khadga would stay behind.

Tulba began his journey. Beating his drum, he
summoned his leopard spirit and rode eastward. The leopard moved
rapidly, though from time to time, it slowed and left the trail to inspect
a thicket or to rest. But Tulba was in a hurry. He cried out and whipped
the leopard with a leather thong. I ducked as the thong whistled overhead. *Maybe*, I thought, *I'm sitting too close.*

Suddenly, Tulba became agitated. "Out of the way, out of the way,"
he began to shout, "I'm coming through!" Suddenly, his body was
thrown across the room, and he lay unconscious. Khadga sprang to his
feet to help him and found his body scratched with thorns.

"What happened?" I asked, completely dumbfounded.

"It was a shaman from Maikot," Khadga explained. "They ran into
each other, and the other shaman was carrying a load of thorns to the
underworld."

Now the journey resumed, and Tulba reached the cavern entrance.
One look at his face told me everything I needed to know: this was not
a pleasant place. Inside, he was attacked by demons. He screamed in
terror, and Khadga kept hammering the drum for him, banging around
his head. Tulba was too busy to drum, taken up with fighting, flailing,

and holding his arms up to deflect incoming blows. He writhed on the floor, he convulsed, he cried out. Finally, he stood before Sepa Serong, the lord of the underworld, and began to bargain. They settled on a price—the blood of a large male goat.

Tulba snatched the soul and ran. He made it to the cave entrance and out into the open. He cracked his whip, shouted, and arrived at the house out of breath. The journey had lasted a couple of hours, and he was as limp as a washrag. "The patient will get better now," the shamans explained.

The patient died the next day. But the shamans fared just fine; they feasted on goat meat for several days. I'm reminded of some doctors back home.

* * *

I never knew what to make of the shamans. Somehow, their primitive religion seemed a good fit for these wild people—an untamed religion for an untamed people. Their mountains were alive with the presence of unseen beings, and shamanism seemed a reasonable way to express it. Just a few nights in the high wilderness was all the convincing I needed. Faintly, strangely, off in the nighttime distance, one could almost hear the miniature bells on the collars of hunting dogs belonging to the *ban-ngaora* (an imp-like forest creature of Kham folklore). A single hit from one of their tiny darts and you would be sick for a long, long time. Sitting on the mountainside, my companions and I would hold our breath and shudder in silence as they passed through the forest below.

Perhaps I had already failed in my calling. Weren't missionaries supposed to be cocksure that one message—ours—fits all? I still believed in the gospel, but I questioned whether it was practical for these people. Theirs was a different world. One thing I *was* sure of was that it wasn't my place to decide for them. I wasn't qualified. They understood and felt their religion deeply; they would have to judge its relative merits. I would have to wait.

In the meantime, I was translating portions of the Christian Scriptures for Hasta Ram. We started with Jesus' parables, primarily because they are easy to translate. But I also chose the parables because of their profound and universal application. They contain deep wisdom for anyone willing to listen. And Hasta Ram proved himself willing; the parables were a source of endless delight to him. After a while, I began to believe that perhaps I was translating for the sake of this one man alone. Nancy and I decided that that was okay.

Hasta Ram's view of shamanism was simple: he didn't like the shamans, and he didn't like their religion. He regarded most aspects of their practice as pure cunning and deceit. He wasn't alone. Even shamans accuse their rivals of being charlatans. And the view of most villagers is ambivalent: on the one hand, they fear the shamans, and on the other, they despise them. Many a folktale ends with the punch line that "demons and shamans come from the same nest." Demons cause illness, giving the shaman his livelihood, and the shaman obtains blood sacrifice for the demons, keeping them alive.

* * *

One aspect of shamanism that took me by surprise was the way it touched on universal themes, some familiar to me from the Scriptures. Once a year, as prescribed by the shamans, villagers rid their households of bad luck and evil omens. A male yearling sheep is selected to "bear the evil away." But before it can qualify as a sin bearer, it must be twice purified. The sheep is first doused in the river, and then it is taken to the highest point of the village, where water and ointment are poured over its head. Its wool is dyed purple along the spine, and garlands are put around its neck.

Meanwhile, the women of the village assemble on the flat rooftops lining the village's main thoroughfare. In their hands, they hold winnowing trays containing soot, sweepings from the firepit, thorns, and other symbols of evil. The men lead the purified sheep from the top of the village, and as they descend, the women dump the contents of their winnowing trays on or beside the sin bearer, declaring, "May all evil directed at me come to naught like soot and ashes."

The sheep is then led to *Bul Nai*, a special altar at the entrance to the village, where it is slaughtered. The village is thus cleansed of evil. The sheep's head, set on the altar, is a reminder to all who enter.

In addition to this scapegoat ritual, there are several other undercurrents in shamanism that seem to anticipate core themes of the Christian experience. The notion of "God with us" through the incarnation of Christ is one such element. Mircea Eliade, a prominent specialist on shamanism, notes that the well-being and psychic integrity of the community in a shamanistic society depends on the notion that *"one of us* is able to help in the critical circumstances produced by the invisible inhabitants of the unseen world."

A yearling sheep selected to bear away evil

Even I have felt this strange sense of mystical presence. Once, driven out of the mountains by heavy snows, I was forced to take refuge in the remote Kham village of Ranma. The inhabitants kindly gave me a porch to sleep on, up near the top of the village. At about three in the morning, before the moon had set, a shaman emerged on a rooftop below, beating his drum and quietly chanting. Strangely, all seemed well. I lay in my sleeping bag, peering out at a world of snow-covered mountains and uncertainty, struck by the fact that someone was awake, someone watched for us, and that he was one of us.

Perhaps this was the connection that Hasta Ram had felt drawing him on throughout his life—the feeling of a "man in the heavens." What he had once felt as a shadow was becoming for him Reality: that "man in the heavens" was the One who had borne his sins away and now interceded on his behalf. Nurtured on shamanism, he now saw beyond. I too was beginning to see things at a deeper level than ever before. A contrasting perspective helped: "He that keepeth thee shall not slumber. Behold, he that keepeth Israel shall neither slumber nor sleep" (Psalm 121:3–4).

* * *

We had been living in the village of Shera for a couple of years when the shamans made an announcement that the spirit of a deceased shaman had failed to re-emerge. Nine years had passed, the maximum allowed. If, in nine years, a shaman's spirit does not seek rebirth, the community of shamans is required to hold a special ceremony at the shaman's gravesite, urging it to move on.

No one can choose to become a shaman of his own accord. He must be chosen by the spirits. Typically three years after a shaman's death, but no more than nine, the chief spirit, or *gel*, of the deceased shaman "touches" an unsuspecting young boy of the village. The boy falls into a fit of mild possession. If the *gel* approves of the boy, he will touch him again a few days later. If not, he will move on, probing others, until he finds a suitable candidate.

Once the spirit settles on a candidate, the fits of possession increase in severity with each visitation. Eventually, the boy begins to exhibit crazed and hysteroid behavior, and in some cases these visitations result in suicide. The candidate experiences terrifying dreams; he is attacked by animal spirits who maim and dismember him.

*A boy winces as a possessing
spirit touches him*

This period is typically referred to as the "call." It is a dangerous time, and if someone is lucky enough to survive it, he emerges a true shaman—one who has managed to overcome and regulate his psychosis. His attacking spirits become his new source of power.

* * *

In Shera, the community of shamans finished their incantations at the gravesite of the deceased and then moved on to a small open field in front of our house. All day long, we watched them, amused and entertained, as they called up spirits and spun off into fits of possession. The ceremony had the air of a festival—banging drums, jangling bells, and bouncing shamans.

Suddenly, a shaman was possessed by a leopard spirit. He began to viciously attack the crowd, biting and clawing. People in the crowd howled with delight, especially when someone else was bitten. Another was overcome by a monkey spirit and began to swing from trees and the rafters of houses. Yet another was possessed by the serpent spirit and wriggled across the ground, thrashing and flailing. We watched from a safe distance—we thought—the rooftop of our house.

The day passed, and night fell. We witnessed some pretty extraordinary things from our front-row seat! After supper, Nancy put the boys down, and in a couple of hours, we too went off to bed. As we lay there, just beginning to doze off, we suddenly heard a hideous chatter coming from the other room. We sat bolt upright in bed, spines tingling. Who got into the boys' room? How? He must have come in through their window.

We grabbed our flashlights and rushed in to confront the intruder. When we got there, he was already gone. All we could see was Daniel, standing in the middle of his bed. His face was severely contorted, and we suddenly realized that the chatter was coming from him.

"Daniel, Daniel, wake up," we shouted, scared out of our wits. "Wake up, wake up! You're having a nightmare."

Daniel pointed a finger behind us. "Look out," he screamed. We whirled around. There was nothing there.

"Oh, David, oh no, it's an evil spirit," Nancy cried, half whimpering. I knew she was right.

I held Daniel tightly, and Nancy put her hand on his head. "In the name of Jesus," she cried out, "we command you to leave. You have no right over him. He belongs to God." I added my voice to hers.

After Daniel calmed down, we prayed with him again, then sang his favorite song, "Jesus Loves Me, This I Know," and tucked him back into bed. He slept peacefully through the rest of the night.

Nancy and I lay awake for a long time, listening to Daniel's breathing. We talked, we wondered. We were frightened and confused.

* * *

We were also unprepared for what happened the next night, and the next, and the next. The visitation of the spirit became a regular occurrence. The spirit was peevish, underhanded, and deceitful, the wiliest serpent you could ever imagine, a slinking, slithering demon. He never rushed his quarry. He always began by making himself attractive, causing Daniel to giggle and respond with pleasure. Then the steel trap would snap shut, and Daniel would scream out in terror.

As time went on, the spirit became more and more resistant: we had to struggle in prayer, agonizing, pleading for the mercy of God. We took turns, Nancy and I, one keeping watch one night and the other, the next night. Daniel saw leopards, he saw serpents, and all tried to devour him. He was crazed, and his eyes were filled with terror. He was being called by the *gel*, but we didn't know it. Only later would we learn that, according to shamanistic lore, no one shakes "the call." You accept it, or you die.

We grew exhausted. Nightly, as we lay down to sleep, whether early or late, the *gel* and his devouring companions would arrive, taking advantage of our weakened state. It was hard to pray. Especially when it seemed to do so little good. As the weeks wore on, Daniel even began to sing strange chants in the night.

Nancy and I felt a deep disappointment in God. We had followed the footprints of his angel to this place, and now that we were here, it felt like he had abandoned us. Couldn't he deliver his servants from local spirits? What kind of Good News was that? We must have misread the signs.

* * *

We returned to Kathmandu, confused and broken. The dreadful spirit followed us. We called our friends together, people with many years of commitment to the gospel, people who had seen it all. We explained our situation, and upon their advice, we all decided that we would devote the next three days to prayer and fasting. We were reminded of Jesus' words to his disciples, "This kind cometh not out except by prayer and fasting" (Mark 9:29).

On the evening of the third day, we came together again, a united body of believers. We brought the sleeping child into our midst. We saw no evidence of an evil presence now. But we knew the slinking spirit's cunning; we had watched his sinister behavior for six months now. We knew he was hiding, fearful of his own end.

Collectively, we laid hands on Daniel and cast the spirit out in the authority of Jesus' name. Through prayer, we bound it in chains and forbade it to return. After several hours of sustained prayer, our friends returned home. Nancy and I went to bed, bracing ourselves, cringing from habit, waiting for the spirit's arrival. He didn't arrive that night. Daniel slept soundly. The next night was the same, and the next night again. That was the last we saw of the dreadful spirit.

Several years later, after I knew a great deal more about the subtleties of shamanism, I inquired about the shamanic line that the shamans had attempted to revive on that fateful day in Shera. The *gel* had been "terminated," the shamans told me, never to resurface. They were unaware of the exhausting struggle we had been through. It was many more years before I would tell them what had happened.

Chapter 11: What, Give up Speaking Kham?

I heard the wailing of sirens... people were running into doorways to shelter, a group of policemen burst out from around a corner, thrashing the fleeing pedestrians with long sticks. One could smell the odor of gas and of something burning. I tried to find out what was going on. A man sprinting by with a stone in his hand yelled, 'Language war!' and rushed on.
—*Ryszard Kapuscinski,* Travels with Herodotus

Every language is a unique and collective human genius, as divine and endless a mystery as a living organism.
—*Kenneth Hale*

In May 1984, about a decade and a half after my first sight of the Himalayas, I was trekking across the rugged backcountry of Rolpa District, the southern Kham area, with my porter, Satal Singh Kham. No one travels through these parts for fun. In the southern half, it's intolerably hot and humid, and the track goes straight up or straight down across the grain of the mountain ridges. We were on our way to Taka village, still a week's journey away, and Satal Singh had agreed to carry my backpack. The year before, he and his brother, Bom Bahadur, had resettled with their families in Dang Valley, one of the *duns*, or inner valleys, just north of the hot and flat Terai, and Satal Singh was happy for the chance to get paid for making a trip home.

Numerous Khams, looking for a better future, had resettled in Dang in recent years. Population in the mountains had increased dramatically

in some regions, but arable land remained pitifully limited. In desperation, many decided to get out while they still could. Land in Dang was relatively cheap, the bazaar town of Ghorai could be reached within a couple of hours from anywhere in the valley, schools were closer and better, and regular bus service gave them easy access to the rest of the world.

How well the Khams will benefit from this pattern of resettlement remains to be seen. I benefited immediately. Finding reliable porters in bazaar towns had always been an enormous problem. The biggest hurdle was to find someone with enough courage to go beyond the Hindu lowlands, where the definition of civilization seemed to be that the inhabitants spoke Nepali and you could still get a bowl of rice. Who knows what could happen "out there," people would say, with a vague wave of the hand toward the mountains. They had all heard exaggerated stories about bandits on every pass, stories made more plausible by regular reports that the mountain dwellers were even beef eaters.

Such complaints were doubtless motivated in part by fear, but they were also part of a well-rehearsed script for demanding higher wages. If you were lucky enough to find someone willing to accompany you, it was always for an exorbitant price, and even then, you could expect a mutiny for higher wages on some lonely, fog-swept pass halfway to your destination. It happened without fail. But I was, by this point, no naif. And I still held the purse strings. My response had become a well-rehearsed script, too. I would storm and fume for a while to let them know how unhappy I was, and then I would play the trump card, refusing to pay them until they got me to a village. No one turned back without his wages. Once in a village, I felt no twinge of remorse about letting them go. I could always find a more dependable and willing replacement.

All those problems came to an end when Kham speakers began settling in Dang Valley. Satal Singh, in fact, accompanied me on more than a dozen expeditions. He was more than just a porter; he was a friend whom I knew I could count on. I had no doubt that he would die before he abandoned me. He didn't look very dangerous; he was short even for a Kham, no more than five-foot-two. But his frame was like that of a bull terrier. His face was oval-shaped, made more oval by a bowl-shaped haircut. His eyes played tricks on him sometimes, rolling up for no apparent reason; that, combined with an impish smirk, meant that you could never quite tell if he was making faces at you or not.

Satal Singh's voice was odd—high-pitched and airy, something like a pump organ with a wheezy valve. When he was serious, and especially when he was a bit argumentative, he would wrinkle his brow and punctuate his most important points with short bursts of air through his nasal cavity. It sounded like he was trying to dislodge something from the back of his nose. It was a distracting and unpleasant quirk.

Satal Singh and I stopped at a small, trailside teahouse for our regular morning meal of *dal bhat* (rice and lentils). We were still in southern Rolpa, an area once inhabited by Kham speakers who, in an earlier generation, had abandoned their native tongue in favor of Nepali. The population was mixed, partly Kham stock and partly Nepali castes. As we sat in the shade of the veranda waiting for our meal to be cooked, Satal Singh began telling me a humorous story of his late uncle's encounter with a bear.

There's nothing quite as funny as a story told in Kham. The rhythm of the language, peppered with clip-clopping, whistling, and rattling onomatopoeia, is enough, almost by itself, to make you laugh. I kept breaking into howls of laughter as the cadences broke over me and I visualized the whole comic scene in my mind.

Suddenly, we were interrupted by a stranger who had been eyeing us from the other side of the veranda. "Tell your story in Nepali so we can all enjoy it," he said, rather pompously.

Satal Singh whirled around with an invective that surprised both me and the stranger. "Why should I stop speaking Kham?" he answered with hostility, obviously interpreting the man's request as a challenge.

Now it was the stranger's turn to be offended. "It's all a bunch of gibberish; what good is it?" There was contempt in his voice.

Satal Singh was on his feet in an instant. "You poor devils," he said with feigned pity, "you've let the Brahmins talk you into giving up your language, and now you want me to give up mine. I'll never do it. When you lost your language, you lost your land and everything else worth having. We'll never do that. We still have our language."

Satal Singh started snorting through the back of his nose, and I knew then that he was serious. He crossed the veranda in a few quick steps. The startled stranger was eyeing him uncertainly, and I found myself clamoring to defuse the situation, forcing both of them to sit down and listen to reason. I was afraid that they would soon come to blows.

Satal Singh

* * *

Language is the soul of a culture. Every language represents a different window on the world, a different way of seeing things, a different way of categorizing reality. Benjamin Lee Whorf, an American anthropologist and linguist of the early 1900s, went so far as to say that different languages have "different conceptual universes," and that every language provides a "unique guide to reality." He concluded that "one's language constrains the way one thinks." Most modern linguists, myself included, believe in at least a weak version of Whorf's hypothesis. Kenneth Hale, for example, argues that every language is a "unique and collective human genius, as divine and endless a mystery as a living organism." The loss of a language, then, is the loss of a unique human genius and diminishes our world as surely as the loss of a biological species. My Kham friend Satal Singh seemed to agree. Take someone's language away, and you've destroyed a big part of him.

* * *

Kham, along with about sixty other languages in Nepal, belongs to the Tibeto-Burman family of languages. In fact, Kham retains a number of conservative grammatical features most closely resembling far-flung languages like Tangut from Inner Mongolia, Gyarong at the north end of the China-Tibet border, and Rawang from northern Burma.

Tibeto-Burman, most scholars agree, had its beginnings in the deep folds of mountains running north and south between the headwaters of the Yangtze, the Mekong, and Salween Rivers, now in upper Yunnan province of China (the so-called "Three Gorges"). Slightly south and west, the Irrawaddy descends into Burma. From their original home-land, Tibeto-Burman speakers began a series of outward migrations that rarely went out of sight of the mountains. One group, the Tanguts, did leave the mountains and traveled as far north as Inner Mongolia. They had the misfortune of settling on Genghis Khan's expansion route to the west, and in the thirteenth century, they were wiped out for standing in the way. An entire library of Tangut books written in Chinese characters was discovered hidden in the ruins of a Buddhist stupa by a Russian scholar in the early 1900s.

Linguistic evidence suggests that there were several westward migrations into the regions of the Nepali Himalayas. Nobody knows exactly when they began, or what routes they took, but it is fairly safe to assume that the migrations into Nepal moved westward along the Tibetan plateau before penetrating the Himalayas to the south. There they encountered a lush, well-watered land almost devoid of human population. Kham and Magar were likely among the earliest migrations, both reaching their present homeland in western Nepal well before the time of Christ or of Buddha. Other Tibeto-Burman migrations pushed into eastern Nepal, where today there are more than thirty distinct Tibeto-Burman languages, known collectively as Kiranti. The Tibetan migration was the last, sometime before the eighth century, a rapid

expansion across the entire Tibetan plateau north of the Himalayas. In recent centuries, numerous Tibetan populations have also penetrated southward through the Himalayas.

Most Tibeto-Burman people groups were pre-literate, oral societies, the notable exceptions being those who spoke Tibetan and Burmese. Possession of literature may, in fact, account for the rapid expansion of these two groups. Burmese has been written for almost a millennium (Tibetan, even longer) and has spread far beyond its original mountain homeland. Today, Tibeto-Burman languages, at least three hundred in all, are spoken along a two-thousand-mile corridor stretching from northern Vietnam to northern Pakistan.

* * *

The Pahari language now known as Nepali is a relative newcomer to

the central and eastern Himalayan regions that were once the exclusive preserve of Tibeto-Burman languages. Nepali entered into the regions of the Nepali Himalayas from the opposite direction of the Tibeto-Burman languages; it is derived from ancient Sanskrit, and belongs to the Indo-Aryan family of languages. As such, it is related to Hindi, Panjabi, Gujarati, Bengali, and numerous other languages of the Indian subcontinent. It doesn't take a lot of linguistic savvy to figure that one out: anyone who has heard the languages spoken side-by-side can guess at their common ancestry.

But what surprised and intrigued everybody 250 years ago was that Sanskrit (and, by extension, all its daughter languages like Nepali) was actually related to ancient but familiar European languages—Greek and Latin. Sir William Jones, writing in 1786, came to the conclusion that:

The Sanskrit language, whatever be its antiquity, is of wonderful structure; more perfect than the Greek, more copious than the Latin, and more exquisitely refined than either, yet bearing to both of them a stronger affinity... than could possibly have been produced by accident; so strong indeed, that no philologer [linguist] could examine them all three, without believing them to have sprung from some common source.

Even after thousands of years of separation from their common ancestor, there are still numerous words in modern Nepali that resemble their European counterparts; not loan words, but words that come from the same cradle— words like *tri,* "three"; *sat,* "seven" (*siete* in Spanish); *kamij,* "shirt" (*kamesa* in Spanish); *mech,* "bench" (*mesa,* "table" in Spanish); *paidal,* "foot" (*pod* in Greek); *hirdaya,* "heart" (*kardia* in Greek), to name just a few.

Sometime around the ninth century, a tribe of Aryan people known as the Khas, living in the hilly, sub-Himalayan regions of northwestern India, began migrating eastward across the Mahakali River into the mountainous regions that now make up western Nepal. In the twelfth century, they founded the Malla kingdom of Jumla, which at its zenith in the fourteenth century covered a large tract of land from the plateau of Tibet to the plains of India.

In the same period, during the twelfth and thirteenth centuries, the Khas immigrants began to absorb, even welcome, numbers of Rajput Hindu immigrants from Rajasthan—high-caste Brahmins and Kshatriyas fleeing Muslim oppression in Moghul India. Over time, ethnic and linguistic differences between the disparate waves of immigrants began to fade and eventually vanish. It is assumed that the early Khas language, of which we have no record, incorporated countless features from Rajput. The resulting hybrid, preserved in fourteenth-century inscriptions, is clearly the precursor to modern Nepali.

The Aryan immigrants, enriched by the civilizing contributions of the Rajput Hindus, came with superior agriculture, superior tools, and a more developed civilization. In addition to priests and artisans, many of the newcomers were of the warrior caste (the Kshatriyas). It is not known how warlike the Aryans were in the early years of their expansion, but they slowly began to change and even supplant many of the local languages and cultures.

Kham, situated in the western third of modern Nepal, would have been one of the first Tibeto-Burman languages the Aryans bumped into on their eastward trek. Though the higher-caste Aryans, the Brahmins and Kshatriyas (or Chhetris), never settled in the high, remote regions of the Kham homeland, they certainly would have traveled through some of those regions and left their indelible mark on the language. Perhaps more linguistically influential were the lower-caste *kamis* and *damais* (blacksmiths and musicians), who, finding ready employment as artisans in the remote Kham villages, settled down there. Through the centuries, Kham borrowed scores of words from the Aryan immigrants, mostly from their material culture, so that today a full 25 percent of the Kham vocabulary can be traced to Indic sources. Some terms are very, very old, no longer found in modern Nepali, and may hearken back to the original Khas language.

Evidence suggests that Kham, in the not-too-distant past, covered a much wider geographical area than it does today. Numerous

villages, ridgetops, and landmarks in the warmer climes to the south and east bear unmistakable Kham names: *Harjang,* "Cattle Hump"; *Lumsum,* "Mortar Stone"; *Rihzanam,* "Little Water Village"; *Libang,* "Bow Meadows"; *Singlah,* "Firewood Hill." To the modern inhabitants, these are only labels; no one seems to recognize that the names might actually mean something.

Today, Kham survives only in the remotest parts of Rukum and Rolpa

Districts, where villages cling to the sides of two massive outgrowths of high, mountainous terrain that extends for fifty miles off the western and southwestern flanks of the Dhaulagiri Himal. No roads reach the region. Recent satellite photos have shown that less than 2 percent of the land is under cultivation, and to cultivate even that tiny fraction, the inhabitants have to farm on terrain with as much as forty-five degree slopes—that's one hundred vertical feet for every hundred feet hori-

zontal! This tract of land is too high, too arid, and too rugged for rice cultivation; barley and potato cultivation is hardly sufficient to feed the local population. Of necessity, there is a great dependence on livestock, chiefly sheep and goats, nimble on their feet and prized for their wool.

So it is unlikely that the Aryan invaders drove the hapless inhabitants out of their original homelands into the harshness of the mountains, and also unlikely that they engaged in intentional glottocide, the destruction of a people's language. Rather, the Khams already inhabited

the mountainous regions, and because there was nothing there to attract the newcomers' greed, the Aryans were diverted to easier and richer prizes. The rugged and hostile environment of the Khams became, thus, the salvation of their language and culture.

The picture that emerges from eastern Nepal is less fortunate. Eastern Nepal is home to numerous Tibeto-Burman languages, known collectively as Kiranti. Though the Kiranti languages were touched only recently

by the Aryan expansion, they have had less to insulate them. Many of them have very small numbers of speakers, and their tribal areas take in no more than two or three intersecting valleys. These people have always had to depend on an extra language, a *lingua franca*, to transact necessary and regular inter-tribal trade. Before the arrival of the Aryans, that *lingua franca* was Bantawa, a widespread Kiranti language. But once the Aryans had settled beside them, Nepali soon became the *lingua franca* of the region. Today, with all primary and secondary education conducted in Nepali, many children speak their mother tongue only with their parents, and many others have ceased to use it altogether. Linguistic extinction is rapidly approaching.

Chapter 12: The Perils and Challenges of Literacy

Knowledge without justice ought to be called cunning rather than wisdom.
—Plato

Ten years before my trek across Rolpa with Satal Singh, in the mid-1970s, Nancy and I had already determined that we would attempt a literacy program in Kham. One might say, in fact, that Satal Singh's hostile reaction in the teahouse was due, in part, to the success of that program.

We had, by that time, done sufficient language study to come up with a good working orthography. It was based on the Devanagri script used in Nepali and several northern Indian languages. If the Kham people had had any contact with reading at all, it would have been in this script.

So we were careful to ensure that the characters used had the same phonetic value as they did in Nepali and that there was as little intrusion of novel symbols as possible. We wanted to build on what some already knew and also to make it possible for new readers to make an easy transition to Nepali. So क was the symbol for "k" in both Nepali and Kham, त was the symbol for "t," and म was the symbol for "m." Where Kham had sounds that were nonexistent in Nepali, however, we had to craft new or modified symbols.

Back in Taka-Shera, I decided to take our proposal to the *ghat buda*, the council of village elders. If I could demonstrate that their language was writable, maybe they would begin to perceive it as a *pakkaa*, bona fide language, more on a par with Nepali. Hasta Ram, my friend and language teacher, made the arrangements and agreed to go with me. In fact, I was counting on him to present the idea. There was less chance that way of making a serious blunder. We went prepared, armed with a familiar folk story pleasingly written in the proposed script.

We met at Nar Bahadur's house, up near the top of the village, with its broad, sweeping view of the valley below. When we arrived, everybody was already there. They were sitting on blankets and lounging in a semi-circle, some with their backs propped against the wall.

Although they tried not to show it, they were intensely curious about our proposal. There had been rumors for years that the reason Nancy and I were in the village was to uncover deposits of gold, or better yet, diamonds and rubies.

Only Nar Bahadur sat fully erect, his usual bearing. It seemed somehow to match his equine face and long, straight nose. He wore a faded red turban, cocked slightly to one side. He sported an impressive mustache for a man of his race, something of which he was justifiably proud. He always fidgeted with it, especially when he was thinking, twirling the tips between his fingers.

He welcomed us with a typical Kham greeting, a restatement of the obvious, "You've come."

"Yes," we replied, "we've come."

I took my place in the circle. Everyone feigned indifference. From where I sat, I could see row upon row of flat rooftops descending below me to the bottom of the hill. Directly across, only a few hundred yards away, were the towering cliffs of *Nokya Haang*, a favorite harvesting ground for wild honey, extracted under great peril. Off to the left, little more than two miles away were the black crags of *Nar Shing*, 5,500 feet above us. The whole world was like an immense IMAX screen, right in our faces; it was almost too much to take in.

Nar Bahadur took the lead by pulling a *sulpa*, a straight smoking pipe, from his inner vest pocket. No clay model, this one, but lovingly carved from a choice piece of gnarled rhododendron wood. He took a metal pick from a string around his neck and poked it into the intake hole to dislodge old, dried tobacco. He blew into it and slapped the bowl sharply against the palm of his hand. Then, to free up his hands, he wedged the *sulpa* between the toes of his right foot. From his other vest pocket, he pulled a rolled leather pouch and began to unwind it. He extracted a bit of tobacco and kneaded it between his right thumb and the palm of his left hand, then he filled the bowl and packed it tightly.

A typical pipe

Nar Bahadur motioned to the left side of *Nokya Haang* cliffs and began to talk about a deer that had been cornered there yesterday by hunting dogs. He had watched it all from his porch. As he talked, he put his pouch away and dug into his outer vest pocket for a tinder box and striking steel, placing the pipe between his toes again.

"Somehow, the deer managed to get away," he said, and then as though for emphasis, he struck the steel against the flint. A spark flew, and a wisp of smoke

Lighting up with flint

rose from the tinder. He deftly placed the smoldering tinder onto the pressed tobacco. He was in no hurry. However curious his listeners, there was a protocol to follow. These things were not to be rushed.

Still talking, he put his tinder box away. Then, gently holding the pipe between the two forefingers of his right hand, he cupped the bowl with his left hand and began to suck and puff until there was a steady flow of smoke.

Sitting across from Nar Bahadur were Bahadur and Bhadiraj.

Bahadur was *pradhan* that year, the village headman. Bhadiraj was *upa pradhan*, his assistant headman. At election time every two years, Bahadur and Bhadiraj exchanged offices; it had been this way for years. It was reported that Bahadur was wealthy. Not only did he have a lot of land but he was an astute moneylender. Everyone owed him money, and the lending rate was high enough to ensure that nobody ever got out of debt.

Bahadur, to be sure, didn't look wealthy. He was a squat, bandy-legged man, who usually wore an old *lungi* wrapped around his waist and a pair of flip-flops on his feet. His front teeth were gapped and tobacco-stained. On his head, he wore a black Nepali cap, a *topi*, that gave every indication of having been there for twenty years. It was so grimy in places that it looked waxed. It perfectly fit the curvature of his head. When he talked, he would sweep it off with one hand and scratch his closely cropped head with the other before sliding it back on.

Bahadur liked to chew, but he was a terrible spitter. Today, he sat on the outside edge of the circle, opposite Nar Bahadur, in a place where he could spit off the porch. From time to time, he craned his neck side-ways and swung his chin outward in an attempt to lob the tobacco juice clear of his leg. Tobacco stains on his *lungi* testified to the fact that he'd missed at least once today. His shirt sleeve, too, was stained from wiping his mouth.

As usual, Bahadur joked a lot and kept everyone laughing. All of us knew, though, that Bahadur's jokes were intended to demonstrate a serious point—a skill that he'd honed through years of practice.

Bhadiraj, Bahadur's deputy, spoke Kham with the slowest drawl I have ever heard. Whenever I was around him, I had a hankering to yank the words out of his mouth. Even his laugh was a slow, drawn out guffaw. Something about Bhadiraj made me wary of him. He smiled too much and was too polite. I was never sure he could be trusted.

He had a fresh, calico-print *topi* on his head, the latest fashion statement from Kathmandu. But he didn't know how to wear it. The crown was pushed all the way out, making it look more like a dunce cap. It tilted forward precariously, resting just above his brow. Perhaps that was a deliberate affectation, so that everyone could see the Hindu topknot at the back of his head. Bhadiraj liked to keep up appearances.

Though he didn't chew tobacco, Bhadiraj was a skillful spitter, a perfect foil to Bahadur. He projected neat little squirts of clear liquid straight through a gap between his two front teeth. It even made a precise little spurting sound—*pppt*. Today he would have to refrain; he was a long way from the edge of the porch.

Across from me was Ranya, the oldest man in the group. Ranya exuded class. He had a strong face, with high cheekbones, and wisps of white whiskers coming from his chin. He was the portrait of a Mongolian gentleman, and my camera loved him. In all the years I knew him, he wore a heavy black felt cloak, complemented with a cuffed top hat fabricated from the same strip of wool. Ranya was gifted in understanding differing points of view, an invaluable asset in bringing a group of men to a consensus. He always delivered his final verdict with a deep, rumbling voice that carried a great deal of weight. It was clear to me why Ranya was part of the *ghat buda*.

But I could never understand how Jhuparya got onto the council. He was a big oaf of a man with a protruding brow that made him look like a Neanderthal. (*Jhuparya* was, in fact, a nickname that meant something like 'overhanging brow'. I never knew his real name.) He always wore a dirty white turban tied sloppily on his head and on the verge of coming undone. He had a sepulchral, booming voice. Unfortunately, his booming was usually off-topic.

There were other men there, too, but I remember only Hakalya, sitting in the corner, leaning against the grain box. He wore a wool skull cap, the trademark of a mountain shepherd. His hands were strong and bony, and his strong bare feet gave one the impression that he was capable of traveling with ease in any kind of terrain. His strong face and solid jaw hinted further at his tough character. He said little, but when he did speak, he was always worth listening to.

It took almost an hour, but eventually the meeting got under way. Hasta Ram and I carefully presented our case. Since even those on the council could barely read or write, we were sensitive to their concern that their youngsters, if educated prematurely, might challenge their authority. So we assured them that we would teach them first.

Hasta Ram read the story and explained some of the spelling conventions. Bahadur seemed a bit confused at first, then a little amused, his eyes twinkling. I had no idea what he was thinking as he swiped the *topi* off his head and slid it back on.

Hakalya, usually quiet, was the first to speak. "What's the point of learning to read folk stories?" he asked. "We already know them by heart."

I was a bit surprised, but before I could form a reply, Bahadur followed with a question that revealed what he had been smiling about. "Sahib," he said, "if we learn how to read, will we ever be white?"

Everyone laughed. Ranya looked embarrassed.

Not understanding what he meant, I asked, "What do you mean, 'Will we ever be white'? Being white is not what it's about."

"That *is* what it's about," Bahadur insisted. "We'll always be black because our hearts are black."

Everyone laughed again. Hasta Ram squirmed in discomfort. Bahadur was clearly agitated now; he aimed a big wad of tobacco juice at the edge of the porch and missed. It splatted across a timber, and he wiped his mouth on his sleeve.

I don't remember the rest of the meeting except that Bahadur's remark was considered final. We all got up to leave, and on the way home, I asked Hasta Ram, "What happened?" He was shaken and apparently figured that my question didn't merit an answer. He remained silent. It was several years before I fully understood the meaning of Bahadur's words.

* * *

Before the restoration of the Shah kings to power in 1951 by King Tribhuvan, ending one hundred years of hedonistic rule by the Rana prime ministers, education of the masses had been an extremist idea deliberately opposed. The British historian Daniel Wright, writing on

Nepal in 1877, said, "The subject of schools and colleges may be treated as briefly as that of snakes in Ireland. There are none." In 1951, only 1 percent of the population was enrolled in school. King Tribhuvan changed all that, and by the time of his death in 1955, education was becoming fairly common; schools had been constructed in all major administrative centers.

Using education as a vehicle for unification, the basic mantra in all public schools was "We are all Nepalis," and the language used by the eighteenth-century conqueror Prithvi Narayan Shah was declared the official language. Originally known as *Khas Kura* ("Khas language") and later as *Gorkhali*, after the name of Gorkha District, from which Prithvi Narayan launched his military campaign in the 1740s, the language was now increasingly being referred to as *Nepali*.

Today, Nepali is the official language of government, commerce, and education, though this reality is unpopular in some parts of the country, especially in areas dominated by larger ethnic groups. Official Nepali education ran roughshod over regional and cultural sensitivities, despite their venerable history and sophistication. The great cities of Kathmandu Valley—an example of that history and sophistication—were built not by Nepalis, but by Newars, an ancient race with their own language and a rich literature dating back to the fourteenth century. Newar architecture is unique in South Asia, claimed by some to be the source of the ancient oriental pagoda. Yet despite their continuation as a vital and vibrant ethnolinguistic group today, the Newar identity is only reluctantly recognized in any official sense.

Before Prithvi Narayan Shah took the throne in 1775, the northern Kham villages were part of the ancient Shah kingdom of Rukum. The Shahs of Rukum had migrated from Jumla, the Malla kingdom farther west, and after its demise were part of a federation known as *Baise Rajya* ("the twenty-two kingdoms"). Their hold over the Khams was a loose one and, more importantly, of little practical concern to them. The Khams of that period were barbaric, to be sure, but they kept to themselves and posed no real threat. Besides, they were beef eaters, and their land was of little value. They just weren't worth getting in a fuss over.

Over time, Khams became aware that they were slowly being
marginalized by the political system that now ruled Nepal. A few of
their men were able to make up for the inequity by joining the British
Gurkhas in India, but even that was a long shot for most of them. Most
young men, having spent much of their lives in sheep camps, lacked
confidence when speaking Nepali. So they didn't venture out much.

When an opportunity for education showed up in the 1960s, some
of the wealthier families recognized their chance and sent their sons
to Baglung, five days' walk to the east. In a few years, schools were also
available in Burtibang, two or three days' walk away.

The results were disastrous. A generation of malcontents was born.
Back in the villages, the new breed was too good to dig in the soil or
chase after sheep. And jobs were unavailable for the newly "educated"
even in the cities, unless one were a Brahmin or a Chhetri or had influential contacts. As the Nepali anthropologist and social critic Dor
Bahadur Bista observed, "Scholarship in the Sanskritic tradition is
associated with privilege and never with labour... To be educated is to
be effectively removed from the workforce."

So, many students returned home and became village thugs, perfect-
ing the criminal practices they had witnessed in the towns. They were
all engaged in the illegal drug trade, something the villagers accepted
at first—at least they had a ready market for their hashish crop. But the
criminal behavior didn't stop there; this new breed of thugs forged alliances with the police in district headquarters and formed local mafias,
running extortion rings in every village. Villagers were called upon to
pay timber tax, house tax, trail tax, pig tax, and even dog tax. Shamans
had to pay drum tax.

Those who resisted found themselves in jail. The uneducated villagers were easy prey to the stratagems of an administrative and legal
system distorted by their educated assailants.

Most honest, hardworking villagers were thus understandably wary
of Nepali education and wanted no part of it. In Kham, as in many
Nepalese languages, the word for "smart" is synonymous with the word

for "deceitful." The adults, given a choice, preferred their children to be dumb and honest.

In Maoist-controlled areas in the mid-1990s, the first item of business was a settling of scores against the thugs on behalf of the aggrieved villagers. A local hooligan who bullied the villages of Taka and Shera for as long as we were there, was tortured, his limbs hacked off one at a time. Others were flayed alive or had chili pepper rubbed into their wounds. Pleas for mercy were answered by swift decapitation.

* * *

Bahadur—the man who had asked me, "If we learn how to read, will we ever be white?"—was, for all appearances, just a simple villager. He had never heard of most Hindu or Buddhist philosophers, and he had certainly never heard of Plato. The only sages he knew were the home-grown variety—the occasional wise man who grew up in the village. But he had arrived independently at one of Plato's basic conclusions, that education is useless if it doesn't create a better citizen. The goal of literacy is education, and the goal of education is good citizenship.

Too many literacy programs, especially those for tribal societies, fail to take these principles beyond superficial levels. Everyone knows that motivation is the biggest obstacle to a reading program, but few such programs hold out to their readers anything more than health pamphlets or homilies on better agricultural methods. These are good things, God knows, but how will such technical tracts inspire people to want to read? Any attempt, no matter how well-intentioned, to create a new-and-improved citizen through milk-and-water platitudes masks a vulgar condescension. It assumes that because people are new to literacy, they are new to the most important questions of life—that they are incapable of serious inquiry. To use a modern term, it "dumbs down" where it should inspire.

How much better a literacy effort that treats people in preliterate societies as full adults, and their language as capable of expressing the best philosophical and religious notions of the ages. If we want to preserve people's languages, and if we want them to be literate in those languages, how about giving them something worth reading— something ennobling, something that stirs the emotions and fires the passions? Although I did not understand it on the day of our meeting, this was Bahadur's challenge.

If we want to preserve people's languages, and if we want them to be literate in those languages, how about giving them something worth reading?

Chapter 13: On Translation

The translator labours to secure a natural habitat for the alien presence which [he imports] into his own tongue and cultural setting.
—*George Steiner,* After Babel

The limits of my language mean the limits of my world.
—*Ludwig Wittgenstein,* Tractatus Logico-Philosophicus

By the same act whereby [a speaker] spins language out of himself, he spins himself into it, and every language draws about the people that possesses it a circle whence it is possible to exit only by stepping over at once into the circle of another one.
—*Wilhelm von Humboldt,* On Language

The history of language is not so much the story of people misled by their languages as it is the story of a successful struggle against the limitations built into all language systems.
—*Peter Farb,* Word Play

Over time, I began to have a nagging feeling that maybe the Christian Scriptures couldn't be translated into Kham. It's not that Kham was lacking in virility or strength. It was almost too virile, too vigorous. Gods and demons lurked close to the surface, and if one wasn't careful, certain solemn passages began to sound creepy or even to take on the feel of a shaman's rite. Why in the world was Jesus putting spit on the blind man's eyes, and what was Jesus doing inviting his disciples to drink his blood? And any talk about receiving the Holy Spirit as a "baptism by fire" made it feel like the eyes around the campfire had moved in just a bit closer. Ordinary words came loaded with associations of magic.

Hasta Ram, it's true, took delight in our simple renditions of the parables of Jesus. The earthy metaphors of rural Palestine suited Kham well; the herding of sheep and sowing of seed are better suited to Kham than to modern English sensibilities:

> Behold, there went out a sower to sow. And it came to pass, as he sowed, some fell by the wayside, and the fowls of the air came and devoured it up (Mark 4:3–4).

> I am the good shepherd. The good shepherd lays down his life for the sheep (John 10:11).

Kham excels here. This is the stuff of everyday life.

But even some of the parables presented difficulties. What about the rich man who sounded like a delusional schizophrenic?

> And he began reasoning to himself, saying, "What shall I do, since I have no place to store my crops?" And he said, "This is what I will do: I will tear down my barns and build larger ones, and there I will store all my grain and my goods. And I will say to my soul, 'Soul, you have many goods laid up for many years to come; take your ease, eat, drink and be merry.'" But God said to him, "You fool! This very night your soul is required of you" (Luke 12:17–20).

So why did God call him a fool? Why, of course, because he *was* a fool—he sat around talking to himself!

It was impossible to tell where the next unexpected challenge would come from. I liked to call them "exegetical surprises." The Bible commentaries poured out oceans of ink explaining the mismatches between Greek and English, but who would have guessed at the mismatches between Greek and Kham? They were everywhere.

Slight differences in grammatical structure sometimes yielded unexpected meaning differences. Take the famous passage: "It is easier for a camel to go through the eye of a needle than for a rich man to enter the kingdom of God" (Matthew 19:24). There have been different opinions on whether Jesus was referring to a gate in Jerusalem known as "The Needle's Eye" or not, but that's immaterial here. The plain sense is clear enough. Compared to one feat, the other is easy.

I couldn't make Hasta Ram understand. We spent hours discussing it, but it all ended in frustration. Finally, with a bewildered look of defeat on his face, he said, "But I don't get what's easy about either one!"

"Oh, but they're not easy," I responded. "They're hard!"

"Well, then, why don't you say that they're hard?"

"Isn't that what I've been saying?"

"No, you've been saying that one is easy, and the other is easier."

Finally I understood the problem. It's the way the comparative is formed in Kham. The form of construction in Kham says literally, "More than X is easy, Y is easy." So we restructured the passage to read, "It is *harder* for a rich man to enter the kingdom of God than for a camel to go through the eye of a needle."

There's not a single commentary that would have alerted me to that.

* * *

Kham culture takes a perverse kind of pleasure in passages that may or may not have been funny in the original. When Jesus says, "If your eye offends you, pluck it out; it is better to go into life with one eye than to be cast into the fires of hell having both eyes" (Mark 9:47), Khams are unable to repress a laugh. They love hyperbole; their own speech is peppered with it. The passage in Mark 9 about tying a millstone around somebody's neck and casting him into the sea is one of their favorites. "Good, he must have had it coming!" Who knows, when Jesus uttered these sayings in Aramaic, they may have been funny, too. But in the context of Kham culture and discourse, they are naturally funny.

I remember traveling with half a dozen Kham men on a broad trail several hours from the village. It began to rain, and we took immediate shelter in a small herder's hut. Suddenly, around the bend came a woman bearing an enormous timber on her head with the aid of a tumpline. Clearly, she had been thinking about stopping, but seeing us, she pretended to have another destination in mind.

As she passed, one man said loudly, "Wow, what a fine umbrella she has, don't you wish we had one, too?"

"Oh yes," another replied, "not only an umbrella, it can even serve as a bench when she gets tired. How very nice!"

"And not only that," said a third, "it's long enough that she can even use it for a bed when it grows dark!"

"Better still," said the first, "it's long enough that she can sleep on one end and burn the other end for fire!"

I felt bad for the poor woman. Hoping to put her load down, she had encountered a bunch of rowdies. I don't think, though, that they were trying to be mean. They couldn't help themselves. Something about the Kham language usage inclines the people to see life as if it were a comic strip. They rebel against bland diction. Everything is exaggerated for effect.

But it's all right to go ahead and pour it on the bad guys: they deserve it. So everyone sits up when Jesus starts out, "Woe unto you, Pharisees!" Every punch prompts great satisfaction. Heads wag and bodies lean. They can't help but think about their overlords, the Brahmins and the Chhetris. This is good stuff!

Some of the early criticisms of Wycliffe's fourteenth-century English Bible translation could certainly have been directed at me, too: "The gospel pearl is cast abroad, and trodden under foot of swine; that which was before precious both to clergy and laity is rendered as it were the common jest of both. The jewel of the Church is turned into the common sport of the people, and what was hitherto the principal gift of the clergy and divines is made for ever common to the laity."

* * *

Compared to the linguistic virility of Kham, the rhetorical cadences of New Testament Greek seemed sterile and lifeless. Not only were they awkward and unpleasant to the Kham ear, they seemed to force Kham into a straitjacket. Some passages were downright impossible. What is one to do with "To whom God would make known what is the riches of the glory of this mystery among the Gentiles; which is Christ in you, the hope of glory" (Colossians 1:27)?

Where does one even start?

It has long been recognized that "not everything that can be said in one language can be said in another"—at least not with the same force or with the original association of meanings. All translation is a compromise, and the greater the difference between two languages, the more severe the problem becomes. Kham and Greek, like Kham and English, are worlds apart.

I wasn't the first to notice or to struggle with problems of equivalence. Beginning in the third century B.C. and continuing over the next two centuries, the Hebrew Scriptures were themselves translated into Greek, a version that came to be known as the Septuagint, "the work of seventy scholars." One of the scholars associated with the latter stages of this translation, a grandson of Jesus ben Sira, wrote down a few of his observations about the translation process. "Those things said originally in Hebrew," he said, "have not equal force when they are transferred into another tongue."

All of the European languages, Greek included, abound in abstract nouns. In grade school, you'll remember, we learned that a noun designates "a person, place, or thing." But in order to include abstractions too, the definition has to be expanded: a noun is thus "a person, place, thing, or idea." Common nouns that name concrete things, like stones or trees, can be pointed to; they can be counted, weighed, and manipulated. Abstract nouns are a bit less wieldy. Can anyone point at love except as a concrete act of love? Can mercy or forgiveness be weighed?

Abstract nouns typically name actions or states or events. But this is stolen turf that rightfully belongs to verbs: "I love you," expresses an emotion; "He forgave me," bespeaks an action. Both are the rightful province of verbs. In a "normal" language like Kham, concrete things are named by nouns, while processes or events are still expressed by verbs.

It's only when philosophers and poets have felt the need to get a handle on such notions by manipulating and talking about them in the abstract that the need has arisen for abstract nouns. It's as though we can understand some things better by isolating them, stopping them dead in a freeze frame. But in Kham, there are no freeze frames, and I was forced to deal with biblical concepts in their original, non-abstracted state, the way they occur in the real world, at the full speed of motion.

I remember well some of those early translation efforts, when Hasta Ram and I began to learn how to improvise, to be true to the original meaning without marring the pure diction of Kham. One day we were translating one of Jesus' short homilies on prayer, where he says that prayer doesn't do anybody any good if you continue to harbor a grudge in your heart.

And when ye stand praying, forgive, if ye have ought against any: that your Father also which is in heaven may forgive you your trespasses (Mark 11:25).

Khams are human in every other way, so I was pretty sure that they held grudges against one another. But I couldn't recall having heard anyone talk about it. Hasta Ram and I discussed this, we looked at the Nepali version of the passage, but we weren't able to make the necessary connection.

"You know," I said, "somebody does something to you that he shouldn't have done and you don't like it."

"You're angry," Hasta Ram replied.

"Yes, you're angry," I say, "but it's different from just anger. You avoid him; you want him to fail; you don't like him."

"Oh, you hate him!"

"Well, sort of, but not quite."

I created all the hypothetical situations I could think of, trying to elicit an appropriate term, but nothing was forthcoming. In the end, I set the passage aside, disappointed, intending to take it up again another day.

Deep down, though, I kept thinking, "How in the world can I translate the gospel into a language like this? Their language might be enjoyable to speak and hear, but it's somehow lacking. Love, hope, faith, forgiveness, mercy: these aren't grand notions from advanced philosophy, they're just basic human concepts. If the Khams can't talk about these, how will they understand theological notions like justification or redemption?"

On such days I felt like tossing in the towel. Even the so-called "good stuff" sounded wooden, and the cadences were usually off. *Just admit defeat,* I thought, *and go home.*

One afternoon, several weeks later, I was sitting on the veranda of Hasta Ram's house. A neighbor came bursting in, complaining and fuming about something. I couldn't tell what about at first, but I knew he was mad at somebody else. As the two men talked and Hasta Ram tried to settle him down, the neighbor finally declared, "He'd better watch out, may the demons tear him to shreds! I've got him strung up in my heart!" The verb he used was the same verb you'd use for stringing a fish by its gills.

Inattentive until that point, I suddenly woke to the conversation. "What do you mean, he's 'strung up in your heart'?"

He whirled and looked at me with a surprised look on his face, as if to say, "Who are you, and why do you care?" He mumbled an evasive answer. I think he thought I was going to take the other person's side. Or maybe he just thought I was crazy. People were getting used to me asking questions that didn't make any sense.

Hasta Ram began to laugh. He knew what I was up to. The next day, we went back to the drawing boards with Jesus' injunction about prayer: "If you have anyone strung up in your heart..."

Wow, that sounds kind of good, I thought, but then I stopped. I was in trouble again. I still didn't know how to say "forgive him." Then, with a flash of insight, I made the big leap: "Unstring him! How about 'unstring him'? Would that work?"

Hasta Ram looked at me, a bit dazed. "Yes, that works," he said slowly, apparently unable to figure out why I was so excited. "You mean

Fishing with dams and traps

that's all you've been trying to say? Why didn't you just say so?"

So it turned out that Kham could talk about bearing grudges, about forgiving, and about a host of other things that humans find reason to talk about. But their expressions were somehow more immediate, more vividly expressive of human experience. Bearing a grudge chokes up the human heart. Not only does it immobilize its object, "stringing it up" by its gills, it also tangles up the grudge-bearer's heart. Forgiveness brings relief to both parties; both go free.

Nothing abstract here. Jesus' words are full of practical instruction. "Unstring and be unstrung," he says. And so it is with much of the Kham translation. It makes good sense. Jesus may not have spoken this plainly since he first said these words in Aramaic!

George Steiner sums it up best: "The translator labours to secure a natural habitat for the alien presence which [he imports] into his own tongue and cultural setting."

So many translations kill, literally, rather than giving new life to a text.

This was one of our first lessons in how to do translation. Improvisation was at the heart of it, and we gained new ground only by subtle and nuanced negotiations. We kept at it for sixteen years, one verse at a time, one line at a time. The more we translated, the better we got. By the time we finished the New Testament, our early work appeared so terribly crude compared with our later work that we didn't even try to revise it. We threw it out and started over. All of our efforts for the first four or five years had been no more than practice.

David and Hasta Ram hard at work

Chapter 14: Disappointment in God

No wound? no scar?
Yet, as the Master shall the servant be,
And piercèd are the feet that follow Me;
But thine are whole: can he have followed far
Who has nor wound nor scar?
—Amy Carmichael, "Toward Jerusalem"

"They were the darkest years of our lives," we said later of those early years in the Kham villages. Disappointments were everywhere. True, Hasta Ram had found delight in the gospel, and we took much comfort in that, but we had to resign ourselves to the fact that we might be translating the Bible for this one man alone. That might have been okay if everything else had been going well. But it wasn't.

Steve and Daniel were doing much better than we were; they had learned how to adapt. The villages were full of bullies, so much of their waking life was devoted to establishing and maintaining the proper pecking orders. Who could beat up whom? When they were older, just to survive, our boys had to learn to fight—but they developed their own style. If either boy was pounced on, the attacker had two to deal with. Daniel's job, being younger, was to tackle the assailant by the legs and to hang on for dear life while Steve, the older, gave the guy a good pummeling. Back in Kathmandu, Nancy and I were sometimes embarrassed when one of our boys bloodied the nose of a colleague's child. But we were also perplexed: should we have one code of conduct for the village and another for the city?

In those early years, it seemed our worst disappointment was in

God. We felt that God had managed to trick us. He had led me over the mountains with angel tracks. *Surely,* I thought, *he must be here. I followed his tracks to this place!* What's more, he had led me directly to Hasta Ram, a man who had been inquiring about the gospel for years. But now that things had gotten rough, God was nowhere to be seen. He had skipped town. Maybe he'd gone south with the sheep. He sure wasn't here!

The walls of Jericho weren't crumbling the way we had supposed they would. In fact, just the opposite was happening: we were crumbling. We found the people tiresome and irksome, often offensive. They were rude to us, they pulled on us, they poked at us, they demanded from us. And we weren't taking it too well.

When Daniel was viciously attacked by an evil spirit, as the *gel* of a deceased shaman latched onto him and wouldn't let go, we prayed, we pleaded in prayer, we spent whole nights in prayer, but we were powerless. Where was God?

Then in the following year, both Nancy and I were struck by a severe illness. We had returned to Kathmandu a few months earlier to get help for Daniel. By summer, we ourselves had come down with hepatitis B. We recovered fairly quickly—we thought—but were still in a weakened state when the debilitating fever hit. It was August. We lost all strength, and after about ten days, the fever attacked the heart, dragging us, it seemed, to death's very door. A couple of months later, we still moved very, very slowly, and the slightest exertion made our chests hurt.

Our colleagues helped out with the boys, and by late November we were ready to return to the village. Or so we thought. Back in the village, my health continued to improve, but Nancy began to grow worse. The pain in her chest drained all of her strength away, and on Christmas Day, 1972, Nancy asked if I would take over the household duties "for a few days" until she got better. The days dragged on into weeks, and we began to think that Nancy might die in this horrid, rat-infested place. One side of her body began to grow numb, and she was unable to move. A cold terror struck at her heart. "I don't want to die out here. Not here, Lord."

The shamans held a séance, unsolicited, for Nancy in the village, then came to the house and announced the cause of her intractable illness: Nancy had been cursed by a witch. What? Cursed by a witch? Do witches hold sway over God out here?

Not only was God apparently deaf to our prayers, but his Word seemed lifeless, even impotent. We had hoped for more, but nobody cared about the passages that Hasta Ram and I were translating. As we would complete a short passage to the best of our ability, which in hindsight was still not very good, Hasta Ram would take it into his village, the great village of Taka, and gather together anyone who was willing to listen. Very often, the village *ghat buda* with Bahadur, Bhadiraj, and Ranya, would be there. Hasta Ram would read through the passage, explaining what it meant.

There were no outright rejections. Hasta Ram was never ostracized for his new faith. The villagers listened, but always from a polite distance. Sometimes they even declared that "those are nice words," but there was no real spark of comprehension, no stirring of the soul, nothing that indicated that they might want to stake their lives on it. And why should they? Was there anything here that might actually help them? I couldn't say. My own faith was at a very low ebb.

Hasta Ram reads on his rooftop

* * *

Meanwhile, Nany's health was failing. Yet we managed to get her out of the village when she was at her worst. Her rescue was really quite remarkable, a timely reminder that maybe God still did care about us.

On January 22, 1973, I wrote a note and gave it to Hasta Ram's eldest son to take as quickly as possible to the government wireless in Musikot. From there, the message would be transmitted to our mission office in Kathmandu. The note read:

"Nancy very ill. Please send plane immediately. Airstrip ready."

The next morning, at about nine o'clock, we heard the sound of an airplane coming down the deep valley. Unbelieving, I rushed out of the house and saw the plane already beginning a tight loop over Taka village across the river. I plunged into the river, the freezing water up to my waist, and crossed to the other side. Running up the hill, I could see that the plane had already landed on the little makeshift airstrip we had constructed in the cornfields.

With lungs bursting, I hurried toward Bob Peterson, one of our pilots, who was getting out of the plane. "How did you get my note so fast?"

"What note?" he asked.

"I sent a note yesterday," I replied.

Then Bob explained that he had just delivered a planeload of goods up in Dhorpatan, two days' walk to the east. While there, he said, "God spoke to me to come down here and see how the Watters are doing."

"But how did you know that the airstrip was operational?"

"I didn't."

Bob wasn't supposed to land on that strip. It was treacherous, and only one man had been checked out to land on it earlier that winter. Bob wasn't that man.

Now I could see the hand of God, unmistakably. I had sent Hasta Ram's son only the day before. He couldn't have arrived yet; in fact, he wouldn't have passed out of our valley yet. He made it, I learned later, on the day after the plane, but the message he carried never arrived in Kathmandu, at least not in our office. We still have no idea what happened to it.

* * *

Eight months later we were ready to go home to America. Nancy had gotten a little better, but she was far from well, and we had been confined to Kathmandu for that whole period.

During that time, the person who helped Nancy most was Princess Glenda Dorji from Bhutan. Her husband, Prince Lendhup, was the queen's brother, and the Dorjis were living in exile in Kathmandu, the result of alleged palace intrigue.

Nancy and the princess became very close friends, and they spent many hours together, mostly chatting and planning dinner parties. For our eighth wedding anniversary on September 10, 1973, the Dorjis hosted a wedding party in our honor and invited some of their titled acquaintances who happened to be in Kathmandu at the time—maharajas from India, diplomats from England, royalty from Nepal and Bhutan, and even an actress from Hollywood. What a contrast from life in the village!

* * *

Shortly afterward, we flew back to the States for a year's furlough and settled in the California Bay Area so that I could attend linguistics classes at Berkeley. We knew no one. Nancy's medical condition was difficult to diagnose, given financial and insurance constraints, but a public welfare clinic was able to determine that she had an erratic heartbeat.

Nancy has remained weak ever since; thirty-five years later, she was diagnosed with dilated cardiomyopathy, assumed to have started "way back there," as a complication of her prolonged, life-threatening bout of hepatitis B.

Now we could add insurance woes and a frustrating medical process to our list of disappointments, but mostly, we were disappointed in God.

A letter arrived from Hasta Ram that summed up our sense of futility. "I have come to the conclusion," he said, "that no one will ever come to the gospel. I made one friend, but he died within two months. I have tried everything, but to no avail. Now I go to the hillside daily and I pray to God. Maybe he will do something."

Yeah, maybe, I thought. *Or maybe not.* I had grown cynical.

* * *

February 1974 was a watershed month for us. We had decided that we probably wouldn't go back to Nepal. How could we? There was nothing there for us. We had already failed.

One Saturday afternoon, after Nancy had spent a particularly discouraging week in bed, we felt inclined to kneel beside our bed and pray. This was a different kind of prayer for us. We realized that the heaviest burden we carried was not the burden of illness, but the burden of disappointment. We decided to give it all to God.

Once we started to acknowledge and lay down every source of discouragement, it became easier, and we were suddenly feeling a whole lot lighter and a whole lot freer. Our step quickened that day, and several months later, on April 24, we wrote a letter to our headquarters in Santa Ana, California. Following is an excerpt:

We had an encounter with God that Saturday afternoon.

We gave our burdens to Him. It was a heavy load that Nancy was carrying—the illness plus the burdens. I'll never forget how she gave them away. She named them one by one—all the disappointments, the worries, the wounds; and as she did, with tears streaming down her face, she held out an open hand to God saying, "And Lord, take that one too! And this one too, Lord! And Lord, don't forget this one!" Before long we were sobbing with relief from the lifted burdens, and our souls were bursting with revival. Praise God! There really is a balm in Gilead! There really is a river whose streams gladden the city of God! There really is a tree of life whose leaves are for the healing of the nations!

Nancy in Kathmandu

Chapter 15: The Prophets of Baal

Then they... called on the name of Baal from morning until noon saying, "O Baal, answer us." But there was no voice and no one answered. And they leaped about the altar which they made. And... Elijah mocked them and said, "Call out with a loud voice, for he is a god; either he is occupied or gone aside, or is on a journey, or perhaps he is asleep and needs to be awakened."

And it came about when midday was past, that they raved until the time of the offering of the evening sacrifice; but there was no voice, no one answered, and no one paid attention.
—*1 Kings 18:26–27,29, KJV*

In September 1974 we returned to Nepal, and by October I was back in the village again. I had gone ahead of the family to ascertain the condition of our house and also to rebuild the airstrip that we had originally built in October 1970. Rebuilding the airstrip was an annual affair. It sat just below the village of Taka in the middle of what looked like an ancient lakebed and was the only flat piece of ground for several days' walk. The area was used primarily for growing maize; fortunately for us, the soil was not moist enough to grow barley, so it went fallow throughout the winter months. We were given permission to use it as a landing strip between harvest in mid-October and plowing in mid-March—about five months.

There were dozens of small fields, all sloping gently upwards. For every increase in altitude of five or six feet, a terrace wall separated the upper and lower levels. To make the area useable as an airstrip, all we had to do was collapse the walls along a forty-foot slot, wide enough to

Rebuilding the airstrip was an annual affair

An inventive boy makes a toy plane out of cornstalks

accommodate the body of a plane (the fifty-two-foot wingspan of the Pilatus Porter extended over the walls in places), and then slope the terraces evenly. Eleven hundred feet was the limit; after that we ran into rough terrain and large boulders. When we built the strip for the first time, it took three hundred men six days to complete.

Our house in Shera had all but collapsed, the earthen roof soaked through from the summer monsoon. There was no one to care for it and, since it was unoccupied, no fire to keep it dry from the inside. Rather than repair it, I decided to leave Shera and build a new place in Taka. Taka was where Hasta Ram lived, and there were faint glimmerings of interest in the gospel there.

I was anxious to get back to work on Kham, so I gave myself only a month to build the new house. It proved to be much easier than the previous construction in Shera had been. Hasta Ram was my general contractor, and before long he had half the village organized into various jobs: there were quarrymen, stone carriers, masons, timber cutters, and timber haulers. Since I had the hand tools, I appointed myself the chief carpenter. I squared timbers, built wooden stairs, and made door- and window frames. The choicest timbers I used for floor joists and ceilings, and the roof was made of tin flown in from Kathmandu. I could hardly keep up with the masons. Everyone worked efficiently and smoothly, and the house was completed in just a month and four days.

* * *

The house was built on a small plot of land in about as scary a place as anyone could hope to find—a choice location for a Halloween party. It belonged to Hasta Ram, but lay outside the village boundaries, a notion with considerable religious significance. "Outside" in the minds of the villagers meant the haunt of evil and all sorts of unpleasant things, and most people avoided walking there after dark.

The demarcation line between "in" and "out" was a small stream that meandered across the valley floor and plunged off the far end. In numerous shamanistic ceremonies, such as "casting away the evil," the evil is deposited on the "other" side of the stream, the side we had decided to live on. The footbridge that crossed over the stream directly in front of our house was a kind of no-man's land, neither "in" nor "out." At midnight, it is believed, the departing soul of a dying person can sometimes be overtaken here, and if the right deal is made with the lord of the underworld, the soul can be coaxed back into the dying person for healing. A small rest area to the left of the bridge was known as *bulnəi*, "The Resting Place of the Corpse." It was there that the dead paused on their way to the netherworld. On the right side of the bridge was a large boulder, the dwelling place of a large demon or troll. You could hear him tumbling stones at night.

I wasn't aware of all this when I started construction. If I had been, I might have thought twice. It was during the building of the house that I first got wind of it. People kept expressing their disbelief that I would even think of building a house in such a place, and they warned me that I would have to do a "really big" sacrifice. We brushed off their comments and said that they shouldn't worry. We would be just fine.

The family arrived in November, and we moved into the house. People arrived the next morning to see if we were still alive. They wondered if we could hear the troll at night. Over time, their incredulity seemed to diminish; I don't know whether they had decided we had big magic or were just plain lucky.

* * *

On May 11, 1975, after we had been in the house for more than six months, a hurricane-force wind came howling down the valley funnel and across the ancient lakebed. It bore straight for the house. Everything began to shake, and the noise was like a freight train. Suddenly all was silent, and we found ourselves looking up at open sky. The tin roof had torn off the house, taking with it the heavy timbers that anchored it to the stone walls. We were eating supper at the time, and Nancy had made up a nice batch of chocolate pudding for the boys. Not knowing what else to do, I said to Nancy, "I'll have another bowl of pudding, please!"

It was already a bit late at night for the villagers to venture out, especially near the demon rock, but they all showed up the next morning. "We told you so," they said knowingly.

* * *

I hired some local craftsmen, and we started replacing the roof the same day. We made it more solid this time, using the trusted village materials of stone, slate, and mud. On the third day of construction, with about two more days to go, a large group of villagers arrived in the little marsh next to the demon rock. They were carrying a small, squealing piglet, and stuffing its head into the mud anywhere there was a small spring of water. They even stuffed it under the demon rock. I sat on the roof watching, wondering what they were up to. I was further mystified when, every time the men pushed the piglet's head into a hole, the women began shouting hideous obscenities.

The weather that spring had been very, very dry, and the maize that had been in the ground for a couple of months was parched and shriveling.

"They're making rain," my workers explained to me.

"Making rain?" I said in disbelief. "How does that make rain?"

"Well," they answered, "this is how we infuriate the water gods.

Water gods don't like pigs, and they don't like vulgarity much either. If they get angry enough, they'll strike out with lightning, thunder, and even rain."

I found this wonderfully amusing. "Hey, you guys," I called out to the rainmakers. "Could you wait until I get my roof on before you make it rain? It's just a couple more days!"

I laughed, and they laughed back. *At least they appreciate my jokes,* I thought.

From the valley they carried the piglet up the slopes, more than five thousand feet, to the top of Nar Shing mountain. I could see them making their way in the distance. At the top of Nar Shing they sacrificed it on a stone altar and threw its flesh to the sky gods. Then they turned and ran back.

They were running hard.

When they were halfway down the mountain, the clouds began to swirl. Thunderbolts were hurled to the earth, and the rain burst forth in torrents. The trail down the mountain turned into a river. The laughing rainmakers were soaked through to the skin. Nancy and I scrambled, trying to cover what we could inside the house.

I was dumbfounded. Who was laughing now? My story was the story of Elijah and the prophets of Baal in reverse. What happened?

Nancy enjoys the upstairs fireplace

Chapter 16: New Beginnings

He is the owner who delights in His flock. For Him there is no greater reward, no deeper satisfaction, then that of seeing His sheep contented, well fed, safe and flourishing under His care. This is indeed His very "life." He gives all He has to it. He literally lays Himself out for those who are His.
—Phillip Keller, A Shepherd Looks at Psalm 23

My alphabet starts with this letter called yuzz. It's the letter I use to spell yuzz-a-ma-tuzz. You'll be sort of surprised what there is to be found once you go beyond "Z" and start poking around!
—Dr. Seuss, On Beyond Zebra

The old things didn't matter so much anymore; our biggest disappointments seemed to be behind us. At least we hoped so. God had given us a new outlook on life, and it was okay that the translation we were doing was primarily for the benefit of one man. The work was stimulating, and the old Gurkha warrior and I had developed a deep friendship. There were so many things to do and so much to learn that there just wasn't room in our lives for boredom or disappointment, much less self-pity.

From November 1974, when the family joined me in the village, until June 1975, when we returned to Kathmandu for the monsoon, Hasta Ram and I hunkered down and worked on translation. We had already, in the previous year, completed a concordance project. Nancy was doing well and, like the rest of us, loved being in the village. To reduce some of the physical stress on her, we hired a middle-aged Tibetan man, Barchya, to help with household chores, even cooking. He came to us looking pretty thin, and within a few months, his cheeks were becoming remarkably chubby.

We had a little storeroom off to the side of the kitchen where we kept our supplies of sugar, flour, rice, *ghee*, and a few canned goods. We weren't aware of how liberally Barchya was using *ghee* until we'd already gone through a whole biscuit tin of it (about two-and-a-half gallons). I reached into the store for a backup one day and found the second tin nearly empty, too. Bare finger marks clawed their way to the bottom, and nothing was left on the sides, either. The old boy had single-handedly polished off a whole bucket of lard!

After a morning of school, the boys are free to play with friends

* * *

One night Nancy was called up to the village. A young woman had been laboring in childbirth for about twenty-four hours. The baby wasn't budging, and now the mother was in a dangerously weakened state. She was in pain, and her eyes were filled with fear. All the men had already been expelled from the house, and now the old ladies controlled the firepit as they exchanged terrifying tales of childbirth. "So-and-so went on like this until her guts burst," one would say, only to be outdone by another.

"Do you have a place to put the child?" Nancy asked, and they handed her a pile of filthy rags. Then they gave her a black string woven from the hair of the mother. It was for tying off the umbilical cord. Nothing else would do, they told her.

In the dark room filled with smoke and soot, Nancy could hardly see. She had her flashlight with her, mostly to read her medical manual. She had never been trained in midwifery. Eventually, she realized that the baby was turned wrong, and through extensive effort, combining massage with probing and pulling, she managed to correct its position. A healthy baby girl was born just before daybreak. On the way home, in the early light of dawn, Nancy prayed for her.

* * *

Two days later, the young woman's husband appeared at the house with a basketful of cloth sacks. When Nancy opened the door, the man fell to the floor, grasping her feet and touching them to his forehead, the gesture of an indentured slave whose life belonged to another.

Tears came to Nancy's eyes as she called out to me, "What am I to do?"

"As hard as it is, just accept," I answered back. "He wants to thank you."

So, trying to hold back a flood of tears, Nancy accepted his gifts. He unwrapped a bag full of barley, then another full of cornmeal, then he gave her a ball of popped amaranth seeds laced with honey, and finally a half-dozen eggs. Bowing again to the floor, he took off his topi, removed three one-rupee notes, and handed them to Nancy.

"It was the most humbling gift I ever received," Nancy now recalls.

The baby girl is now a grown woman and calls us "Mother" and "Father."

It's no small thing to live with a primitive people, to learn their language and thought processes, and to participate in a way of life that is soon to pass. You begin as an outsider, but if you stay long enough, there's no end of opportunity to laugh with those who laugh, to weep with those who weep, and to become a part of them.

* * *

The best days of my life were spent traveling with the semi-nomadic shepherds on the western flanks of Dhaulagiri. Many Khams still practiced a transhumant manner of life, maintaining permanent villages in the deep river valleys, but traveling most of the year to already established grazing lands in the high mountains. On numerous occasions, I roamed with them in their summer pastures all the way to the foot of the glaciers.

In this northern part of Kham country, an area of about six hundred square miles, there are only a handful of tiny villages, all Kham. This is their grazing land. The upper limit of forest extends to about 11,500 feet in this part of Nepal, and above that is a swath of rich grassland extending upward until black shale and rock begin to dominate the landscape at about 14,500 feet. The grassland is carved up into natural amphitheater-like bowls, each separated from the others by towering spires, ridges, and high walls of black basalt. One of the biggest challenges in this high country is learning how to navigate the rugged terrain. I was lost once for two days. But being lost doesn't matter, if you're properly outfitted for a two-week stay.

In my opinion, the most beautiful place on earth is the bowl-shaped mountain basin of Chokotya, perfect in form. The basin floor, as green as Ireland in the summer, sits at over 14,300 feet and is surrounded by great cathedral spires of basalt rock. Beyond it, as a backdrop, are the snow-capped, 24,000-foot peaks of Churen and Putha. Hasta Ram first took me there in a snowstorm in May 1973. At first we could see nothing, and then, as if by magic, there it was—a sight so glorious that it took our breath away. The beauty of the place drew me back again and again.

* * *

Caring for sheep is a demanding task, and for a shepherd to prosper is no accident. It comes as the result of careful planning and diligent

The bowl-shaped mountain basin of Chokotya

Cathedral spires of basalt surround the valley

work. Just to keep a sheep camp supplied is a major undertaking. The shepherds live in a *pherwa*, a structure that looks like an Iroquoian wigwam, except that it is built not of bark but of goat-hair blankets stretched over a bow-like frame. Goat-hair blankets repel rain better than sheep's wool, but they are heavy, bulky, and hard to carry.

All the accoutrements of the camp have to be transported—pots, pans, woks, plates, jugs, milk buckets, churns, fire tripods, and axes—but pack animals are foreign to Khams. Men carry everything. Well, almost everything.

The Tibetan Mastiffs—big, shaggy dogs the size of small bears—are fastened during the day to heavy, iron chains and staked to the ground. The dogs are tenacious, fearless, and highly alert guard animals—and they've been known to kill. While on the move, these big sheepdogs carry their own chains wrapped several times around their shaggy bodies.

Sheep sometimes carry small packs of salt when the camps move. Sheep don't do well without salt. Deprived of this crucial mineral, they lose appetite, become weak, and fall prey to illness or disease. Depending on the size of the flock, at least one man in every camp is

detailed to nothing but the transportation of salt. If a shepherd has the wherewithal to pay for the labor, he may move salt in stages to the village during the winter months so that he doesn't have to move it so far in the summer. Otherwise, he has to transport it all the way from the Terai on the backs of men. When they reach camp, the sheep are "salted," and the men are immediately sent off on another trip.

The camps have to be self-sufficient for long periods of time, and the food supplies come all the way from home, sometimes a week or ten days away. Cornmeal and potatoes don't cook at high altitudes; water boils at temperatures too low. In fact, just to get water to boil at all, the men have to pump air into their choking fires with sheepskin bellows. So the camps have to be supplied with great quantities of pre-roasted barley flour, called *muhr manam*. The barley is roasted in the village, then ground on stone querns. *Muhr manam* doesn't need to be cooked: you just add boiling water or tea and it's ready to eat. Cornmeal is made into cakes, about the weight and consistency of an Olympic discus, and fried in oil or sheep butter.

Sometimes in the summer, several shepherds will combine their flocks into one large herd, with as many as two thousand head, to facilitate high-altitude grazing. In late August, when the herds are split up again to go their separate ways, the men always know which sheep are theirs. Only rarely do disputes arise. It is hard not to think of the familiar words: *"I am the good shepherd, and I know my own."*

The shepherd's most important task is to find good pasture. Khams call it *usuu usuu*. It means "breath" or "firstfruit." If they can help it, they don't graze in the same pasture two days in a row; they are in constant search for the firstfruits. When they move into a new area, they set up camp and move outward each day in a different direction like spokes of a

The good shepherd

wheel. When an area has been grazed in this manner, they move on to a new pasture.

A Kham proverb says, "A shepherd sleeps with his ear turned toward the sheep." I was in a sheep camp one July in the area known as The Seven Wildernesses. Though the calendar said it was summer, it didn't feel like it, at least not while the cold rain was coming down. At these altitudes, even in the summer, the temperature under the clouds hovered just a few degrees above freezing, and rain was always mixed with sleet and snow.

The herd, which combined two smaller flocks, had about three hundred sheep in it. The sheep were in a skittish mood that night and frequently spooked, rushing off into the darkness and driving rain. The owners got up repeatedly, first one, then the other, wrapping themselves in wool blankets and braving the miserable cold. Finally, when nothing else could be done, both shepherds went out and settled down among the sheep, singing lullabies and making reassuring sounds. By morning, they were nearly dead of hypothermia.

Shepherds caring for their sheep

One acquaintance of mine wasn't so selfless and paid the price. He had driven his sheep long and hard all day, and that night he slept too soundly. Before he could wake himself, a pack of Himalayan wild dogs had brutally killed 116 of his sheep. "Wolves kill for food," the Khams tell me, "but wild dogs kill for pleasure."

When Hasta Ram and I translated the twenty-third Psalm into Kham, it evoked all sorts of astonishing images of the sheep camp, and of the selfless devotion of our Heavenly Shepherd in caring for his sheep. Just as for English readers, it remains one of the Khams' favorite scriptural passages.

* * *

Sheep camps are wonderful places for learning language. You're bombarded with images and smells that are impossible to forget and, amazingly, there are Kham expressions for all of them. If there's no noun or verb, there's an ideophone for every experience or sensation. Ideophones are partly onomatopoeic, that is, they imitate the sound associated with the event. *Bang* in English imitates the sound of a gunshot, and *splish-splash* imitates the sound of stepping into a puddle. But in Kham, all sorts of events have associated sounds. Feelings have sounds, tastes and smells have sounds, and sights have sounds!

Have you ever heard the sound of a delicate alpine flower, or the sound of a fawn crouching in a bush, or the sound of a majestic mountain peak? I hadn't either until I went to the sheep camps and learned how a language can express such things through the subjective feelings of the beholder as he encounters them.

Khams say, for example, that a cavern goes *dwang dwang*, or the sound of a growl is *ngarr ngarr*. There was something intuitive about those sounds that I could readily grasp. But what did they mean when they said that a field in bloom goes *tara wara* or fluffy wool goes *gwaa gwaa*? Stiff joints go *khagara khogoro* and pockmarks on the face go *barja burju*. Salty food makes your mouth go *chachata*, and lemons make it go *chyachyar chichur*. The sound of mental shock or dismay is *chyang ching*, and the sound of embarrassment is *zuu zuu*. Of course, these things don't really produce sounds, but the effect in your brain is like a little bell going off. Is there anyone who has experienced a sudden mental shock and not heard *chyang ching* in the back of his mind?

In English we distinguish between different kinds of smells—fragrance, stench, aroma, etc. Kham has only one word for smell, but several ideophones. Rotten meat smells *chyachya chichi*, roasted meat smells *mhur mhur*, and liquor smells *phang phang*. But in what way does an uphill trail go *jhor jhor*, or thick fog go *kap kup*? We can agree that the sound of strangulation is *kik kik*, but in what sense does the scorching sun go *hip hip*? And did you know that when you sit on your haunches, you're going *chom jom*, or that when you sleep with your arms spread out, you're *chocho lala*?

All of this figures in translation. In English it's sufficient to say that a donkey caravan "plods along," but in Kham there's no word to properly describe "plodding along." Instead, one says that the donkey's head bobs *ngatyao ngatyao*. In the biblical story of a boy cast to the ground by an evil spirit, the English says, "he stiffened out." In Kham he goes *khyanggya khengge*—which is what an animal skin does when it becomes hard and brittle. Likewise, in English, when Jesus heals a blind man and asks him to come, the blind man "casts his cloak aside." In Kham he tosses his blanket *hya hyi*, which is what a person does with anything that encumbers him. Revelation 8:5, for another example, is filled with apocalyptic sounds: the thunder goes *gar*, the lightning goes *myalyak-ni-myilyik,* and the earthquake goes *chanaa-chanaa*, the same ideophone used to describe sifting rice in a winnowing tray.

* * *

A goat-hair pherwa *tent*

A night sitting in a goat-hair *pherwa* is spent talking. The men laugh, tell stories, and debate right and wrong. Their hands are usually active, too, spinning rope, repairing a cracked jug, or concocting medicines to nurse the weak and the fallen sheep. When I was with the shepherds, I sat with notebook and pencil in hand. I learned. There's no better place in the world for talking philosophy and the stuff of life. Their wisdom is practical, not abstract; it's homegrown and finds expression where man's ideals meet real life.

Shepherds in their pherwa

On occasion, a stranger might pass through. Travelers who brave the tumbled expanse of high alpine meadows make every effort to arrive at a sheep camp before dark for fear of the Tibetan Mastiffs, which are let loose to guard the sheep after dark. I have stayed in sheep camps myself on many occasions; there's no other place to go.

To accommodate a traveler, the shepherd pulls a few stakes at the end of his tent and stretches the goat-hair blankets as tight as he can get them. It might be inconvenient, but the shepherd can't turn him out. It's usually well worth it, too. Travelers bring news and sometimes even a stray animal they've found. But the law of the wilderness hospice is foremost: next time, you might be the traveler in need of shelter.

A beautiful metaphor has grown out of the practice of alpine hospitality. The verb *thu*, meaning "stretch," used primarily in the context of "stretching out the tent," also means "to stretch out one's heart toward another." The other person could be anyone; you take him under your protection and care, making his interests your own, and do what you can to help him. Either that, or you close your heart to him.

When Hasta Ram and I first began translation, I was often troubled by what I thought of as the 'impoverished' state of Kham. There seemed to be no single word equivalents for all kinds of things: love, forgiveness, mercy, and a host of crucial biblical concepts. The Nepali word *maya*, which is often translated "love," has been borrowed into Kham as a weak kind of word and really means nothing more than affection. Is this what Jesus meant when he said "Love one another" or "Love your neighbor as yourself"? Not likely. Living with the people at an intimate level, I was beginning to discover that their language was not impoverished after all: the Khams could talk about the central realities of life, and with considerable nuance of meaning.

Of course, it was still not possible, in Kham, to talk about love in the abstract, the way one does in Greek, and especially the way the Apostle Paul does in 1 Corinthians 13: "Love is patient, love is kind, and is not jealous; love does not brag and is not arrogant..." But the fact remains, if love has these characteristics, then the person who loves also has these characteristics. So in Kham we made our grammatical adjustments accordingly: "*He who stretches out his heart toward another* [he who loves] bears patiently with all things good and evil, he maintains a heart of kindness. When another receives more than he does, he does not get a poison eye [he is not jealous]. And when he receives more than another, he doesn't get haughty and all puffed up [he is not arrogant]."

The result is not so pithy nor so aphoristic as the original, but it's full of practical instruction. We translate this way not because we're trying to be folksy but because this is the way the Khams talk. This is their language.

When Khams are called upon to perform acts of love and sacrifice, their response is typical of people anywhere: either they seal their hearts off or they "stretch them out" in acts of altruism. To respond with love was nothing new to them, but to make it a commandment of life was new: "This is my commandment, that ye love one another" (John 13:34). More startling still was the fact that God would act that way toward us. His love for us becomes the standard, the central definition of what it means to "stretch out one's heart."

The Khams' language, it seemed, anticipated the coming of Christ. It is a language permeated with longing for the One who could reconcile them to God. C.S. Lewis talks about "gleams of divine truth" evident in cultures around the world, at first unfocused, but then centering upon

Christ, their intended object. The metaphors of Kham, too, appeared to be ready-made to receive none other. It is clear to me, in fact, that this language never reached its full potential until it found expression in Christ.

Chapter 17: A Small Spark

"They say Aslan is on the move—perhaps has already landed."

And now a very curious thing happened. None of the children knew who Aslan was any more than you do; but the moment the Beaver had spoken these words everyone felt quite different. Perhaps it has sometimes happened to you in a dream that someone says something which you don't understand but in the dream it feels as if it had some enormous meaning—either a terrifying one which turns the whole dream into a nightmare or else a lovely meaning too lovely to put into words, which makes the dream so beautiful that you remember it all your life and are always wishing you could get into that dream again. It was like that now. At the name of Aslan each one of the children felt something jump in its inside.

—*C.S. Lewis,* The Lion, the Witch and the Wardrobe

Hasta Ram and I were making good progress. We had already translated the Gospel of Mark, The Acts of the Apostles, and the First Epistle of Peter. Now we were beginning Genesis. It didn't make a lot of sense to talk about the Son of God when we hadn't said anything about God, and it didn't make a lot of sense to talk about sin when we hadn't talked about the origin of sin. Genesis was meant to supply some of that.

We returned to the village in October 1975 with trial printouts of Mark's Gospel and First Peter and carried on with the translation of Genesis. After finishing Genesis, we decided to go on with Exodus.

There are so many passages in the New Testament that make reference to important events in those two books. They're foundational to an understanding of the gospel—the Creation, the call of Abraham, the giving of the Law.

One January morning in 1976, three months into our stay, Hasta Ram arrived at the door with three men. One was from Hasta Ram's village of Taka, another was from the village of Bacchigaon, just behind Taka, and the third was from Upper Shera, across the river. They had some "urgent questions," Hasta Ram explained.

Nancy served some tea. Bishnu, the oldest, was the first to speak. "We want to be baptized," he said.

This was completely unexpected, and I didn't know how to respond. I had already resigned myself to the fact that no one would ever show any real interest in the gospel.

"Baptized?" I responded. "Whatever for?"

"We read in the Bible that when someone believes, he gets baptized," he explained.

I turned to Hasta Ram. "All of you?" I asked.

"Yes, all of us."

"Have you explained to them what it means?"

"No, I was hoping you would do that!"

I was dumbfounded. The day I had been waiting for was now upon me, and I didn't know what to say. Were they thinking that baptism would save them?

"Well, how *does* one lay hold on God's salvation?" one of them asked.

I thought back to all the things we do in the West prior to baptism. We kneel at the altar, we raise our hand, we go forward, we walk the sawdust trail. All such rituals were badly out of context here and seemed ludicrous at best. I thought about the *Four Spiritual Laws* I had learned about in a seminar somewhere: "God loves you and has a wonderful plan for your life..." If I said that to these men, they'd think I was smoking something.

"Come back in three days," I said, "and I'll explain it to you."

They thanked me, got up politely, and left.

For the next three days, I locked myself in the upstairs room. I pored over the Scriptures, and I began formulating an answer. I wrote it all on paper until I was satisfied that my answer was an adequate one.

* * *

Three days later, the men returned—Hasta Ram, Bishnu, Danthya, and Panchya. I began to talk. I began with original sin and the fall of man. I explained that God had made provision for our sin and that he promised to send a Redeemer. I talked about the birth of Christ and his life among us preaching the gospel and healing the sick. I talked about his crucifixion and all that that means. I talked about our hope of eternal life through him. All this took a couple of hours.

Then, I gave them a strong warning. "If you believe," I said, "you become liable for imprisonment in your own country. In Nepal, it is illegal to become a Christian, so my advice to you is to think very carefully about what you will do. Are you willing to suffer imprisonment for your faith?" At the time, both conversion and proselytism were illegal, punishable by one or six years, respectively.

David and a new believer

All of them responded in the strong affirmative. "Yes, we understand," they said. "This is what we've been looking for all our lives."

* * *

I understood, then, that the men who had come to my door were looking for a threshold experience. They wanted to be able to point back to an event, to a time when everything had changed, the day they had believed and committed themselves to the gospel. So why not follow the biblical pattern of declaration?

Their next question was, "How is one baptized?"

In many languages the word "baptism" is just transliterated—*baptisma*, or some such thing. But in our translation of the New Testament, I had wanted something that would connect meaningfully to the Kham culture. We chose a word that hearkens back to some of their own rituals, a word that means "to become purified." When Khams go "outside the village" to bury the dead, for example, they do not return before entering the river and washing the impurities of death from their bodies.

I showed them the word in the gospel and reminded them of its meaning in their own culture. Then I went on to explain its meaning in the Christian context. "In some traditions," I explained "they pour water over the head to signify the pouring out of the Holy Spirit."

"But in many traditions," I went on to say, "they submerge the person completely in the water to signify that he has died to the old self and is risen into a new life."

"Well, I don't see why we can't do all three," they said in one voice.

I thought for just a few moments. "There's no reason not to," I said. "They all have meaning. We'll do all three." The Kham ritual would be the cultural bridge for the other two.

That evening, after dark, when the villagers were staying close to their fires, we went down to the stream that is viewed as a boundary between this world and the world to come.

Hasta Ram went first. Stepping into the cold water and acting out the Kham ritual, he scrubbed his legs and declared, "As this water cleanses the impurities from my body, so Christ has cleansed me from my sin."

Then, I stepped in with him. I submerged him in the cold, dark water and declared, "I now bury you with Christ to signify the death of your old self, and I raise you to newness of life."

Finally, asking him to kneel, I filled a *bopka* with water and poured it over his head, saying, "Now receive the Holy Spirit."

Hasta Ram broke into spontaneous prayer. Then, standing on the shore, he wrapped himself in a blanket while I performed the same ceremony with the other three men.

Trembling from the cold, we went to my house to warm ourselves by the fire. Nancy served us hot tea. All of us burst out into prayers of thanksgiving. The Kham church was born that day.

Before leaving that night, we all decided that we would go to Hasta Ram's house the next evening to read the Scriptures and to discuss the gospel.

* * *

When the men came together the next evening, they had an eagerness about them that I had not seen before. This was something new: they were embracing the gospel, and they were staking their lives on it.

After that first night, Hasta Ram's three friends brought their wives. The night after that, they brought some of their friends, too. Within a week, their numbers grew from ten to twenty to thirty, and then to fifty. There was nothing stopping them now. There was an urgency about them that

Hasta Ram's wife and infant son

couldn't be explained; everyone was suddenly desperate to know about the gospel.

The meetings would start just after dark. The core group, which had settled at about thirty or forty, would arrive first. As they packed the room, a hush would fall upon them as they sensed the presence of God in that little place. With no coaxing from anyone, they would remove their *topis* from their heads and bow in silence. Latecomers would crowd onto the outer veranda and the stone stairs leading up from the cattle yard; they all wanted to hear.

Hasta Ram would clear his throat and pause a few moments until all was silent. "We've come here to meet God," he would say quietly. Then he'd pause for more silence. "This is not a festival," he would continue. "We are not here to drink and to revel, to party and to dance. We have come to meet God." No one breathed. He would open his books to a passage from the Gospels, usually a parable of Jesus, and begin reading in Kham:

The sower is one who proclaims the word of God.

The seed that falls along the trail is like anyone who, as soon as he hears the word of God, Satan comes along and snatches away all that was sown in his heart.

In the same way, all that falls upon the rocky outcrop is like anyone who hears the word of God and receives it with joy, but because the word did not take root in his heart, it lasts only a short time. As soon as persecution and trouble come as a result of the word, he loses heart.

All that falls in the midst of thorns and weeds is like anyone who hears the word of God but goes on fretting and worrying, thinking, "What will become of my life? How can I accumulate more and live a life of luxury?" Such things swallow up the word, and these people become sterile and useless.

All that falls on good, rich soil is like anyone who hears the word of God and accepts it well. He is like seed that produces much fruit, some thirty, some sixty, and some a hundredfold (Mark 4:14–20).

Everyone sat as though mesmerized. These rough, wild, boisterous mountain men and women, people that we thought would never bow the knee to Christ, listened with rapt attention. These were people who made crude jokes even at their own religion. But now as the tears coursed down their leathery old cheeks, they heard things that warmed their hearts, words that "sounded like the voice of our grandfathers." They recognized the voice of the Shepherd.

Within a few weeks that little spark was fanned into flame as everyone in the village was desperate to hear. The core remained the same, but the outside periphery changed every night. Within a month or so, the whole village had passed by that door and listened. Things would never be the same again.

Every evening, as Hasta Ram would finish his talk, the listeners would beg for a second passage, and then for a third. They couldn't get enough. Finally, in exhaustion, Hasta Ram would beg, "Please, my friends, that's all for tonight. Come back again tomorrow night."

Then, he would stand and pour out his heart to God in prayer. Everyone wept, and when it was time to leave, they would all embrace one another and say, "I can't wait till tomorrow night." This went on every night of the week, two or three hours at a time, for a period of four months.

Word spread quickly that the people of Taka had "the words of God in a book." People came to listen, and often, having heard no more than a sentence or two of the Gospel in their own language, they were captivated. Some looked startled as they listened, like they'd heard it all before but weren't quite sure where.

One evening, a man from the Kham village of Maikot arrived at the entrance to the village. Maikot is a very long day's walk to the north of Taka, up over a 12,000-foot pass. "Where do they meet to listen to God's talk in a book?" he asked.

The villagers showed him Hasta Ram's house, and he sat near the edge of the open room. I was there that night. He sat in attentive silence: at first amazed, then mesmerized. Finally, the meeting ended, and a few people prepared to go. Others began talking about the weather. Speaking for the first time, the man from Maikot asked, "Is that all that God said?"

"No, God said other things, too," the people told him. "We have a whole book of things here."

"Look," the man said, "I have just this one night, and then I have to go back to my sheep. I'm ready to stay up all night. I want to hear everything God said!"

Chapter 18: Contract Terminated

Remember that God called us [SIL] as an institution very different from any other institution in the world known to me, to go abroad and work for our translations and scientific output. Linguistics is done, not because it helps translation. It does help translation, but we also do scientific work for the will of God.
—Ken Pike (former President, SIL International),
    Pike's Perspectives

For several months, from January into April 1976, Hasta Ram was a busy man. He shared the gospel in Kham with hundreds of people who crowded into his house for several hours each evening. He felt their sense of urgency and was doing everything he could to address it. Then, for several hours each day, from mid-morning into mid-afternoon, he worked with me on translation. It was demanding work, and we had to be alert. In addition, he still had his family, his fields, and his cattle to think about.

In April of that year, Hasta Ram was stricken with a severe illness. We thought at the time that he was having a heart attack. He complained of pain in the chest, and began to experience numbness on one side of his body. We cut our stay in the village short and managed to get him out with us on the last flight that spring. At Shanta Bhawan Hospital in Kathmandu, physicians determined that the real issue was not heart-related at all, but a bowel obstruction, and they easily cured his problem.

Since Hasta Ram was in Kathmandu, I decided to keep him in town for a month or two so that we could complete our translation of the book of Exodus.

We were living at the time in a wonderful old Rana palace at the edge of the city. The house belonged to a high-ranking official of the Royal Nepalese Army, and he occupied one of four apartments in the house. Another apartment was occupied by Raju and Bina (pseudonyms), who became our close friends.

Bina was lesser royalty, a granddaughter of a prominent Prime Minister and cousin to both Queen Aishwarya and Queen Komal. Raju, her husband, was a young army captain. He eventually advanced very far up the military ladder, with close connections to King Birendra and, after Birendra's untimely death, King Gyanendra.

Raju's position enabled him to help Nancy and me in ways that no one else could have, as we attempted to secure a modicum of justice and equality for the Kham people. For the time being, however, he was only a captain, working his way upward.

* * *

David and Hasta Ram work on Exodus

Since our arrival in Nepal in 1969, Nancy and I had been living and working under a contract between the Summer Institute of Linguistics (SIL) and the state-run Tribhuvan University. There were other SIL linguists in the country, too, not only from the U.S., but also from Australia, New Zealand, Canada, the U.K., various European countries, and Asia. All were working in minority languages—Newar, Chepang, Magar, Gurung, Tamang, Sherpa, Sunwar, Khaling, Jirel, Tharu, and others. Most, with the exception of Newar, and to a certain extent Sherpa, were without alphabets or literature.

The contract between SIL and the university was a remarkable one. The Kingdom of Nepal was an official Hindu state, the only one in the world, and conversion to any other religion was considered a crime. SIL, on the other hand, is in many ways an evangelical missionary organization, with the translation of the Christian Scriptures into minority languages as one of its primary goals.

SIL's other mandate, however, "the documentation, development, and preservation of minority languages," is what makes it unique among missions and allows it to enter into contracts with governments, to operate within secular universities, and to have consultancy status with international organizations like UNESCO. Unfortunately, SIL's Christian motivation also makes it a target of vilification and criticism. "SIL's linguistic research," the critics say, "is only a front for doing missionary work."

This is not true. Linguistics and the linguistic rights of minority peoples have always been a sincere focus of SIL. More languages have been documented by SIL than by any other organization in the world. Its members are actively involved in writing dictionar-

Linguistics and the linguistic rights of minority peoples have always been a sincere focus of SIL

ies, grammars, literacy pamphlets, and much more. Secular linguists from all over the world regularly access the SIL website for linguistic fonts and a variety of innovative software applications for the study and documentation of unwritten languages.

As in any developing country, there has always been a liberal intelligentsia in Nepal ready to test the limits of the monarchy and to push for democratic reforms. But in the late 1960s, they hardly dared to speak. There had been experiments with democracy during the 1950s, and even democratic elections. But late in 1960, King Mahendra carried out a royal coup and dismissed the newly elected government. Two years later, he promulgated a new constitution and had hundreds of democratic activists arrested, along with Members of Parliament and the newly elected Prime Minister, B.P. Koirala. Koirala spent the next eight years in prison. Democrats of all stripes in those days spent sizeable chunks of their lives in prison, and many in the university, too, felt squelched in the new climate. Just about everyone who wasn't a Brahmin or a Chhetri was stung by the policies of a government intent on suppressing their cultural and linguistic rights.

When SIL arrived in Nepal in 1966 with a gleaming track record as a champion for the linguistic rights of minorities all over the world, the university recognized them a possible ally. Justifiably cautious of a Bible translation agenda, they first signed a limited two-year contract involving just four research teams. "How rabid in their evangelicalism were these people?" they wondered. At the end of the two years, they were pleased with the results and extended the contract for another four years, opening the door, even, for additional research teams. Nancy and I were in that second wave.

The contract was renewed for another four years in 1972. Now, in the summer of 1976, it was up for review again. We began to get hints that all might not be well when our flying program was grounded in May of that year.

Throughout the early 1970s, Tibetan Khampas, operating out of Nepal, had mounted a resistance movement against the Chinese in Tibet, running guerrilla attacks across the northern border. Even the CIA got involved, with secret airdrops of arms and ammunition. All the locals knew about this; when the planes missed their target one night, we saw the blinking lights on their parachutes.

Our own flight program

The timing of these events coincided regrettably with our own flight program. Whether anyone actually believed that we were involved in supporting the insurrection is unclear. We felt confident that we would be cleared of any suspicion: after all, on every one of our flights was a government "observer" whose job was to make a detailed report of where we went, what we did, and what we carried. But in the end, with questions about our work being planted on several fronts, suspicion remained.

By this point, the work of SIL had come to the attention of almost everyone in government, and not everyone was as liberal or open-minded as those who sponsored us at the university. There were plenty who opposed democratic change, and any hint of empowerment for marginalized peoples was quickly crushed. Not surprisingly, government seats went to the royalists, not to the democrats. The Crown was everywhere.

Khadga Shah, one-time Director of the Centre for Nepal Asian Studies, thoroughly trounced a research proposal I made in the '80s to produce a dictionary of Kham. A highly placed Rana who was trying to help me push the proposal through explained to me later: "I should have seen it coming. There are three things sacrosanct in Nepal—the Crown, the Hindu religion, and the Nepali language. Your proposal indirectly undermines all three." (Khadga Shah was King Birendra's brother-in-law; both were killed in the June 2001 royal massacre.)

There was always an undercurrent of tension between the liberal intelligentsia and the royalists. A semblance of democracy existed in the countryside, but only a semblance. Every two years, villagers were free to elect their own representatives to seventy-five district-level *panchayats* (councils), and then the district *panchayats* elected representatives to fourteen zonal councils and on up to the 125-seat Parliament or National Panchayat. But the National Panchayat itself was presided over by a Prime Minister hand-chosen by the king. Moreover, district parliamentarians could not go against the decisions of a Chief District Officer (CDO), also hand-chosen by the king. Nothing could be truly democratic as long as the royalists were in charge. And they, of course, made sure that it stayed that way.

In Kathmandu, Nancy and I once rented the house of a CDO. There was something shady about him; he struck me as a first-class syco-phant—servile and conniving. He liked to follow Nancy around the house with a silly grin on his face, rubbing the palms of his hands and popping his knuckles. It was hard to tell what he was thinking, but he was always anxious for a handout. Hasta Ram was shocked that a man of such political stature should behave like a "village blacksmith." We were careful not to offend him, but it was good to eventually move out of his place.

One day in early summer 1976, while the SIL contract was still pending, I ran into our CDO landlord in town. "I'll be getting a promotion soon," he said to me with a devious but self-congratulatory grin.

"Congratulations," I answered. "How did it come about?"

"You know the two SIL ladies working in my district, don't you?" he asked.

"Yes."

"Well, I forwarded a report on them," he volunteered.

"What kind of report?" I asked, displaying a little alarm.

"The CDOs of districts where SIL has been working have been asked by the palace to write a report. In particular, we were asked to comment on religious proselytizing. So I gave them what they wanted," he said, feigning helplessness.

* * *

On June 10, 1976, our Director, Dick Hugoniot, was given notice that the SIL contract would not be renewed. Furthermore, we were given only three months to pack up and be out of the country. (The ladies of our CDO landlord's district were given just two weeks.) There were no appeals. Three charges were made: "preaching, proselytizing, and anti-government activity." Though we asked for a clarification of the charges, none were given. The newspapers always assumed that "anti-government activity" was an explicit reference to a connection with the CIA and the supplying of arms to the Khampa soldiers. How wrong they were.

In a letter written on Royal Palace stationery and dated October 12, 1976, the Private Secretary to His Majesty the King wrote to

Richard Hugoniot, the Director of SIL projects in Nepal. Copies went to the Vice Chancellor of Tribhuvan University, to the Secretary of the Ministry of Foreign Affairs, and to the Secretary of the Ministry of Home and Panchayat. We felt, at least, like we were partially exonerated, but it was too late. Among other things, he said:

> I am commanded to thank you and all those, who on behalf of the Summer Institute of Linguistics served Nepal and her people in different capacities in keeping with the policies, plans and programmes of His Majesty's Government... I am commanded to add that your good will for Nepal and her people will always be remembered with gratitude.

The refusal of the government to renew our contract was a big blow for all of us. We had come to love Nepal and its people, and now we were being asked to leave. Our good friends at the university grieved as much as we did, but there was nothing anybody could do. We archived our work as efficiently as possible, printing up word lists, reports, descriptions, and even short Bible portions. This would be our last chance.

* * *

Just a few months before, we had discovered a technological marvel—the Friden Flexowriter. Flexowriters weren't actually new, but they were new to us. A prototype had been around in WWII, and the U.S. Army made use of them in Vietnam. When the military upgraded some of their office systems, they auctioned the old equipment off, and we were ushered into the "computer" age!

Flexowriters were like player pianos or braillewriters. As the operator types on the keyboard, not only does the text appear on paper, as with an ordinary electric typewriter, but the machine also punches tiny holes in a roll of paper tape. Different hole alignments code different keys. The machines had a paper tape reader as well as a paper tape punch, and by running both simultaneously, you could transfer the correct information onto a new tape, being careful to skip over errors and retype them correctly. The tapes could be stored, and anytime you needed a fresh printout, all you had to do was "play" the paper tape.

During playback, the machines nearly beat themselves to death. The keys would hammer away at a constant rhythm, and every seventy or eighty keystrokes, the carriage would slam back for a new line. Carriage return tension was set at ten kilos. The machines were built to be heavy-duty in order to survive all their pounding, and had to be bolted to their tables. The tables, in turn, were bolted to the floor. A bank of three or four Flexowriters all working at the same time sounded like muffled jackhammers clanging inside the room. It made your head ache.

In Nepal, of course, we used Devanagari script, not Roman, so the slugs on the type-bars had to be changed. We managed to buy type slugs from an Indian typewriter manufacturer, and, pulling off the old ones, we soldered new ones in place. On occasion, during playback, slugs would work lose and zing across the room. It took a technician working the floor full-time to keep the machines in repair. But the time and effort they saved us was enormous. The paper tapes became our archives.

Chapter 19: Saying Goodbye

I never wanted to go away, and the hard part now is the leaving you all. I'm not afraid, but it seems as if I should be homesick for you even in heaven.
—*Louisa May Alcott,* Little Women

"Good-bye, dear little house of dreams," she said.
—*Montgomery,* Anne's House of Dreams

I immediately set about trying to get a passport for Hasta Ram. I desperately hoped to collaborate with him for a few more months, but that was now contingent on our getting him out of the country. Passports were exceedingly difficult to acquire in those days, and depending on how heavily you bribed, the waiting period was reported to be about six months. As with everything else in Nepal, though, if you knew someone, you could expedite the process.

Hasta Ram and I paid a visit to a Magar friend, Balaram Gharti, who, when I first met him six years earlier, had been a member of the National Parliament. He supported me then in my choice to do research on Kham and he had shown some interest in my progress. Though he couldn't speak Kham himself, he traced his ancestral roots to Kham. He had risen in the ranks since then and was now Secretary of Defense.

Secretary Gharti was cordial, as he had been on previous visits. If anyone would have known about CIA allegations, it would have been him. But he said nothing, indicated nothing, and expressed no doubts. "And, yes, of course," he would be happy to help Hasta Ram get a passport. He wrote a few letters, made a few phone calls, and we had the passport before the week was out.

When I tried to get a visa to take Hasta Ram to America, the American embassy turned us down. Somewhat disappointed, we went to the British embassy, where we presented Hasta Ram's credentials as a British Gurkha during World War II. They were quite happy to give him a nine-month visa to England, and our whole family as well.

* * *

Hasta Ram needed to make a trip home before leaving for England. I wanted to go along, too. I couldn't just leave without bidding farewell. What would our village friends think?

The idea of my going back to the village when everyone else was preparing to leave the country caused, understandably, a bit of consternation in the SIL directorate. But when I reminded them that my hunting rifle was still stashed out there, they were suddenly more agreeable. Although the rifle was duly licensed in Nepal and I renewed the license every year, it was unnerving to think what our enemies might do with a story about my possession of a weapon if they ever found out. So I was dispatched to the village, along with Hasta Ram and my good friend Dag Wendel. We would be gone for almost a month.

Back in the village, we met with the believers and explained our plight to them. "But," we assured them, "Hasta Ram will be back in six or seven months."

They all wept and likened themselves to orphans. "We try to meet together," they complained, "but it's not at all like having Hasta Ram here. None of us reads very well, and we're unskilled at speaking or praying. Our numbers have already dwindled, and now without our parents, whatever will become of us?"

We felt their loss and encouraged them to get together often even if they didn't feel like it.

* * *

Dag and I left Hasta Ram in the village for another two weeks and headed north into the mountains. It was the middle of summer, albeit also the middle of the monsoon season, and I wanted to visit as many sheep camps as I could. We traveled to the foot of the glaciers, all the way to the northern extreme of the Kham grazing lands. Putha and Churen towered above us, both around 24,000 feet in altitude and separating us from the northern district of Dolpa. We continued east all the way to Dhailya Khagar.

There were no trails in these mountains. Nobody went up there if they were trying to go somewhere. Everything dead-ended in glacial walls. So early each morning, before the monsoon clouds began to develop, the shep-

Putha and Churen tower above the tents

herds of one camp would carefully point out our route to the next. We jotted the landmarks down on paper, noting at each one whether we should continue straight or turn left or right. Once the clouds rolled in and we were on our own, we had only our notes to rely on. But sure enough, late every afternoon, an hour or two before dark, we would hear the welcome bleating of sheep in the fog ahead. The shepherds would then "stretch out their tents" and take us in. At one camp we were able to provide fresh blue sheep meat. It had been a long shot with my rifle, but I had been lucky.

Only once did we get lost, and that for two days. There was no bleating of sheep to be heard; the silence was so profound that it made our ears ring. The altitude (on one high ridge we reckoned we had reached eighteen thousand feet) intensified the sensation. Flies could hardly stay airborne, the air was so thin; they had learned to get around in full-throttle kamikaze dives.

I was surprised during this trek to find flocks of sheep from almost every Kham village grazing these alpine regions, even those belonging to southern dialects. The Gamales, in fact, a southern group of Kham, occupied the northernmost camps. I knew then that this would be as good a place as any to collect research data on dialect variants.

* * *

Back in the village, with my research data in hand, I was taken up with issues of linguistic diversity. I was slowly becoming aware that there were numerous dialects of Kham. Every village speaks a bit differently from its neighbors, and everyone knows immediately where a person is from as soon as he opens his mouth, but some dialects, it turned out, were so distinct that the inhabitants of Taka and Shera could barely make out what was being said.

With my adventuresome traveling companion, Dag Wendel, right at hand, I made preparations for us to make a short foray south into the Gamale Kham areas of northern Rolpa. For two days, we crossed over high ridges and through dense forests. Trails that looked promising at first fizzled out into nothing; they went nowhere. In a few places where we did find trails, they were so vertical that they literally climbed trees, going from one branch to the next. Hasta Ram's second son, who traveled with us, called them "monkey trails."

Some locals will certainly remember us for years to come. As Dag and I descended down the Gamale side of the ridge, trudging through trackless forest, we came upon a lone young woman collecting firewood. With the look of a startled deer, she let out a shriek, tossed her load aside, and ran in panic down the mountainside. Dag, who sported a long, shaggy beard, was in the lead. He had been clowning around that very morning and was still wearing long strings of grey-green tree moss from his beard. Who wouldn't have bolted in panic? This woman's tale of her encounter with a yeti is probably still being told and retold.

Gamale Kham, though obviously sharing a common ancestor with the Kham language that I had been studying, was very, very different. Having traveled through dense forests for two days, I could now see how the languages had diverged so much. There had been no social intercourse between these two groups for a very long time. I had the impression, too, that the Gamales were far less developed than their northern cousins. Some of their homes were as basic as the cliff dwellings at the Gila National Monument in the U.S., and the women spoke no Nepali. Most people still wore clothes woven from the hemp-like fibers of the *puwa* plant. Many women shaved the front of their heads and braided the hair at the back in a long, single "Chinese" braid. They were not accustomed to strangers, and the women and children hid when we approached.

Eventually I was able to piece it all together, but the linguistic puzzle was complex, and this was my first eye-opening foray into the world of Kham dialects. Kham is made up of three major groups—

Parbate Kham (which is what is spoken in Taka and Shera), Gamale Kham, and Sesi Kham. Parbate Kham further splits into Western Parbate Kham and Eastern Parbate Kham. One only needs to look at the verb in each of the major groups to appreciate how different they are. The fully inflected verb for the sentence "You beat me" is *jeponake* in Western Parbate, *yecosng-ken̄* in Gamale Kham, and *tupdang-cya* in Sesi Kham. Who would guess that they are even related? Within each of these varieties is a veritable Babel of dialects.

A Gamale Kham woman

Chapter 20: Leopard-Eagles

Traduttore, traditore. ["Translator, traitor."]
—*Italian adage*

Nancy went ahead to England with Steve and Daniel; Hasta Ram and I followed a few weeks later, arriving in mid-September 1976. We went to the Wycliffe Centre in Horsleys Green, Buckinghamshire, where we moved into their family living quarters, an old, renovated army barracks dating back to WWII. Steve and Daniel suffered terribly. Accustomed to running free in the mountains of Nepal, they suddenly found themselves in an English school, wearing black patent leather shoes, dress trousers, neckties, and cardigans. Daniel cried every morning for weeks. One day he had to stand with his face in a corner for an hour because he had said that he had a "bloody nose." "No, you don't," came the stiff rebuke from the Headmaster, "you have a 'nose bleed,' you nincompoop! Don't forget it!"

* * *

Hasta Ram and I worked hard from the middle of September to the end of January. We assumed that this would be our last time together, and in those months, we drafted the New Testament Epistles of Romans, Philippians, and Colossians. Apart from First Peter, this was the first time that we had worked on epistolary material, and it was exceedingly difficult. Cultural mismatches were everywhere. Romans was full of strange lexical collocations that must have posed a challenge even for the Greek mind: "the old man," "the body of sin," "sin becoming

Translating at Horselys Green, U.K.

alive and killing me through the commandment," "circumcision becoming uncircumcision," "baptism into death," and so on.

But the cultural mismatches didn't occur only in the realm of religious thought. Ideas that we might think of as simple and straightforward also posed problems. What is more obvious and rational for the western mind than the classification of animals? It doesn't take a rocket scientist to notice that mammals are warm-blooded, that they give birth to living young, and that they nurse their offspring. Reptiles are pretty much the opposite: they are cold-blooded, they lay eggs, and they don't nurse their young. So in the scientific, rational West, we talk about mammals as distinct from reptiles, birds, fish, insects, and so on. Is there another way to think about them?

Well, yes, Khams see things differently. It's not that they don't observe the same traits that we do; it's just that the distinction between giving birth to living young or laying eggs doesn't matter a lot to them. Babies are babies. They're more concerned with other factors, such as "is the animal naughty or nice?" Their classification system comprises things like *laa-gaa*: "leopard-eagles," *syaa-baa*: "deer-pheasants," *baza-biza:* "bird-rats," and *rwihza-wanza:* "bug-worms."

"Leopard-eagles" cause harm; it doesn't matter if they're mammals or birds. They prey on the domain of man, stealing his chickens and sheep; they are what we would call predators. "Deer-pheasants" are the opposite, providing food for man; these are the game animals. "Bird-rats" are the little critters, things that scurry around on the forest floor and flit through the village. "Bug-worms" are the creepy-crawlies, things that make your skin crawl. They're mostly bugs, snakes, and lizards, but they also include a few unexpected creatures like the river otter (which is regarded as a slimy creature, similar to Gollum from *The Lord of the Rings*).

So what were we to do with a passage like Romans 1:22–23, in which a Greek classification is assumed: "Professing themselves to be wise, they became fools, and changed the glory of the incorruptible God into an image made like to corruptible man, and to birds, and four-footed beasts, and creeping things"?

Any attempt to translate this passage verbatim in Kham, which we tried, only makes it seem that *four-footedness* is the point of the passage. Khams have no such classification, and the mere novelty of singling out "four-footed" beasts makes it a highly marked expression, the focus of assertion. It's like saying, "If only they had made images of three-footed beasts, it wouldn't have been so bad. But these fools made *four*-footed beasts!"

The point of the passage is clear enough: "professing themselves to be wise, they became fools." This is not a treatise on biological classification; it's a statement about the foolishness of idolatry. Even the Khams laugh at the idolatry of the Hindus, so when the passage is rendered in their language, the absurdity is heightened: "In those very things in which they claimed to 'know it all,' they became totally ignorant. In place of the glorious, living, and eternal God, they made images of man, animal-beasts, bird-rats, and bug-worms, and worshiped them instead of God."

Who but a fool would stoop to worship a bird-rat or a bug-worm?

* * *

Much more difficult were the passages in Romans dealing with deep theological notions such as justification by faith.

Khams weren't at all impressed by the idea of God doing tricks with the books, getting someone else to pay up and then writing "Paid in Full" in the balance column. It smacked of pure Brahminical deception.

Then came the big surprise. As I was translating Romans and looking at it through the lens of another language, I came to realize that the Apostle Paul's notion of justification is about a lot more than juggling books. It's about *real* righteousness; it's about pleasing God the way Abraham did; it's about the law of the Spirit of life.

Paul asks the question, "Do we nullify the law through faith?" His answer is, "Of course not! On the contrary, we establish the law." How? It connects us with God in a manner such that we can start living by risk (i.e., faith) and quit being tied up in knots about whether we're doing it right or not. In Romans 4:5, Paul seems almost to encourage reckless abandon. The creativity that comes by risking it all produces some truly good works, and God is pleased with that.

Remember the servant in Luke 19 who carefully tied his silver coin into a clean handkerchief and presented it back to his master in mint condition? His master wasn't pleased at all. He was pleased with the servant who tossed his coin into the ring, didn't worry about tarnishing it, and turned it into ten.

Though justification is a legal term in Greek and English, there's nothing in the epistle to suggest that justification is merely about being right "on the books." It's about being right before God. What does he value, what does he consider righteous? God reckons the man who has faith as righteous, not the man who tries to keep all the laws. In fact, "Faith [itself] is reckoned as righteousness" (Romans 4:9). Wow!

Even preliterate Khams understand this. They know that trying to be perfect by keeping the laws doesn't work. (The "laws" in question don't have to be written legislation; they can be ritual, taboos, whatever.) Eventually you slip up. The better way is the life of faith. This is good news even in Kham!

* * *

Our efforts began to work their magic. Hasta Ram was always a Kham purist. Nepali loan words "made his ears hurt," he used to say. He fairly insisted on certain archaic forms of speech. Only later did I appreciate his wisdom. He had infused the text with an intangible authority. Scholars have noted that even the Authorized (King James) Version of the Bible in English was already slightly old-fashioned from the first day of its publication in 1611. The language was not Jacobean, but grounded in Tudor idiom. By archaizing their style, George Steiner claims, the translators produced a sense of déjà vu. The foreign text was felt to be "not so much an import from abroad" as it was "an element out of their native past." It was "inwoven with the past of English feeling"; it had "a feeling of at-homeness."

How many times have I heard Khams say, with startled looks on their faces, "It speaks with the voice of our grandfathers!"

* * *

In January 1977, Hasta Ram and I traveled to West Germany, where we worked with a Greek exegete and consultant who checked our translation for naturalness and accuracy and made suggestions regarding how to improve it. We returned to England a month later, and Hasta Ram returned to Nepal on February 21.

* * *

There was still a question of what Nancy and I might do next. In the months following our departure, our SIL Director, Dick Hugoniot, contacted friends in the Nepali government and the university. They were very apologetic for what had happened and made sure that he understood that, although we could not work in Nepal as an organization, we were always welcome as individual scholars. It wouldn't be easy; they wouldn't be able to accommodate us officially, but we should feel free to come and go and to collaborate as academics. Dick shot off a letter to us, and we decided to try. We wouldn't have the support and services we had before, but we knew the country now and we could try working out our own arrangements.

After a family romp through Europe on a three-week Eurorail Pass—France, Spain, Switzerland, Austria, West Germany, Denmark, Sweden, Norway, Belgium, Holland, whew!—we visited my parents' home in the little town of Daggett in the Mojave Desert of southern California. We were there, in the home I had grown up in, from April to September. One of the Nepal Flexowriters had been shipped to the

SIL office in Huntington Beach, California, and we went down to get it.

Nancy and I began punching paper tapes on the Flexowriter in my parents' garage. The old machine rattled and shook, and within a few months, we had published four titles: Genesis, Exodus, The Parables of Jesus, and Romans–Philippians–Colossians. The format was pocketbook size, five and one quarter by six and three quarter inches.

During the same period, we were able to visit all of our supporting churches in Southern California—Barstow, Daggett, Yermo, Newberry Springs, Hinkley, and Baker. We asked for confirmation for the journey we were about to embark on, and they stood solidly behind us. Now it was up to us to see how it would all turn out.

Taking the train through Europe

Chapter 21: Bumping into God

The gates of heaven are lightly locked,
We do not guard our gain,
The heaviest hind may easily
Come silently and suddenly
Upon me in a lane.
    —G.K. Chesterton, "The Ballad of the White Horse"

In the 1970s and '80s, Nepal was beginning to come of age. In centuries past, Nepal had been a feudal kingdom that depended on the monarch for everything—its laws, its aspirations, its well-being, even its view of itself. But now the Nepalese people were beginning to develop new ideas, some of which had been acquired abroad. Throughout the '60s and '70s, hundreds of Nepalese students left the country and studied in India, America, and the U.S.S.R. They came back with notions of self-governance and a desire to contribute to a new national life and consciousness.

Although Nepal was a multi-ethnic, multi-linguistic, and religiously diverse state, the king's sovereign powers were based on the Hindu institutions of divine kingship and a hierarchical caste order. Whole classes and ethnicities were excluded from governance. The social and political framework of the state had long been based on the "old boy network" of royal patronage. In exchange for loyalty and service, known as *chakri*, the king dispensed far-reaching privileges to rightly connected individuals of high caste. The most common privileges were tax-exempt land grants, or *birta*, which entitled the owner to mobilize local labor forces and to appropriate a wide range of non-agricultural revenues based on customs, duties, and fines. A land grant from the king, for all practical purposes, was equivalent to a small fiefdom.

This system of royal patronage worked well so long as the *birta* owners were the only ones with access to education. Once education became more widespread, the old system became hopelessly outdated. Education brought a new self-awareness and knowledge of the world. But self-expression was stifled, and this only added to the sense of frustration. The newspapers were heavily censored; all that you could read about was His Majesty the King. One got the impression that he was the only presence that mattered: in his "great, beneficent vision for the people," he inaugurated a water tap, he graced a meeting of ever-grateful subjects, he granted royal audience to some lucky foreign diplomat. But people were growing impatient.

After King Mahendra scrapped democracy, suspended the newly elected government, and banned political parties, he launched his own "single-party democracy" in 1962 known as the *Panchayat* System. He turned his attention to a project of national development known as *Gaun Farka Rastriya Abhiyan* or "Back to the Village National Campaign." In place of democracy, he would promote development— development of agricultural banks, cooperatives, hospitals, forests, roads, dams, hydroelectricity—and, best of all, he would get foreign aid to fund it.

It all looked so good. International non-governmental organizations (INGOs) and development agencies rushed in. But the old patronage-based system of privilege for loyalty didn't cease, it only shifted. In place of land grants, the king was now dispensing privileged administrative positions, and the richest spoils were awarded not to the competent but to members of the political and religious establishment. The new favoritism extended to the lower levels of civil servants and outward to the newly formed rural administrative tiers. And it was all legitimized by Western democratic nations. Corruption became rampant, and those outside the system began to raise their voices. Such dissenters were quickly silenced, though, and many went to prison.

Few outsiders were even aware of the political dissent. Tourism was thriving, with new hotels and guest-houses popping up all over. Private business was booming: you could buy almost anything in Kathmandu. Cigarette and whiskey billboards lit up the night sky with their promises of a "*Safalko* [successful] Life." But democratic politicians and intellectuals had mostly gone underground. The ones who hadn't were in jail. It just wasn't safe to oppose the status quo. Though we had numerous friends at the university, they couldn't afford direct association with us, nor could they sponsor our linguistic research projects. Language and religion were especially volatile issues. We would need to be a part of the underground and cast our lot with the beleaguered villagers. Hopefully, we thought, a day would come when we could all come out in the open.

Many years later, when it was safer to write openly, K.P. Malla, a Newar linguistic activist and recognized member of the Nepali intelligentsia, wrote:

Tourism was thriving:

New Road

Ghora Pani

Patan Durbar Marg

I see no harm in translating any word of God in Nepalese languages. Our own scriptures prescribe that the women and slaves who dare even listen to the Vedas should be punished by pouring hot lead into their ears. The SIL makes no secret of the fact that they are good, God-loving and God-fearing Christians who work in collaboration with the Wycliffe Bible Translators in providing portions of the Bible in the languages of the people with whom it works... The Hindu seers, intending to transform the whole world into Aryans or "the nobility," have yet to translate the Rigveda into Nepali, and the day when one can read it in Hayu or even Tamang language is likely to dawn only when the Himalayas have all melted down the Bay of Bengal...

He went on to say that "At a point in our social history when the whole society and the field of the Social Sciences are in ferment, it is consoling to have at least some God-fearing linguists round the corner."

* * *

Nancy and I returned to Nepal with the family in September 1977—only a year after we had been forced to leave. SIL no longer had an official presence there, but we entered as tourists, at least for an interim period, to see if we could manage in the current climate. Tourist visas were good for a month, and then they could be extended twice within the country, for a total of three months.

Religious dissent was treated even more cruelly in Nepal than political dissent. Simply to become a Christian was punishable by one year in prison and to be guilty of proselytizing was punishable by six years. Though the Christian population was still very small and scattered, many believers were languishing in prisons across the country. The anti-conversion law had been on the books for more than a hundred years, but this was the first time that anyone in government had seriously attempted to enforce it—yet another sign that the royalists were panicking.

In late September, we applied for a family "trekking permit" from the Central Immigration Department in Kathmandu and were granted permission for a one-month trek lasting to the end of October. The permit entitled us to hike from Tansen, a hill town on the bus route to India,

On the 240-mile family hike to Taka and back

out to Rukum District in midwestern Nepal. The distance between those two points was about 120 miles (not the way the crow flies but the way the peasant walks). Nancy had her thirty-third birthday on the trail and celebrated with a freshly cut cucumber that she had to share with a villager's pet monkey.

Back in the village, we met with Hasta Ram and the newly formed church. Fourteen months earlier, when we were saying our goodbyes, they were distraught and likened themselves to orphans. "Without our parents whatever will become of us?" they had asked. But a handful of them had promised that they would continue to meet and to read the Scriptures. We were amazed to discover that they had not only survived, they had baptized six new men.

What was the source of their confidence, turning them from frightened children to bold evangelists? They were anxious to tell us. Several months after we had left for England, taking Hasta Ram with us, the tiny group met one evening to read and pray. It was winter, and they sat around the firepit inside the inner part of the house. They wondered if God was with them or if perhaps he had gone to England with Hasta Ram and us. They felt alone.

"Suddenly," they said, "a large white dove, a wild one, flew in through the low doorway and, completely unafraid, settled in our midst. We were startled and didn't know what to do. We had never seen such a thing before."

Fearing that a dog or a cat might kill the bird, they gently put a basket over it, as they do with their chickens, and weighted the basket down with stones. Taking their Gospels, they turned to the passage in Mark 1:10 that says "The Spirit [of God], like a dove, descended upon [Jesus]." They knew then that God was with them and rejoiced through the night, singing and praising God. No one went home that night, and the next morning, they released the dove. It flew directly off into the forested mountains, and they never saw it again.

"If God is with us why are we despondent?" they asked themselves, and from that day on, they began to speak with new boldness.

God was beginning to show up in unusual ways, after having been missing in action for a long time. Where had he been earlier, when we had cried out to him? But this seemed to be a question only I was asking. The view of these new believers was much less complicated.

"We live at the foot of the snows," they used to say, "and even our own king had never heard of us. But the King of Kings knew us, and one day he visited us."

* * *

One of the six newly-baptized men was Tipalkya, the old hunter. Tipalkya was already the self-proclaimed *sastri* or "religious storyteller" in the village. If anyone could tell the Hindu epics or stories from the Ramayana, it was Tipalkya. But now, he said, those tales sounded like no more than the chatter of radio news: "this happened here" and "that happened there." He was captivated by the gospel. One truth, however, was almost too much for him to comprehend, "that God should take up his abode in me." How could that be?

One day he traveled alone deep into the mountain wilderness with his muzzle-loading musket slung over his shoulder. He broke out above the tree line and was making his way across a patch of open grassland. When he came to a charcoal pit that had been dug by the blacksmiths, he hunkered down for a few moments to take in the slopes ahead. Suddenly, he spotted a she-bear descending across a rockslide toward him. She hadn't seen him yet, and he quickly hid behind a large boulder. He put a new firing cap on the powder lock and waited.

As soon as the bear came into close range, he stood and fired. The bullet struck her in the side, but this only infuriated her. Yelping and snorting, she came running. Tipalkya deftly stepped aside like a matador fighting a bull, and she tumbled into

Tipalkya loads his musket

the charcoal pit. But then she turned and came running uphill at him again. With the bear between him and the forest, he had to run for a point across the hill, where he had spotted a tree that was just big enough to climb. In seconds, the bear was on his heels, and he could almost feel her breath. As he reached the tree, he tossed the musket aside and leaped high for one of the branches. It broke, and he crashed to the ground.

The bear was on him in a flash. As he reached for the *kukri* in his waistband, he looked up into the bear's eyes. The bear returned the gaze. Then, she let out a terrified yelp and ran the other direction as fast as she could go. Dumbfounded, Tipalkya sat and watched her go. Eventually, he pulled his pipe from its pouch, loaded it with tobacco, and began smoking. *Surely, God must have taken up his abode in me,* he thought. *That bear wouldn't be afraid of me. But she saw God in me, and that's what made her run.*

Another man was baptized a few months later, bringing the total to a dozen. His name was Kami, and his home was *Shyapara Pup*, the cliff-caves just north of the village. Kami was in the line of succession to carry on his grandfather's

He pulled his pipe from its pouch

shamanic calling. For years, he had had a recurring dream: a great serpent would appear in his pathway and say, "Worship me, and I will give you all that you need." Eventually, he began having dreams of a house of light, high on a mountain. He watched Hasta Ram and others enter the house with joy. One day he asked, "Whose house is this?" and he heard the reply, "This is God's house." For many nights in his dreams, he tried to get there, but he was thwarted by cliffs and darkness and always the serpent saying, "Worship me!"

One day he found his way to the worship house in the village. There, he heard Hasta Ram expounding from Genesis 3 the story of the temptation of Adam and Eve in the garden. Kami learned the identity of the serpent. He had already seen the "house of God" in his dreams, and he decided that his goal in life would be to climb the cliff and reach the Celestial City. He became a pilgrim along with the rest of us, "seeking for a city which hath foundations, whose builder and maker is God."

Through the years, the Kham Christians continued to be the same remarkable people they had always been. As in their former life as animists, they still sensed the supernatural all around. But now, in place of spirits, ghosts, and goblins, they came to see God's presence everywhere, and they bumped into him often in the little lanes of life. God had invaded their consciousness, and he was there to stay.

Chapter 22: Messing with the Wrong People

The fact of Christianity being a translated, and translat-ing, religion places God at the center of the universe of cultures, implying free coequality among cultures and a necessary relativ-izing of languages vis-a-vis the truth of God. No culture is so advanced and so superior that it can claim exclusive access or advantage to the truth of God, and none so marginal or inferior that it can be excluded. All have merit; none is indispensable. The vernacular was thereby given the kiss of life.
—*Lamin Sanneh,* Whose Religion is Christianity?

"Visa runs" became a way of life for us. We kept them going every three months for a year. Lingerers in Nepal used to stay indefinitely that way—by exiting the country one day and re-entering the next. Hippies and missionaries used the same strategy, though it was generally fairly easy to tell them apart. If you wanted to save money, you could travel by road to the border town of Raxaul, but this was frowned upon by the border authorities. It seemed cheap, I guess; made you look like a hippie. If you wanted to make a better impression, you could fly by plane to Patna. Either way, whether at the border town or at the airport, you'd only get seven days on re-entry.

If you wanted a full month's visa on arrival back in Nepal, you had to visit a Nepalese consulate, the nearest being in Calcutta or New Delhi. If you didn't have the money to fly to Calcutta, you could always make your way to Patna and then take the night train to Calcutta. We did this a couple of times until we grew weary of it.

Because of a business trip I had to make to the Philippines in the spring of 1978, my visa dates were out of sync with the rest of the family. While I was off in the mountains for two months doing linguistic data collection, Nancy and the boys had to fly to Calcutta.

While Nancy was in Calcutta, she contacted the Gospel Literature Service, a publisher that was doing four Scripture booklets for us— Genesis, Exodus, Parables of Jesus, and three Epistles under a single cover. Genesis and Exodus were finished, they informed her. Would she like to take a few copies with her?

"Yes, of course," she replied, and one of their men delivered a few copies right to the guest-house where they were staying.

Nancy arranged to have the rest of the books shipped to Duncan Hospital in Raxaul, on the Indian side of the Nepal–India border, as soon as the other two titles were printed. It would have been so much easier to ship them to Kathmandu, but Bibles couldn't be shipped to Kathmandu in those days. This was the best we could do.

Nepalese customs officials were paranoid about gospel literature, and they usually rifled through everyone's belongings on arrival, looking for contraband of every sort. (Once, I was startled by a customs officer who asked if I had any "mission-ry stuff." "What kind of missionary stuff?"

"Visa runs," often made by grueling road trips to the border of India and Nepal

I asked, and he replied, "Gears, pulleys, wheels; you know, machine-ry stuff!") But the boys had figured things out ahead of time. They stuffed a few copies of the booklets into their backpacks along with schoolbooks, comics, and games. Nobody even looked.

* * *

In spite of our unconventional comings and goings, our acquaintances in Kathmandu generally treated us with respect. They understood our dilemma. Contact with "dissidents," mostly linguists and anthropologists, was always unofficial, but we also enjoyed spending time with Raju and his wife, Bina, our friends now for two years. Raju was in the army, with an elite assignment, and our relationship with him felt a bit incongruous. How do you balance those kinds of things? He knew we were traveling in and out, but he didn't want to be burdened with too much detail.

Some Nepalese scholars were risking a lot. Dor Bahadur Bista, an intellectual and long-time friend of our institute (it was he who had first supported Nancy and me on our assignment to Kham) was critical of the age-old patronage culture of the royalist elite. It stifled innovation, he said, and was proving detrimental to the economic development of the nation. For development to be effective, he argued, a worker's status needed to be achieved or earned, not given automatically. Otherwise, individual efforts were directed

The Nepali population that has remained untouched by Hindu caste principles is Nepal's greatest treasure

simply at maintaining one's own privileges. He also held foreign aid partly to blame for cultural stagnation. Goodwill aside, as long as aid was being used to bolster the positions of those who perpetuated the system of caste hierarchy, it wasn't achieving its intended purpose.

Mr. Bista held numerous prestigious positions in government, academics, and business, and his insider status gave him deep insights into the culture as well as a powerful prophetic role. One of his most startling assertions, in his controversial book *Fatalism and Development: Nepal's Struggle for Modernisation* (1991), was that "the

Nepali population that has remained untouched by Hindu caste principles is Nepal's greatest treasure."

"This is a very sizeable proportion of the population," he went on to
say. "But presently they live in remote areas, at a little above subsistence
level, with little or no education and no opportunities to develop and
actualize their aspirations. Their values are not the values of hierarchic
Bahunism [Brahaminism]. They do know the importance of hard work,
of endurance, and the role of individual effort in the improvement of
one's circumstances. And they have the positive qualities of strong
cooperative behavior and an appreciation of the general well-being and
importance of the group or community as a whole" (151–2).

Shortly after publishing this work, Mr. Bista disappeared. He was
rumored to have been murdered for his revolutionary views, but the
mystery of his disappearance has never been solved.

* * *

If academics like Dr. Bista were sympathetic toward our work, the
foreign aid community treated us with contempt. Our story was "inter-
esting," and so Nancy and I found ourselves from time to time invited
to cocktail parties. Invariably, though, our host would be embarrassed
for us before the evening was over. More often than not, one of the
other guests, with a bourbon in one hand and a cigarette in the other,
would eventually sniff us out and go on the attack. "What right have
you to tamper with the locals' religion? I know your type—I've read
Michener's *Hawaii*. You destroy indigenous cultures!"

About their own work, such people were always self-
congratulatory; conversations were peppered with the buzzwords of
the day—"development," "human rights," even Mahatma-Gandhi-
style "dissidence." The Rapti Integrated Rural Development Project
of the United States Agency for International Development (USAID)
was pouring millions of dollars into the Rapti Zone of midwestern
Nepal, the zone where we had worked, but we hadn't seen a single
tangible benefit up in the Kham areas. They had set up what they

called "demonstration pockets," and they proudly claimed that in all of them, they could demonstrate "increased income, equity, women's participation, sustainability, and favorable social effects."

What they failed to acknowledge was that their demonstration pockets were tiny enclaves belonging to the king's age-old patronage system. Their so-called "rural development" was actually bolstering the king's power. Payback for this disingenuousness was coming: the Rapti Zone, unsurprisingly, became the heartland of the later Maoist movement.

The American ambassador, L. Douglas Heck, and his wife were notable exceptions to the rule of foreign condescension. Nancy developed a good friendship with Elizabeth Heck, and on three separate occasions, we were invited to the ambassador's residence for

Daniel celebrates his eighth birthday at the U.S. Embassy in Kathmandu

a private dinner; Daniel celebrated his eighth birthday there. They were so impressed by our get-your-hands-dirty approach in Rukum district that they made arrangements to hire a Nepalese Army helicopter and take Ellsworth Bunker, the U.S. ambassador to South Vietnam, along with his wife, Carol Laise, the former ambassador to Nepal, out to the village where we had worked. Unfortunately, a military emergency in Vietnam intervened, and the trip had to be cancelled.

A few months later, in August 1978, the wife of an SIL colleague went to Central Immigration for an extension. She was asked point-blank, "Where are the Watters?" A few days later, the same question was asked of another colleague. It was clear that immigration officials knew who the SIL people were. They deserved more credit than we had been giving them. Since I was away on a linguistic data collection trip, Nancy contacted Mrs. Heck. "What shall we do?" she asked. Mrs. Heck promised to look into the matter.

The next day, the ambassador's wife personally called on Nancy.

"I'm sorry," she said, "but there's nothing we can do. You won't get your next extension. The decision has been made at top ministerial levels; it may even be from the palace itself. The next time you go to immigration, you'll be given a twenty-four-hour notice to leave."

This came as a surprise. Was it a backlash against our planned trip to the village with three American ambassadors? Probably so. Taka-Shera was outside the Rapti Zone's "demonstration pockets."

When I arrived home from the mountains at the end of August, our visas were good for only another four days. We began packing immediately. The four days came and went, and we still had a lot to do. We decided to overstay the visa and pay the fine at the airport. It came to only twenty dollars, and nobody said anything. The day before our departure, the Hecks drove their big, black embassy vehicle to our tiny, unpainted concrete house. Their parting words were, "You have done nothing to be ashamed of. Go with your heads held high!"

On September 4, 1978, we departed for the Philippines, where the family would reside for the next two years.

David, Daniel, Nancy, and Steve at Nasuli in the Philippines

Chapter 23: Just the Man

Knavery and flattery are blood relations.
—Abraham Lincoln

I wrote a letter to Hasta Ram, making arrangements to begin working with him in Kathmandu on February 5, 1979. Immigration had a short memory; it lasted only as long as the bales of records stacked in the corner weren't covered by new bales of records. The officials were meticulous at making records, but once the records were bound into bales, they might as well have been buried in the Pyramids.

I went a few days early, arriving in the capital on the last day of January, and began setting up my narrow, concrete flat near the zoo in Jawalakhel. The floor was made of rough planks; I could see through the cracks into the Tibetan wool and kerosene shop below. Directly over my head was a local whorehouse of some sort; the noises became monotonous. When Hasta Ram arrived, we began work on First Corinthians.

As we worked on translation, we were also making frequent trips into the city, trying to get a visa for Hasta Ram to come to the Philippines. I was beginning to miss my family, and the long absences were taking their toll on both sides. By late March, we were successful, and we made our way together to the Philippines. Hasta Ram stayed with me there until early August.

Before we left Nepal, though, I met a man named Edward (pseudonym) that had become uniquely positioned to represent the plight of the Nepali church in political spheres. Despite being a Nepali Christian, his high government connections both in Nepal and internationally gave him the ability to meet behind many important closed doors and to function as a remarkably bold ambassador of the church.

Levering his influence, Edward often put himself in the mouth of the lion. He had even dared to open a small Christian bookstore in Kathmandu—I went down to see it—and so far he was getting away with it. He even brought Bibles and Christian literature across the border from time to time. I informed him of the Gospel booklets in Kham that would soon be arriving in Raxaul, and he assured me that getting them across would be no problem. "Just leave it to me," he said. "I'll bring them across for you."

The next time I heard of the matter was when Hasta Ram arrived back in Kathmandu on his way home from the Philippines. On August 11, 1979, Hasta Ram sent a short letter from the capital saying, "The books have been held up at the border in Raxaul." He then headed for the village.

In the middle of October, I was asked by SIL to spend six weeks at various locations in South Asia, doing training seminars and providing one-on-one translation consulting for our teams. One leg of the journey led me to Kathmandu, where I called on Edward to find out what had happened.

"Well," he said, "I didn't actually go myself. I contacted some friends who were traveling overland from Europe and asked them to stop off in Raxaul and pick up the books. The books were confiscated, and they turned the van back, too."

"Confiscated on what grounds?" I asked.

"Oh, it was just a technicality, I suppose," he replied. "These guys weren't familiar with how things are done in Nepal, and they got turned back. It's no big deal. I'll go down to the border with you, and we'll get them released. How would that be?"

"Yeah, sure, I'd appreciate that," I murmured.

Edward picked up a calendar from his desk and began calculating. "How about Tuesday, November 6?" he asked. "Will that work for you?"

"I can make it work," I replied. "Where shall we meet?"

"You'll need to run down to RNAC [Royal Nepal Airlines

Corporation] and buy a couple of tickets to Birgunj," he said, "on the Nepal side of the border, just across from Raxaul. Make the return flight for Wednesday. Come back when you've got confirmed seats, and let me know."

I went downtown to New Road the next day and did as Edward had requested. With the tickets in hand, I visited his house that evening. It was after dark, and I rapped on the side door.

Edward opened the door. "Ah, David, welcome," he said as he swung the door wide.

"I have the tickets," I said as I stepped through the doorway.

Inside the room, I noticed that Edward had three guests. Two I recognized: one was a well-known Christian activist; the other, a man who had spent time in prison for being a Christian. The third man, I didn't know, but it wasn't long before I realized that I was in the wrong place at the wrong time. He had been in the middle of an angry tirade, cut short by my arrival. Now he carried on with his barrage.

"I'll have all of you jailed," he threatened. "You pretend to be preachers of the gospel, but in fact, you're a bunch of frauds. If it weren't for the poor in this country, you wouldn't have a crust of bread yourselves. You go to the West and take up offerings for orphans and lepers, but you use it to fatten yourselves." On and on he went.

Finally, he glanced my direction and said to Edward, "Where the hell are you two going, anyway?"

"We're going to the border to clear some goods," Edward replied.

"I don't believe you. You're going down to clear Christian literature."

"No, not Christian literature," Edward protested. "Bibles."

"I want to see them," the man demanded. "I want to see what they look like."

Edward got up obediently, went to his little office off the main sitting room, and came back, carrying two booklets—one red and one blue. (These were the first in the shipment that Nancy had arranged to be sent from Calcutta.)

"Yeah, yeah," the man said. "I suppose the blue one is Genesis and the red one is Exodus."

"How did you know?" Edward asked in disbelief.

"Aw, you Christians are all the same. You always put blue covers on Genesis and red covers on Exodus."

Now I was worried. This guy knew more than he was letting on. Suddenly, I was on the hot seat.

"Those books," he said, turning to me, "are written in a language that nobody can identify. Did you write them?"

"Yes."

"Well, explain that to me, would you?"

So I had to tell him my story. I recounted how we as a family had gone out to the far reaches of Rukum district and had spent the last ten years of our lives learning their language and translating parts of the Bible. After a while, he began showing interest, and he softened a bit. His questions were no longer those of an interrogator; they expressed genuine curiosity.

Suddenly, he turned on the others and said, "Now, that's what I call a positive contribution to this country. That's what Christianity should be about. Why can't you do something like that?"

Turning to me again, he said, "I happen to know something about those books. You're wasting your time if you go with these fellows. They'll only get you into trouble." In a spate of bravado, he explained how much more powerful he was than they. He knew the top police brass; he knew the goons; he knew everybody.

"Wow," I said with a finality that startled even me, "then you're just the man I'm looking for. Why don't you come with me to the border?"

He was shocked. He smiled, then laughed. Of course, he'd just commended me as a shining example to these other men. Had he simply been toying with me? After a bit of squirming, he said, "Okay, I'll go. Have the name on the ticket changed, and I'll be ready."

"What name should I use?" I asked.

"D.B.," came the reply.

Edward let me out the side door. "Be careful," he said. "This guy's justly famous in the Crime Investigation Department. This might be a trap. Just be careful."

But I had followed angel tracks once before, and now again, I recognized the same tell-tale signs.

* * *

D.B. met me at the airport bright and early on Tuesday morning. I was astounded that everyone knew him—everyone on the flight, everybody at the flight desk, and all the security personnel. Police clicked their heels and saluted him. He had a joke for everybody. Only ranking officials approached him with confidence; everyone else stood in self-conscious huddles, wondering what to say or do.

He snapped his fingers, and a policeman came running. He pulled a few hundred-rupee notes out of his wallet and instructed the man to run over to the international departure lounge and come back with some duty-free cigarettes—"some of those long, sleek brown ones," he said. "And while you're at it, bring some cowboy ones, too." He was referring to Marlboros.

He turned to me with a grin. "This is where all negotiation starts in Nepal. Anything to get them on your side."

Soon the passengers had boarded the plane, and we were off. Forty-five minutes later, we were in Simra, the airport town just outside of Birgunj. We hopped onto a pedal-rickshaw: "You've got to ride on a rickshaw," D.B. said. "There's nothing like it. These guys can pedal all day—Hey, rickshaw-*wala*! Can't you pedal a little faster?"

Then, turning to me, he asked, "Have you ever been to a Sher Punjab restaurant? They've got the best down here. Omelets in the morning filled with tomatoes, onions, *jira* [cumin], and all kinds of spices. Buttered *naan* [flatbread] in the evening served with *gosht* [mutton] and curry. You'll love it. But

A typical roadside restaurant

first we've got to find a hotel—Hey, rickshaw-*wala*! Do you know of a decent, cheap hotel near the border?"

A few minutes later, we checked in. It was cheap, but it was hardly decent. The sheets hadn't been changed for ages. They were grimy and splattered with blood where people had been swatting at mosquitoes. The mosquito nets were musty and made me grab for my asthma inhaler.

"Well," D.B. said, "we've got plenty of time right now to run down to customs and see if we can't find your books. We ought to have them back by afternoon."

A half hour later, we ambled into the main office of the Customs building, and D.B. asked for the chief by name. When the man appeared, a look of surprise crossed his face, and pressing his hands together, he said to D.B., "Sahib, *namaste*. What brings you here?"

"Please, meet my friend David Watters," he said, and the man bowed his head slightly as he mumbled a polite "*Namaste.*"

D.B. went through great ceremony as he tore open a fresh packet of cigarettes (the sleek, brown ones) and slid one toward the chief. The chief accepted, and D.B. followed it swiftly with the click of a lighter. Then, the chief invited us to his private office, furnished with a beat-up old desk; a few rickety chairs; a dusty, threadbare carpet; and a ceiling fan.

"How can I help you?" he asked, sitting down.

D.B. explained our situation: "My friend here has some books that were held up at the border." Then, he passed on the essential details, being careful to remain friendly and jovial.

"Let me check on it," the chief said, as he began to search through piles of papers. The two men were still talking when the chief's assistant walked into the room, sat down, and began to listen. A frown began to crease the assistant's face.

"No, no," he said. "There's a special directive on those books. I'm responsible for having stopped them. I recognized them for what they were on the day they arrived, and I immediately sent a letter to Kathmandu." Rummaging through the desk, he produced a piece of paper that he waved in the chief's face. "I received a reply here that they're not to be released. I'm to make sure they go nowhere," he said with finality.

D.B. flicked a cigarette toward him.

"I don't smoke," the assistant replied.

There was an embarrassed silence, and nobody said anything. Then, D.B. began bantering with the chief again, telling jokes and amusing little anecdotes. The whole time, the assistant kept staring at me. Finally, he asked, "Don't I know you?"

"I don't know," I replied. "Lots of people know me."

"Where do you live in Kathmandu?"

I spun off the names of several places I had lived.

"No, I guess not," he said, shrugging his shoulder. "Anyplace else?"

"Well, years ago, I lived in a place called Bhurang Khel."

"Did you have a family?" he asked, getting a little animated.

"My whole family was there with me: my wife and two sons."

"So I do know you," he said. "You were renting my father's house!"

Suddenly, D.B. shot straight out of his chair. "Look what you're doing," he said. "You're stopping the goods of your own household!"

"Well, how was I to know?" he said with a look of resignation on his face. "Whatever arrangements you make, I'll go along with."

The chief was staring at the directive from Kathmandu now, and he began to apologize. He was powerless to release the books. "I'm sorry," he said, "but you'll have to go back to Kathmandu and get a release from the Chief of Customs. Short of that, I can do nothing."

Chapter 24: The Practical Lesson

Walk like an elephant.
—Indian proverb

All you need in this life is ignorance and confidence—and then success is sure.
—Mark Twain

The next morning, after a spicy omelet and sweet, sticky tea at D.B.'s favorite Punjabi restaurant, we took the plane back to Kathmandu.

"I'm going to spend today trying to get a jeep to go back to the border, and tomorrow morning, as soon as it opens, we'll go to the Central Customs Office," he said. "It's down by the National Stadium."

"Where shall we meet?" I asked.

"Customs; ten o'clock sharp," he said.

The next morning, I was on the steps of the Central Customs Office ten minutes early. That was mostly unnecessary, except that D.B. was prompt. The office peon, still sipping a cup of tea, showed up at about 10:05, and then workers started showing up ten minutes later. They still had to go out and get their tea. The chief did not arrive until about 11:00, and he already had a waiting room full of people. He knew D.B. personally, of course, and we were given preference over everybody else. I was getting used to this.

D.B. offered one of his Marlboro cigarettes to the chief. I don't know if he considered him more of a maverick than the Birgunj chief, but the gesture worked well.

"I love these American cigarettes," the chief said. "Now, what can I do for you?"

D.B. carefully explained our situation and the fact that customs in Birgunj wouldn't release the books until we had a letter from the chief himself. The chief swiveled on his chair, blew a puff of smoke, and bent forward to flick some ashes into a tea glass.

"I don't know if you realize it or not," he said slowly, "but those books are not written in Nepali. They're written in one of the indigenous languages. We can't let something like that go, now, can we?"

D.B. was ready. "Do you have any idea how many unwritten languages there are in this country?" he asked, not expecting an answer. He had been listening to everything I said in the past two days, and now he was repeating it all. "There are eighty such languages. All these people have been deprived of education. They don't even have alphabets. This is the first time this language has ever been written. Don't you think that's a good thing?"

"Well, I suppose," the chief conceded with a puff of smoke. "But there's something else you need to know. These books contain religious material. And it's not Hindu, either—it's Christian. On the inside cover, it says, 'Gospel Literature Service.' You know we can't let that go."

Again, D.B. was ready: "This man and his family have been living out in a god-forsaken place for ten years so that he could help them. You and I wouldn't live in a place like that. One of the first things he wanted to do was help them learn to read. So what was he going to give them? Hindu stories? He doesn't know Hindu stories. He comes from a Christian country. Besides, they're just harmless little stories about how God created the earth and all the animals and all the birds. What's so bad about that?"

"Yes, but why so many?" he objected. "There are five hundred copies of these books."

"Did you know that there are forty *thousand* speakers of Kham? Five hundred is hardly enough for a few kids!"

"Okay, okay," the chief acquiesced as he crushed out his Marlboro. He rang his bell, and a peon entered. "Bring me a few sheets of official letterhead and the official stamp," he directed. "And, oh yes, bring some milk tea, too."

"So you were with SIL, were you?" the chief asked a few minutes later, as we sipped our tea. "I knew several SILers. They were all good men. Did you know Wayne Aeschliman? He was a great pilot. He flew me to Jumla a couple of times. And then there was Dick Hugonoit. He was always very kind to me."

Thirty minutes later we left the building with an official release, stamped and signed by the chief himself.

* * *

"Come with me to my house," D.B. said, "and we'll have dinner tonight." So I went to his home, where I met his wife and two sons. His wife was a good cook, and we had a fine dinner. "Would you mind if I brought my wife along for the trip tomorrow?" he asked.

"No, I don't mind at all," I said, imagining that her presence might prevent awkward questions.

"I'll take you home tonight on my motorcycle to see where you live, and when I get the jeep tomorrow, I'll come by to get you."

The next day at about noon, D.B. and his wife arrived with the jeep. He also had his mechanic along. Nobody went any great distance in those days without a mechanic. The road went up over the Raj Path, a road justly famous for all its hairpin curves. But down the other side, before we got to the plains of the Terai, the alternator died. Even the mechanic couldn't resurrect it. So we coasted most of the way and had to push on occasion up little hills. All of us pushed, including D.B.'s wife.

We arrived after dark and went straight back to the same musty old hotel. D.B. sent the mechanic off to fix the jeep. "We'll need it in the morning, you know."

The next morning, the jeep was fixed, and as soon as they were open, D.B. and I went back to the Customs office, where we met the same official we had seen two days before. D.B. showed him the clearance papers, all duly signed and stamped. The man was impressed. He called for a peon to take us back and show us where the stuff was stored. After a little bit of poking around, he found what we were looking for and helped us load the boxes onto the jeep.

Five hundred doesn't sound a lot when it's only a number on paper. But when you start packing this number of two different titles—even little ones—into a jeep, it can be a tall order.

D.B. looked apprehensive. "Wow. A lot of books," he said.

"No," I replied, "just five hundred of each."

When we got back to the hotel and I began looking through the boxes, I realized that only Genesis and Exodus had come through. They had been printed in June; Parables of Jesus and the Epistles had not been printed until November. I had hoped that they would all be together, but, alas, they weren't. What should I do? Should I say something?

I turned to D.B. "Guess what, D.B.? Only half of the books are here."

"How can you be so sure? Did you count them?"

"No, it's not a matter of counting. I had four titles, and only two are here."

"What do you mean, four titles? Wasn't it supposed to be Genesis and Exodus?"

"Well, yes, it was supposed to be Genesis and Exodus," I said, "but there were also the Parables of Jesus and a few Epistles."

"Good God," D.B. exclaimed, "why didn't you say something earlier?"

"Well, I just assumed that they were all here; why say anything?"

"So where are they? They're not in the warehouse; we collected the full shipment. There was nothing else confiscated."

"Well, if they've been shipped at all," I said, "they'll be stored over at the hospital in Raxaul. That's where I had them sent."

A slight look of amusement came across D.B.'s face. "You know," he said, "you haven't been very smart in the way you've tried to bring those books across. You were bound to get caught. What you need is a good, practical lesson on how to smuggle Bibles into Nepal without getting caught!"

Not sure what to say, I just stood there.

"Well, are you ready?" he said. "Let's go."

This time we drove straight past Customs and headed for the border gates. D.B. parked the jeep beside the guardhouse and walked inside, flicking out a long, brown cigarette. The Immigration officer accepted, and D.B. offered a light. "So when do you get off duty, Son?"

"I'm off in another hour," he replied.

"I need to talk with a certain Immigration guy, and I think he works here. Who follows you this afternoon?"

"J.P. Regmi, Sir."

"Where did he train?"

"Central Academy in Kathmandu, Sir."

"Oh yeah, that's the man. He may not remember me, but I met him at the Academy once. How's his family doing these days?"

"Oh, they're doing pretty well. His wife wasn't too well there for a while, you know, but she's doing better after the surgery."

"Oh yeah, I remember. Gall bladder, wasn't it?"

"No, hysterectomy, I believe."

"Well, I've got to run now. We'll be back later this afternoon."

* * *

Back at the hotel, D.B. got on the phone and started phoning his buddies at the Police Academy. He wanted everything he could get on J.P. Regmi—someone he'd never met in his life. He was soon provided with the man's rank, his graduation date, his struggles, his family life, everything. Even his drinking problem.

Two hours later, we drove back to Immigration and parked the jeep.

"J.P. Regmi?" D.B. asked as he pulled out a cigarette for him.

"Yes, Sir," he replied as he accepted.

Soon, the two men settled into a conversation. Regmi seemed a bit surprised that he couldn't even remember this guy, when he must have had an intimate conversation with him in Kathmandu. This man even knew about his wife's surgery!

"Well, you did have a bit too much to drink that night," D.B. said. Soon he turned his inquiries to the Immigration official on the Indian side, Regmi's counterpart.

Then D.B. grabbed the phone, dialed the Chief Customs Officer, and mumbled something about "We'll be picking up some other stuff, too. Just tell the man at the gate to let us come through." Then he talked the Immigration official into letting me leave Nepal without an exit stamp. "We'll be back in an hour," he said, "and an exit stamp will only complicate things."

On the Indian side, D.B. repeated the whole act: the cigarettes, the friendly chat, and all the rest.

"You have a steam locomotive that comes into Raxaul, don't you? Well, my friend here grew up around steam locomotives, but he hasn't seen one now in years. They've all been replaced by diesels in America. We were just wondering if you'd let us wander off to the train yards for an hour or two, and then we'll be right back. We don't have an exit stamp from Nepal, and now an entry stamp into India will only complicate things."

"Sure, no problem," the Immigration official assured us. "Just check in when you come back."

Off we went, and we headed straight to the hospital. I never did see a railroad. At the hospital, I asked for the Management office and found a British man who might know what I was talking about. As soon as I mentioned "a shipment of Bible booklets," he took me straight to their warehouse.

"The first two titles have already been picked up," he said. "These new titles have been here for just a few days."

What perfect timing!

We loaded the booklets into the jeep and headed back to the border. We passed through Immigration first. The man just waved us on, relieved that we were back without causing him any trouble.

Customs was a bit more difficult. The bar gate came down in front of the jeep, and an eager official came rushing out to open the boxes.

"No, no," D.B. shouted at him. "You're to phone the chief and he'll give you instructions."

The man did as he was told. When he heard what the chief had to say, he looked at the receiver with a bit of surprise and raised the barricade.

D.B. accelerated, and as the jeep rounded the first bend, out of sight of the Customs shack, he turned to me and said, "I told you I could do it, didn't I?"

Chapter 25: This Present Suffering

Why do you want freedom? In freedom your last grain of faith will be choked with weeds. You should rejoice that you're in prison. Here you have time to think about your soul. As the Apostle Paul wrote: "Why all these tears? Why are you trying to weaken my resolution? For my part, I am ready not merely to be bound but even to die for the name of the Lord Jesus."
—Aleksandr Solzhenitsyn, One Day in the Life of Ivan Denisovich

After a year and ten months in the Philippines, it seemed that the worst of the storm had blown over in Nepal, and we decided to return as a family, living once again, if necessary, on visa runs. Arriving at the end of June 1980, we had to exit the country just once, at the end of September, which took us to the end of the year. But the storms were about to take a new turn and increase in intensity.

The first indication was on a scrap of paper written by a Kham named Jaman Singh from the town of Musikot, the headquarters of the Rukum district. He wrote the letter on October 8 and had it borne out secretly by friends to Kathmandu. We received it two weeks later. Hasta Ram was in the city with us, and we were working quietly on Scripture translation, unaware that anything was amiss. The note said:

Dear Brother Hasta [Ram] Budha,
We, your friends and companions, salute you. We are sending you a certain bit of information here. On Sunday, the fifth of Asoj [Sept. 21, 1980], seven of us were arrested and taken to the police headquarters in Musikot. Then, on the day of the

nineteenth [Oct. 5], they put us into prison. When we had to answer allegations, we said, "Yes, we do follow Christ." So far they have not yet informed us how many years our sentence will be. They don't allow us to chat together. They've taken all our reading materials away from us. They won't even allow us to sing the things that are in our mouths. What will become of us?

Therefore, we are writing this letter to you in hopes that we'll receive some word from you... Please send us soon a word that will encourage our hearts... Tell all of our friends and companions, brothers and sisters there that we send our greetings. We bid you all farewell.

Six days later we received a second letter, this one written by Bishnu Gurung. Bishnu had written his letter before Jaman Singh's, but it went by regular post and didn't arrive as quickly. It said:

Dear Honorable Master,

From all us believers, hail to the Messiah. We also extend our greetings to our other masters who are there with you. Thanks be to God our Father. They have arrested seven of us and brought us here to Musikot. We had to bid farewell to the rest of our brethren along with our women and children. We're a little bit concerned, wondering what will happen to us. But whatever it be, we have cast ourselves upon God. Whatever he wants to do is his will. He knows. Thanks be to God. Up until the time that we have written this letter we are sitting in the gloom of the police fortress. But God's glory is with us.

Regardless of what suffering comes in the name of our Lord Jesus, we will endure it. Do not concern yourself. Be of good confidence. We can never repay the debt for all that we have received from our Lord. This present suffering is of no significance. What is it compared to the suffering our Lord endured?

They're deciding our case right now. We already testified. From here on, only God knows. Do not come until your work is finished. Come only after you have completed it. After our next appearance in court, we'll write again. They arrested us on the fifth of Asoj [Sept. 21], and today is the tenth [Sept. 26]. There is not opportunity to write more. We close our letter here. Rest in confidence.

The imprisoned men

The names of the seven men who had been imprisoned were Ram Das Kham, the eldest; Jaman Singh Budha; Sonar Budha; Dantya Budha; Krishna Budha; Bishnu Gurung; and Tejendra Kham, the youngest.

For almost two years, the gospel had progressed quietly and unobstructed in the village, but eventually, some of the local mafia thugs, men who traveled in and out a great deal, learned that it was illegal in Nepal to become a Christian. What better way to extort money? Just threaten the Christians with imprisonment, collect the money, and turn the whole business into a "protection" racket.

But it didn't work that easily. The Christians refused to back down and refused to pay the "protection" money. So the thugs went over the mountains and filed a complaint at the district headquarters, way off in Musikot. They returned with a contingent of police.

The police stormed into the meeting house on a Sunday morning. "Which one is Hasta Ram?" they asked.

The body of believers

"He's not here. He's in Kathmandu," came the reply.

So they identified five elders of the church and took them in his place. Later they added two additional men to go along as helpers, seven in all.

Apparently, dozens of others pushed their way into the center, demanding that they be taken too. Tipalkya the hunter, who was there, wrote later, complaining, "If they were going to arrest us, they should have arrested all of us. And if they don't arrest all of us, they should release the others too."

Like common criminals, the seven were chained together and marched three days over the mountains. Two of them were among the first four who had been baptized, almost five years earlier. After reaching the headquarters and sitting in custody for ten days, their cases were decided, and they were incarcerated. They were given the freedom to go, if only they would sign a statement claiming to be Hindus.

"You don't have to *be* Hindus," they were told. "Just sign a statement that you are."

They refused.

How many times in the history of the Christian church have similar words been spoken? In an attempt to eradicate Christianity from seventeenth-century Japan, officials placed portraits of Christ in front of the converts and demanded that they trample on them.

"We're not telling you to trample in all sincerity," they would say. "Just go through with the formality of trampling. Just the formality! Then everything will be all right."

When news of their incarceration reached us in Kathmandu, we were deeply distraught, especially Hasta Ram. He was the undisputed leader of the church, and to see his men going to prison while he sat free was more than he could bear. It was nearly impossible to restrain him from going out and turning himself in.

"What will they do?" he kept asking. "Did they really understand?"

True, they had taken vows at baptism. They had vowed that they were willing to suffer imprisonment for their faith, they had vowed that if arrested, they would not implicate the rest and would follow the discipline of Christ and the Church. But now that the heat was on, would they stand firm?

Nancy and I were overwhelmed with feelings of guilt. We wept and we prayed. Why hadn't we just left these poor people alone? They lived in their mountain fastness, mostly unaware of the rest of the world. True, theirs was a difficult life, but it was mostly a happy one. Now we'd ruined it for them. We went promising freedom, and now because they were gullible enough to believe what we said, they found themselves in chains—huddled together in a miserable, cold prison cell, away from home and away from the comfort of their families.

"Whatever have we done?" we kept asking one another.

* * *

I thought of D.B.; he was well connected. Could he do anything to help us? It seemed pretty risky. It was one thing to bring Bibles across the border, but to help Christians in prison was something else entirely. But I felt I had to do something to keep Hasta Ram from going out and jumping into prison with them. When I explained to him the possibility of working through D.B., he was ready to take the risk. "Better than just sitting here," he said. I had to agree.

We drove out to meet D.B., and I explained our situation. He liked Hasta Ram immediately, as I expected he would. Some men just have an aura of greatness about them, and Hasta Ram was one of them; he commanded respect.

Without a moment's hesitation, D.B. jumped into action. "The last thing we can do," he said, "is to show any sign of weakness. We have to act immediately!"

He never said *"you* have to act"; he kept saying *"we* have to act." We left his house together. Hasta Ram and I returned to my house across town, and D.B. jumped on his motorcycle and headed for the office of the Inspector General of Police (IGP), the head of the police for the entire nation. "We're good friends," he said.

Before the afternoon was over, D.B. was back at our house, waving papers. He had gotten written permission from the IGP himself to travel personally out to Musikot prison, to inquire into the case, and to come back with records of all the court proceedings.

Within another two days, using the police headquarters' wireless, he had sent a message to the zonal headquarters using the IGP's authority. The message requisitioned a police runner to travel the five days to the district headquarters in Musikot and demand that records of the prisoners' arrests be released. (There are fourteen zones in Nepal, with seventy-five districts within those zones; Rukum is a single district within Rapti Zone.)

There were bi-weekly flights from Kathmandu to Chaurjhari, a small national airport at the western extreme of Rukum district and a full day's walk to the west of Musikot. I bought seats for D.B. on the next flight. He needed to go out personally to collect the records. Besides, he wanted to meet the prisoners.

Chaurjhari is a full day's walk to the west of Musikot, down along the low-lying Bheri River, barely a couple of thousand feet above sea level. The weather there can be unbearably hot, especially for a man who is used to riding around Kathmandu on a motorcycle. But to his credit, D.B. struggled on, climbing upward through the intense heat for 2,700 feet until he got to Musikot.

The next morning at police headquarters, D.B. pretended not to be a friend of the Christians but an emissary from the Inspector General. And, of course, he had letters to prove it. The local inspector was happy to let him "have at it."

D.B. stormed into the prison in a very ill-appearing mood and asked gruffly, "Which of you bastards is Jaman Singh?"

"I'm Jaman Singh," replied one of the prisoners quietly as he stepped forward.

"And which of you is Ram Das?" he asked, and another stepped forward.

"Do you men have any idea that you're breaking the law?" D.B. asked. "Did you know that you're in direct violation of His Majesty's Government? Did you know that you can rot in prison for this? And I'm here to make sure that you do!"

The men said nothing for a few moments while the words soaked in. Then Jaman Singh spoke up, "Sir, we have committed no crimes. We are simply walking in the ways of our Lord Jesus."

"What?" D.B. retorted. "Walking in the ways of your Lord Jesus? You're Hindus. It's illegal for you to change your religion, by decree of the king."

"Well, we have to follow the King of Kings and the Lord of Lords," Jaman replied.

D.B. stared at the men as if he couldn't believe what he had just heard. After a few stiff moments, he relaxed his bearing and said with a hint of kindness, "I just wanted to see if you were real or not. I've come here at the request of Hasta Ram and David Sahib."

"They're okay?" the men responded with excitement. "We were told that David Sahib was in prison and that Hasta Ram had been executed!"

"No, those are all lies," D.B. assured them. "They're trying to confuse you. And I'm here to help you. I want you to know that you are like lights shining in a dark place. Whatever you do, don't let your lights be extinguished."

Before leaving, D.B. hired a local lawyer, Balla Ram, to act as his representative in Chaurjhari during his absence.

* * *

When D.B. arrived back in Kathmandu he said that he had been moved to tears when he saw those seven men being treated like common criminals. They shared their tiny cell with nine others: six were thieves, two were murderers (one had slaughtered seven people in a single day, including an infant whom he had hacked to pieces), and one was a communist activist. They were chained together, bound hand and foot by steel manacles. They slept on thin straw mats on a cold, damp floor. The latrine was a wooden box in the corner, and the highlight of the prisoners' week was when it was their turn to take the latrine out twice a day for cleaning. With sixteen men, your turn came every four days.

D.B. discovered, too, that the courts were looking for evidence to keep the men in chains for six years. To do that, they would have to convict them of proselytizing, so they sent police to the village for witnesses. No one would give testimony. "They mind their own business," came the reply. "They even meet outside the village, and we have to go down to them to hear what they say."

The courts were also looking for legal loopholes that would enable them to confiscate Hasta Ram's fields and to take over the building that the Christians had been meeting in.

Before the week was out, the seven Christian prisoners sent out a secret letter telling of D.B.'s encouraging visit. "A big officer arrived from Kathmandu," they said, "but we can't figure out if he's our friend or not. We thought he was angry with us. But maybe not. Before he left, he said, 'You are like lights in this dark place. Never let your lights be extinguished.' His encouraging words are even now still ringing in our ears!" They signed it, "Your seven believing brothers in bonds, Musikot prison."

The men began talking about their dark, gloomy prison cell as "the house of God," and their chains as "the ornaments of God." Amazing! These were unlettered, unschooled men, but they stood like the giants before and after them: men like Solzhenitsyn, who proclaimed later in life, "Bless you, prison! I have served enough time there. I nourished my soul there, and I say without hesitation, 'Bless you, prison, for having been in my life!'"

* * *

D.B. came back to Kathmandu one week later with all the papers he needed. He had full transcripts of the arrest warrants, the court proceedings, the men's testimonials, and all the rest. He had hired a civil lawyer to defend the men in his absence. As a parting shot, he informed the Musikot court that they should proceed no further until he got clarification from the Supreme Court on their interpretation of this case in light of religious law!

D.B. went to one of his close friends, a liberal-minded Justice who sat on the bench of the nine-member Supreme Court, and confided the case to him. The man wanted to get a sense of Hasta Ram and me, and asked D.B. to bring us to his private residence one evening. The man was a Buddhist Newar, already outside the pale of Hindu Brahminism.

"Though discrimination is only minor towards me," he said, "I understand what it is like to be discriminated against." He was obviously a brilliant man, he knew the law, and he asked for permission to study the documents carefully.

He wanted, too, to get a sense of how the rest of the Supreme Court would respond. How would they stand on issues like this? If ever there was a test case, this was it. In the end, though, he decided not to risk it. All but he were part of the same old patronizing royal culture; they would certainly remain loyal to the system rather than going out on a limb.

In the end, the Justice did the best he could without bringing the whole court into session. He was deeply touched by the men's testimonials, and he remarked on their obvious, genuine character.

"I have dealt with criminals all my life," he said, "and these are not criminals." He was indignant over the injustice of putting such men into prison. "These men should be our future," he said. "Unfortunately, though, there is a law (separate from the national constitution) which states that a person can be imprisoned for a maximum of one year simply for becoming a Christian"—a charge to which all seven had pleaded guilty. That person could then be imprisoned for an additional six years if he were found guilty of proselytizing others.

In the end, concealing his identity from the courts, the Justice gave

D.B. authority to go to the zonal headquarters and force the district court to decide immediately upon the duration of the imprisonment, not to exceed one year from the date of the arrest. In addition, he drew up a writ of *habeas corpus*, pointing out various illegalities in the court proceedings and demanding a suspension of undue restraint. He challenged Hasta Ram himself to fly to Chaurjhari airport and personally deliver the papers to the court, a challenge that Hasta Ram accepted without hesitation.

* * *

The next weeks dragged on and on. There were twists and turns in the courts and appeals that weren't going anywhere; it sometimes seemed that we were not making any progress. Our dear brothers were languishing in prison, and my fear was that the waters would overwhelm their souls (Psalm 124:4). Four of the seven became severely ill, and one was unable to move without being carried. He began asking for hashish to ease his joint pains.

All of us prayed and wept. Nothing expressed my inner turmoil more poignantly during that time than the music of the Russian composer Sergey Rachmaninoff. Some who knew him described him as the saddest person they had ever known. But I heard more than just sadness. I heard triumph, too. I heard defiance. I heard the bittersweet melancholy of a tortured but steadfast Russian soul. It afforded emotional catharsis. This was music that knew deep joy and stubbornly clung to a ray of hope.

The flute and clarinet *adagio* at the beginning of Rachmaninoff's Concerto no. 2, op. 18 dares to climb out of its despair, almost afraid to reach too high. It's the respite of the evening, the hope of the morning. What will the day bring? Maybe more than we can bear. Yet the music reaches; it climbs. The piano and the strings move in with a bit more confidence. Could I do the same? I tried to pray and let the sadness enrich my soul. This is what was happening to my brothers; now I must let it happen to me. I would learn from them what it means to be a disciple of Christ.

Rachmaninoff's later *Rhapsody on a Theme of Paganini* continues with the same melancholic moods, but they are tempered now with something more exultant and laurel-crowned, suggesting reward after suffering. Subtle folk tunes are artfully woven in with the simplest of orchestral garb—piano octaves and solo winds. This music became my prayer to God, "groanings which cannot be uttered."

"How long, O Lord? Wilt thou forget me forever? How long wilt thou hide thy face from me?" (Psalm 13:1).

Chapter 26: Time Afforded

God moves in a mysterious way
His wonders to perform;
He plants His footsteps in the sea,
And rides upon the storm.
—William Cowper, "God Moves in a Mysterious Way," verse one

In mid-November, D.B. made his trip to the Rapti zonal head-quarters in Tulsipur to investigate the particulars surrounding the sentencing of the prisoners. He wanted also, if possible, to set reasonable time limits on their incarceration. By the third week of the month, Hasta Ram flew to Chaurjhari with the writ of *habeas corpus* and papers criticizing certain court proceedings. This was potentially a very reckless thing to do; there was nothing to assure his safety. After all, it was Hasta Ram they had actually been after, and now he was marching unprotected right into their stronghold of Musikot.

Tika Ram, a Kham who lived on the edge of town, saw Hasta Ram coming and rushed to intercept him. "No, no," he urged, "you'll be arrested. Turn around and go back. You can't just walk in here."

"I have committed no crime," Hasta Ram replied. "Show me the district court office. I have letters to deliver."

"What letters? No, you mustn't. Let me deliver them. You mustn't come into town."

With Tika Ram still protesting and tugging on his sleeve, Hasta Ram marched straight into town and into the district court office. He delivered his papers and took another batch over to the police station. "These are for you!"

Across the street, Hasta Ram sat down in a little teahouse and ordered a meal of *dal bhat*, the Nepali staple of rice and lentils. People began to arrive and mill around.

"Isn't that Hasta Ram? What's he doing here?" they were all asking.

"Ha," someone guffawed, "just wait around for a while, and you'll get a good show."

A couple of policemen gawked, not sure what to make of it all.

When Hasta Ram finished his meal, he stood and walked through the crowd. It parted for him like the Red Sea, and nobody, including the police, laid a hand on him. He had come, he had done his business, and now he was going.

* * *

In Kathmandu we waited anxiously. There was no word. Surely, Hasta Ram must have been arrested and put into prison. Hours turned into days, and days turned into weeks. Several times a week, the little iron gate leading into the street at the bottom of our yard would creak open, and we would jump. Usually it was D.B., but he was always without news. We began to despair. I listened to more Rachmaninoff.

Our current three-month visa was about to expire. In fact, we hadn't gone in to Immigration even once to renew it. D.B. had gotten three months for us in one fell swoop, which took us to the end of December. The question was what to do then. With all the arrests in Rukum district, and now with our own names implicated, we would surely be expelled.

* * *

Early in December, my telephone rang. It was Lynn Knauff, the director of the American Peace Corps in Nepal. I had never met her, but she told me that one of their young Peace Corps volunteers had gone missing. "Would you be able to offer some assistance?"

"What kind of assistance?" I asked. I had had no dealings with the Peace Corps and knew nobody there.

"One of our people, a young man named Phil Cyr, has gone missing in Rukum district," she explained. "He had just completed a successful two-year tour in the southern parts of Nepal and wanted do a proper trek before going back to the United States. He left in October and never returned. We've sent numerous teams of volunteers into Rukum, trying to retrace his route, but so far we've come up with very little. It appears that he made it as far as Dhorpatan, but beyond that we don't know. He may even have made it to Maikot, but the locals are tight-lipped. We can't get anything out of them. We understand that you used to live in the Magar parts of Rukum district and that you might be able to help."

I arrived at the Peace Corps headquarters in Kamaladi that same afternoon. I was shown into Mrs. Knauff's office, and we proceeded to chat. "Phil wrote a letter to his parents," she said. "Here, read it. Maybe you'll be able to recognize something that we couldn't see."

As I held the letter in my hand, I couldn't help but think about the anguish and anxiety the parents must have been feeling at a time like this. Phil did talk about Dhorpatan and Maikot, but to me these places appeared to be only the jumping-off points for his trek. He talked about being "drawn by the mountains." How many times had I written to my parents in similar ways but then continued on, far on, to where few Westerners had ever been? I could sense his spirit of

Drawn by the mountains

adventure, and I began to suspect that he had a more elaborate plan than he was spelling out in the letter.

"Once past Maikot," I explained to Lynn, "the trail goes steeply upward till one comes to the Cave of Dulya (a place Gary Shepherd and I spent a cold night, on our way to Tarakot in 1969). Above Dulya one comes to Seng Khola, a stream flowing off the western end of Dhaulagiri."

"What kind of altitudes are we taking about here?" Lynn asked as she pulled out a large piece of white paper and began drawing a rough map based on my observations.

"Well, you cross into Seng Khola at 13,000 feet, and then proceed upstream to about 15,000. From there you can cut north over the pass to Tarakot or cut east up to the Nimkun [Bear Hole] glaciers at the foot of Putha."

"Any way out of there?" she asked.

"Not if you continue east. You have to backtrack to the foot of the falls at Zhigar, cross Lamsar Pass and continue on the south part of the high ridge all the way to Putha Sheep Camp and beyond."

Lynn was impressed. "How many times have you been across there?" she asked.

"Oh, a half-dozen or so," I lied. Sure, I had penetrated beyond the edges on both sides half a dozen times before, but I had been across the center only once, with Dag Wendel back in 1976. The center was quite vast, and most of it was trackless wilderness.

"So where do you suspect he is?" Lynn asked again.

"I don't know," I replied. "What I have detected from his letter is only a wild guess. He could even have gone to Dolpo. But if he had only gone to Maikot, he certainly would have made it back by now. He could be lying in a tent somewhere with a broken leg. I don't think we should call off the search until we've exhausted that possibility."

"So you'll be willing to head up an expedition?" Lynn asked with relief.

"Well, I have just one problem," I confided. I explained to her that my visa was to expire before the month was out and that I was having trouble with renewals. My family and I were staying in Nepal on tourist visas, and on the next renewal we would have to exit the country. Furthermore, if I were going to go at all, I would need to go while the weather was still dry. Precipitation commonly blows in during late December or early January, and if that happened before we set out, an expedition like this would be impossible until May or June.

Understanding the need for haste, Lynn urged, "Bring your passports in, and we'll have them extended to the end of January 1981. We'll do the renewals at top diplomatic levels so they won't go through regular scrutiny."

So I took our passports in, and our visas were extended without a hitch and, best of all, without a trip to the border.

*　*　*

The next day I was called back to the Peace Corps office. There were several people they wanted me to meet. One was a Tibetan from Dhorpatan, the other a Lepcha from Sikkim. Both were unsavory characters, and the Lepcha, I had been warned about before—"some kind of double-agent and drug dealer from the borderlands," I had heard. They were trying to ingratiate themselves regarding the expedition through insidious means. What really was their motive? Did they need a job?

They had purportedly found "wrapping paper with a note on it" just short of Thankur Pass on the way to Maikot. But their claim had little credibility; a young American trained in interrogation techniques discredited them easily: "When you went to retrieve it, did you pick it up with your left hand or with your right hand? Did you step off a bank downward or did you step upward?" Their answers were confused, sometimes contradictory, and they kept glancing uncertainly at one another.

After the two were dismissed, the American team asked me, "What do you think? Will you travel with these guys?"

"No," I said. "They are up to something, and I don't know what it is.

I'll organize my own expedition with men from my own village, whom I can trust and who know the way."

"We can supply you with walkie-talkies," they said, trying to encourage me. "We'll make food and supply drops by helicopter anywhere you need them."

"No," I said, "I'll go as lightly as possible. The only helicopter support I want is at the beginning, to take me to the village where I'll launch the expedition. From there, I'll take four trusted men, and you won't hear from me again until I get back. I'll be back in about three weeks' time, and I'll know by then whether Phil Cyr is dead or alive.

"But about these two guys," I continued. "I'd appreciate it if you could get rid of them."

"How do we do that?" they asked, a bit surprised.

"Well, for one thing, they don't need special papers to go to Dolpo; I do. Tell them you've picked up some possible leads on Phil up in Dolpo and you'd like them checked out. You can chopper them up there and leave them on the north side of the Himalayas until I'm safely back home."

Whether the Peace Corps approached them again or not, I don't know. They showed up at our doorstep several days later, asking Nancy why they'd been left behind and where I'd gone off to. Nancy put on gracious airs, served them tea and biscuits, and told them nothing. Fearing that they might try to intercept me, she intimated that I had gone directly to Dhorpatan with a bunch of men.

Chapter 27: Here He Comes Now!

Deep in unfathomable mines
Of never-failing skill
He treasures up his bright designs,
And works his sovereign will.
—William Cowper, "God Moves in a Mysterious Way," verse two

Sunday, December 14, 1980, was a beautiful day for the helicopter flight to Taka-Shera. Nancy and the boys came along to the Kathmandu airport to see me off, and the American Consul, Nancy Powell (later to become the American ambassador in 2008), was there to make sure that the papers were signed and everything was in order. The embassy had tried to hire an 11th Brigade Nepal Army helicopter, but the only chopper available was King Birendra's drab, olive-colored Alouette III, serial no. RAN-17, used mostly as Nepal Army One. We lifted off a little after daylight.

The Alouette III was used mostly for reconnaissance and small missions and didn't have a lot of capacity. There were two crew members on board, plus an armed guard whose main job, apparently, was to keep villagers away from the tail rotor. I was the only passenger, and by the time I had loaded on the expedition gear—tents, sleeping bags, down pants, down parkas, boots, tennis shoes, primus stoves, fuel cylinders, pot and pans, two bags of rice (fifty kilograms, or about 110 pounds), pressure cookers, and over twenty pounds (about ten kilos) of dried jerky and sausage—there was little room left. I did manage to throw on two small wooden boxes of the booklets that D.B. and I had brought across the border the year before.

I insisted to the pilots that we wouldn't be able to make Taka without refueling in Pokhara, but they ignored my request and we had to land in Dhorpatan. "How much farther to Taka?" they asked.

"At least another half hour, counting the return trip," I replied. "Maybe even forty minutes. Why the hell didn't you listen before?"

"Well, sorry. We're going to have to go back to Pokhara to refuel. There's no way we can add forty minutes to our flight program. We weren't counting on this kind of headwind."

So they dumped me off in Dhorpatan while they flew the hour-and-a-half return to Pokhara to refuel. I went into Dawa's (pseudonym) hotel at the airstrip and had some steamy Tibetan *thukpa* (noodle soup) and a few cups of yak-butter tea. Dhorpatan was always cold. I asked Dawa about the Peace Corps fellow, but he said he didn't know anything. He was jittery.

* * *

It was about one o'clock in the afternoon as we cleared the last ridgetop before our descent into Taka. "Where do you want us to put it down?" the pilots asked.

"In the open field next to the willow tree there," I replied, pointing through the window.

As we whirled slowly downward over 4,000 feet in a straight descent, I had plenty of time to see the villagers rushing out of the village and making their way to the open field. About forty people streamed out of the meeting house. It was a Sunday. I wondered if Hasta Ram would be there or if, God forbid, he had been arrested.

Kham villages always look forbidding from a distance. Giant segmented structures on a cliff-side, they give the appearance of an unblinking insect's eye, and the pilots began to have misgivings about setting down there. "Where's your expedition team?" they asked a bit nervously.

"Don't worry, they're here," I replied.

"Are you sure you want to get out here?"

"Yes, I'll be fine."

As the helicopter landed in the open field, the guard jumped out with his rifle and began shooing people away from the tail rotor. I stepped out into the sunshine and took a quick glance around at the crowd. Two policemen were there. Apparently, the district government had set up a small police post in Taka to monitor the "Christian situation." And there, off to the side, was Hasta Ram with a big grin on his face. I rushed up to him, gave him a big bear hug, and everybody cheered.

After we unloaded the supplies, the pilots started up the helicopter. The big engine shuddered and lurched, and as quickly as it had appeared, the helicopter headed back the way it had come.

* * *

Hasta Ram drew me toward himself and whispered in my ear, "I hope you brought Bibles!"

"Why do you ask?"

"Well, did you or didn't you? If you brought Bibles, I need to call everyone back into the meeting house."

"Well, I did bring Bibles," I replied. "Those wooden boxes right there."

So people shouldered burdens, and we made our way with all the goods over to the meeting house.

"Sahib, I have to tell you a story," Hasta Ram said in front of everybody. "Just this morning, we were talking about what to do about all those Bibles you had stored in Kathmandu. The church is growing, people are showing interest, but all that we have out here anymore are a few tattered remains of the first titles you printed four or five years ago. This morning we organized a few groups of men to make the trip into Kathmandu—to buy rice and to conceal a few Bibles in their grain sacks. Then somebody stood and said, 'Why don't we pray about it? Maybe God can arrange a better way?'

"So I said, 'Okay, wise guy, you stand up and pray, and the rest of us will listen.' So Rentya here stood to pray. While he prayed, we began to hear the sound of a helicopter engine.

"'Here he comes now,' someone shouted. 'Sahib is coming with the Bibles!'

"So we all jumped up and ran, and here they are; we have the Bibles!"

Meanwhile, the two policemen outside were confounded. I was supposed to be the "enemy," but I had arrived with an armed guard in the king's helicopter. Whatever was going on? They avoided me out of embarrassment, but they sent a runner off to Musikot asking for clarification on what to do. One week later, they tacked a summons on Hasta Ram's door, but by then we had already gone.

* * *

We spent the rest of the day and Monday organizing the expedition. The weather was holding up, but we knew that we'd have to leave quickly. I hired three men—Hasta Ram, Lal Bir, and Janga. A fourth, big Karna Bahadur, was to accompany us over the closest ridges before turning back. In the end we couldn't do without his support, and all four men ended up going all the way.

In addition to the food we already had, we added several kilos of potatoes, bought locally, as well as a couple of jugs of sheep *ghee* for savoring the stew. By the time we were ready to go, we were so heavy that we could hardly stagger down the trail. It's a logistical nightmare to outfit a self-sufficient cold-weather expedition for two weeks without resupply.

We traveled the next day to Hukam and then on to Maikot. Since Maikot was supposedly one of Phil's destinations, we spent several hours there asking questions. But no one had seen or heard anything. From there, we moved up to the Caves of Dulya, where a woman lived alone with her small family. She claimed, "Some people say they saw a man with a red backpack pass by, but I saw no one." This was as far as the Peace Corps had reached in their own search efforts, and I suspected that the woman was confusing their questions with what might actually have been observed.

From Dulya we traveled for nine days through desolate mountain wilderness without seeing another human being. We passed into the Nimkun glacier basin and then eastward across the passes, through the trackless wilderness of Putha, Churen, Ghustung, and Chalike. We stopped often to scan the slopes with binoculars for any signs of a tattered tent, a flag, a backpack, anything. But we saw nothing; only a few bands of bharal. Most days we saw upwards of forty animals total, with some herds having as many as twenty-five.

Bharal typically station a single ram at a vantage point to stand guard while the rest graze. At the approach of an intruder, the ram warns the rest with a shrill, high-pitched whistle that sounds like a man whistling down a taxi. The first time I heard this, I got excited, thinking Phil had spotted us and was signaling for our attention. But no such luck.

Passing into the Nimkun glacier basin and eastward

Out across the twin frozen lakes of Barpe and Marpe, we spotted a band of eight bharal skipping their way across the ice. Off went the whistle, and I could imagine a faint voice in the distance: "Now, Dasher! Now, Dancer! Now, Prancer and Vixen! On, Comet! On, Cupid! On, Donner and Blitzen!" It was Christmastime, and I was missing Nancy and the boys.

On December 23, it began snowing. The buildup had been coming for a couple of days. It snowed only about five inches, but that was enough to bedevil us with danger. The new powder concealed patches of hard-glazed ice, making the south-facing slopes of the high passes exceedingly treacherous. Coming down off of Dhailya, we hit a patch of ice that careened us crazily downward for hundreds of feet. Miraculously, we avoided all the big rocks sticking out through the snow. Only Janga hit a small snag on the way down, which tore the seat of his britches out. Goose down filled the air as he turned a somersault and landed upside down in a drift. We laughed so hard we could hardly stand up.

The other big problem was wet clothing. The sun is fierce at 15,000 feet, and the snow would soften even at those altitudes. Then as the sun would dip toward the horizon, temperatures would return to zero Fahrenheit, and our clothing would freeze stiff.

A high mountain camp

For two nights, we spent the first hour in our tents, trying to thaw our boots over the primus stoves enough to get them off. All of us suffered minor frostbite, though all we lost, fortunately, was a bit of skin.

Sunday night, December 28, we were back in Dhorpatan at Dawa's hotel. We had eaten our way through mounds of food: five kilograms of rice per day (that's five kilos before cooking), plus nearly one kilo of sausage and the same of potatoes each day. Dawa was still looking over his shoulder and seemed a bit unnerved that we had arrived before he had gotten out of town. He was making preparation to leave with his horses the next day and was locking up the hotel for the winter.

Hasta Ram and I made our way overland out of the mountains, first five days to Tansen by foot, and then to Kathmandu by bus. When I reported to the Peace Corps some days later, I communicated that Dawa knew more than he was letting on. "You'll find him in Tansen with his horse train," I said.

The U.S. Embassy turned the case over to the Nepali police, and a few days later they arrested Dawa in Tansen. Threatening to spike his feet to the prison floor, they got him talking. He implicated three *kamis* (men of the blacksmith caste) from Bhuji Khola. The men were arrested, and one of them took the police directly to Phil's body, buried under a pile of stones. He was within a few miles of Dhorpatan and had certainly never made it to Maikot.

Nobody knows for sure what the motive for the murder was; probably just plain greed. But I'm still convinced that Dawa was hiding something that he didn't want known, along with the Tibetan and the Lepcha I had met in Kathmandu.

Chapter 28: Fire and Ice

The word of the Lord rang out... everywhere your faith in God has reached men's ears. No words of ours are needed, for they themselves spread the news of our visit to you and its effect: how you turned from idols, to be servants of the living and true God.
—1 Thessalonians 1:9–10, NEB

D.B. warned us that it would be impossible to apply for a visa extension at Immigration. He advised us to travel to India, stay a couple of days, and come back overland, picking up a seven-day visa at the border. There was very little coordination between the border posts and Central Immigration, and chances were good that we would be able to re-enter without a problem. It worked as we had hoped, and we re-entered Nepal on the last day of January 1981. D.B. took our passports into Immigration, where he personally stamped us in until the end of April.

Hasta Ram and I were close to finishing a first draft of the entire New Testament. But things were falling apart in the village. Not only were seven good men in prison for their faith but their families were suffering as well.

"How stupid can you be?" their friends and neighbors were saying. "Hasta Ram tells you to stand firm, and he's off in Kathmandu making money with the Sahib. Don't you get it? He's getting rich off of you. He's as bad as a demon; he's living off of your blood!"

It was inappropriate to pressure Hasta Ram to continue in drafting at a time like this, so I released him on February 10 to return to the village and answer his accusers. He insisted on going. He had, first of all, to encourage the believers and then to silence his critics by showing that he was unafraid. No amount of logical argument would do that; he had to jump into the lions' den along with the rest. His code as a warrior demanded it. Before long, I would have to face similar dangers; I would have to finish the first draft of the New Testament out in the village.

I had promised Steve and Daniel a "proper expedition" before we left Nepal permanently, and it looked like this might be the right time. Nancy had urged me for some time now to "do something significant with the boys to deepen their connection with their father." She had been the primary caregiver. She taught them in school, and she was their point of reference for nearly everything. "It's time for a shift in the center of gravity," she said, wisely and courageously.

This fit well into D.B.'s plans, too. He wanted to introduce me to the Superintendent of Police for the Rapti zone. Rukum district, the district where the Khams lived, was under his purview along with four other districts: Rolpa, Salyan, Pyuthan, and Dang. He had already cooperated with D.B. a great deal, and if he could just meet me, D.B. said, he might be even more forthcoming. It was worth a try.

So D.B., the boys, and I traveled by plane out to Tulsipur, the zonal headquarters. There we would meet the superintendent. It was February 22, and Hasta Ram had been gone for only twelve days. For the boys and me, this was the beginning of an eight-week expedition. Tulsipur lay in the sweltering Dang Valley, an elongated valley of the inner Terai that often saw temperatures over 40°C (104°F). Before we were finished, our hike would take us to over 18,000 feet in elevation and six feet deep in snow.

* * *

In Tulsipur we checked into a simple hotel of stone and mud, and D.B. went off to meet the superintendent. He came back in the evening with good news. We could meet the superintendent two days later in his

own home. There, we'd be away
from prying ears, and we could
discuss anything we needed freely.

"You'll find him an amiable
man," D.B. assured us.

And he was. Sabin (pseud-
onym), the superintendent, had
grown up in Burma. That fact in

Daniel in the hotel window

itself made him less parochial and more open-minded. Some estimates
have it that there are as many as five hundred thousand Nepalis living in
Burma. Their great-grandfathers fought as Gurkhas for the British Raj,
and their fathers fought against the Japanese all across Southeast Asia.
They were able to acquire good land in Burma and settled down there.
Though Hindus, they were surrounded by Buddhists and knew a good
deal about Christianity, too.

For some reason that I couldn't figure out at first, D.B. insisted that
I not speak Nepali too fluently. "Better to stumble a bit," he said. "We
don't want the superintendent to think you've been here too long!"

At the superintendent's house, sitting on wooden chairs in a nice,
expansive lawn, we began talking about the case of "the Christian prisoners in Rukum district."

After an hour or so and several cups of tea, during which time I
spoke only as directed, D.B. began to get to his point. "There have been
unfortunate violations of human rights in this particular case," D.B.
explained, "and these things have come to the attention of Mr. Watters."

The superintendent turned to me. "What all have you heard?" he
asked bluntly.

Not sure how to say it in broken Nepali, I replied perhaps too
fluently, "Well, I understand that the men have been denied any kind
of human decency. They're kept in chains and not allowed to go outside
even for their toilet. They're not allowed to read, and they're beaten if
they sing. All of them have been ill because of the cold and the damp,
and nobody does anything about it."

"So what can I do for you?" he asked.

D.B. answered for me: "Mr. Watters needs permission to visit the prison in Musikot. And he needs a letter from you soliciting help from the police on every step of his journey."

Sabin looked a bit surprised, maybe even alarmed, but he said that he would help out. "I'll write the letter in my office tomorrow," he said, "and D.B. can pick it up for you."

Several years later, it became obvious that the superintendent had known exactly what he was doing, and for that time, all he had needed was the appearance of being duped and coerced. The man was more in favor of democratic reform than he let on.

I had no intention of visiting Musikot, and D.B. knew it. But he got what he wanted. The next day, the superintendent hastily dispatched a messenger on horseback to the prison in Musikot. He wanted the messenger to get there before I did. I don't know exactly what the message said, but apparently it warned that the prison was about to be inspected for human rights violations and that the men should be released immediately.

Who in the world was D.B., anyway, I wondered. He used bluffs a lot, but how did he back them up? What were people afraid of? Government officials everywhere called him "Sahib," and so far he had gotten what he wanted from the highest levels of the police force—from the Inspector General of Police, from the Deputy Inspector General for western Nepal, and now from the Superintendent of Rapti Zone. He had utilized the help of the Chief of Customs and a Justice of the Supreme Court. How did he do it? What were his connections? Who was this guy?

* * *

While D.B. headed to Musikot, the boys and I set out on our expedition. Our route passed over numerous high ridges: one night we'd be in a river gorge, and the next night on a ridgetop at 10,000 feet. It was punishing. By the time Steve, Daniel, and I finished our trip, we had traveled 250 miles on foot and had traversed a vertical distance of more than 100,000 feet.

After a seven days' march through Sesi and Gamale (southern Kham) territories, where I recorded as much grammatical detail on their languages as I could, we arrived in the village of Taka. Much to our surprise, the prisoners arrived back in the village on the very next day. They had been released three days earlier on *tarik*, a kind of parole that required that they report in once a month till the end of their sentencing period.

The police post in Taka had been made permanent now, and a Sub-Inspector (S.I.) was in charge. No one was more pleased about this development than the local mafia. With easily corruptible power so close at hand, extortion would be easy. And who better to harass than the little band of Christians? There was no need, even, to twist the truth. The police had a mandate from the district government to do everything they could to stop the Christians.

The S.I. and one of his sergeants came to the house to check our papers. We gave him our trekking permits and the letter from the Superintendent of Police. As he read the letter, he was visibly shaken. He handed it back and disappeared. We didn't see him again.

We discovered quickly that the men's imprisonment was the number one topic of discussion in every Kham village. Around every hearth the gospel was being discussed, by believers and unbelievers alike. "What does the gospel say, and why is it so bad?" All seven men were considered model citizens, and it baffled everybody that the government should wish to put such men into prison. "Why?" they asked. "What in those booklets is so terrible that it would put a man in prison?" So they began beating a path to Hasta Ram's village to buy booklets and find out for themselves.

Nancy and I have commented since that if we had hired those seven men to preach the gospel in every village, it would not have been nearly so effective as having them go to prison.

The men came back with a new collection of Kham hymns. I was unaware that Kham could even be set to poetry. But it could. Chained to the others in their dark little cell, one man, Ram Das, began to write line after line on gospel themes, and the man chained next to him, Sonar, began putting those lines to tune. One of their guards, a man named Homya, understood that these were good men, and he allowed them as much freedom as he possibly could. He enjoyed sitting at the door and listening to them sing.

> The Son of God, he came to earth, in order for sinners to save.
> You he pitied and me he pitied, and in order to help us, he came.
> Because of sinners his heart was sickened, and he offered up his

life.

> He came to earth, and for three full years he preached to us the
>   good news.

> On Calvary's hill, for the sake of sinners, he spilled his
>   precious blood.
> "I am the one," he told them, "the one to forgive sins, the one
>   to give life."
> Coming to earth, he became a man, down from heaven, Jesus.
> They crowned him with thorns and whipped him, all for the
>   sake of sinners.

> "I am the truth, and I am the life; come to me," he said.
> They killed him on a cross, and in three days he rose again.
> He bore the penalty I should have received, and by him I was saved.
> "I am the way, I am the door; come to me," he told me.

One of the seven men who had just come back from prison was Tejendra. He was the youngest of them, only twenty-two years old. He had never had opportunity to be baptized. Now he, along with several others, applied to Hasta Ram for baptism. Steve and Daniel decided that this was their time, too. What better man to baptize them than the man they called *Kaka* ("Uncle"), the leader of the Kham church? And what better companions than men who had suffered imprisonment for their faith?

Hasta Ram required that the boys take the same vows as the other men that night. Dipped into an icy stream "at the foot of the snows," as the Khams say, the boys declared their intention to follow Christ and to participate in the fellowship of his suffering whenever and wherever they were called upon. It was a day they never regretted. Daniel, nearly twelve, wrote a poem:

An icy baptism

> Lord, I am imperfect yet
> Keep thy conscience in me set
> So when I transgress
> I'll be able to hate my mess.

> Thank you for making me your son
> and strength for the daily race to run
> Make me what you want me to be
> So your glory, one day, I can see.

We remained in the village, living in our old house, for a month. The time passed quickly. Almost every evening, Hasta Ram met with the believers, and we were all greatly encouraged. Every day during the daylight hours, Hasta Ram came to the house, and we spent long hours working on translation. I was determined that we wouldn't budge until we had finished the last *Amen* of the book of Revelation. And when it was completed, the boys and I would celebrate by climbing a mountain. Quite a lot of revision was still needed, but at last we had a first, rough draft that we could work on and polish as opportunities came our way in the next few years.

* * *

Steve, Daniel, and I, along with four porters, left the village on a bright spring morning. This would be their rite of passage into manhood. They had just been baptized with prisoners, and now we had our sights set on a minor Himalayan peak, a 21,000-foot spike off the western end

of the Dhaulagiri massif. In the end we didn't make it, and we had to settle for an 18,000-foot hump. But it was an experience they'll never forget. It was a wet spring that year, and the high country was covered with deep snow. Up in the Nimkun glacier basin, the snow was deeper than a man's head, and we got as far as we did only because the snow had crusted over at lower altitudes. Higher up, we were wallowing.

Nights were terrifying out on the high slopes. Shortly after dark, strong winds would drop down off the peaks and nearly blow us away. One night especially, the wind bent and twisted the tent poles until they were like coat hangers. The tent flapped and snapped like a flag at the end of a pole. The friction of nylon on nylon lit up the tent fabric like a florescent light, and the boys could see, for the first time, that their dad's eyes were as big as theirs.

A couple of days out of Maikot, Daniel began complaining that he had "little white things" inside his shirt.

"Don't worry about it, and they'll go away," I said, not eager to deal with the problem up here in the snow.

When, a couple of days later, I was forced to look inside Daniel's shirt, the inside seams were highways of lice. We didn't move camp that day. We had Daniel remove his clothing and crawl into a sleeping bag while we boiled his clothes in one of our cooking pots. Wringing them out, we hung them over boulders until they were frozen stiff, like dried-out animal hides. We beat them and flapped them, beat them and flapped them, until they were as dry as we could get them. Daniel then had to dry them the rest of the way by putting them on and crawling in and out of his sleeping bag all day. Luckily, his clothes were dry by late afternoon, and he had no more trouble with lice.

Two days later, with ice axes and crampons, we were working our way up a very steep slope not far from the summit. Suddenly, the slope that we had just traversed began to move. Silently and swiftly, it slid off to the lower parts of the mountain. With the afternoon sun warming the deep snow, I decided then that we had had enough. The boys had already proven they were bona fide mountain men; no sense making them bona fide dead men. We turned around and headed for home. Still a hundred miles from the bus road, Steve came down with hepatitis; by the time we got home, he looked like a yellow skeleton. Nancy wept when she saw the boys. After eight weeks out, we finally arrived home April 18, Daniel's twelfth birthday.

Chapter 29: Embracing the Deeper Life

When we mortal men, living amid the realities of earth, enjoy the utmost peace which life can give us, then it is the part of virtue, if we are living rightly, to make a right use of the goods we are enjoying. When, on the other hand, we do not enjoy this temporal peace, then it is the function of virtue to make a right use of the misfortunes which we are suffering.
—*Saint Augustine,* City of God

The family flew out to Calcutta at the end of April and enjoyed a few days of holiday. We had already gone through our three months in Nepal, and it was time to start the visa process over again. Our new visas, issued in Calcutta, allowed us one month, up to May 30, 1981, before we had to apply for extensions. On the very last day, I went in. D.B. figured I might be okay on my own by now; maybe things had blown over. This was the first time I had been to Immigration since the seven men had been arrested in September.

Immigration rules were changing constantly in those days, and it was hard to keep up. The new rule was that passports had to be surrendered for three days before visas could be extended. They were beginning to scrutinize them with more detail. When I went to pick up the passports, I was asked to go upstairs and meet with the Immigration Chief.

Not sure what to expect, but guessing that I was probably in trouble, I went upstairs and introduced myself to the chief: "I was asked to come upstairs to collect my passport," I said, trying to sound nonchalant.

The chief looked me over for a moment and then with a wave of his hand, he asked me to take a seat. "So where have you been?" he asked in a not unfriendly voice. "We've been expecting you for several months now."

"Is there a problem?" I asked.

Without answering, the chief rang his bell and a peon came running. "Bring two cups of milk tea," he ordered. To me, he asked, "You can stay for a few minutes and have tea, can't you?"

"Sure, I can stay for a cup of tea," I replied, not knowing what else to say. Besides, he seemed friendly enough.

People were coming and going. Finally, after the two cups of tea arrived, the chief turned with a bit of amusement creasing his face and asked, "So how did you do it?"

"Do what?" I replied, careful not to say anything prematurely.

"Well, reports about you have been coming in to Home Ministry from Rukum district, and we've been asked to do something about it. Apparently, there are some men in prison out there, and you've been implicated. We knew that your visa was good to the end of December, and we expected you to come in for an extension. But when you didn't show up, we assumed that you had left the country. Now, when we look at your passport, we see that you were here the whole time. So how did you do it?"

Relieved that I didn't have to answer allegations about the men in prison, I responded to the more immediate question. "I'm sure you know that I can't tell you how I did it," I replied. "That would be giving trade secrets away."

He smiled and went on, "We've been directed not to extend your visa and to give you just twenty-four hours to leave the country."

"That's quite impossible," I protested. "I still have to buy tickets, and it's usually not possible to get bookings that quickly."

"Okay, fair enough," he acquiesced. "Here are your passports. You go ahead and work on getting a flight out, but until you leave, you will be required to come in here and check with me every day."

I thanked him, took the passports, and went on my way.

Nancy and I had been thinking about traveling to England on Aeroflot via Moscow for some time now. They had a cheap flight that included two free nights in Moscow for a little over four hundred dollars, so I took our passports into the Soviet embassy and applied for a visa. They retained the passports, which they said they would have to send to Moscow, and instructed me to book my flight out of Calcutta for June 5. I booked out of Nepal for June 4. Then for the next five days, I went into Immigration every afternoon and had a pleasant chat with the chief over a cup of tea. Every day he asked, "So how did you do it?"

From England, we went on to the U.S. and then to Canada, where we lived for the next two years.

Family portrait in Canada

* * *

The 1980s were an extremely difficult time for the Kham church. The Rukum government was hell-bent on trying to eradicate Christianity from their district, and for the next four years, there was not a day that passed when a Kham was not in prison for his faith. The police post in Taka was expanded, and the primary responsibility given them was to monitor and harass the church. Solzhenitsyn characterized this kind of action in his *Letter to the Soviet Leaders*—"setting useless good-for-nothings to hound [the country's] most conscientious citizens." But the church accepted its calling seriously and saw to it that, in spite of it all, they would live irreproachable lives. Eventually, the police began to weary of arresting them. These people could not be intimidated. They seemed almost eager to go to prison. The CDOs and the courts just couldn't wrap their minds around this kind of behavior, and the rumor began to circulate that these people welcomed prison because they had a better diet in prison than they did at home. In prison they got *chokho* (ritually pure) Brahminical food—especially rice. High-caste Hindus, in their self-proclaimed superiority, couldn't imagine that people might actually prefer cornmeal.

Hasta Ram was arrested and imprisoned from the end of June to the end of October 1981. We were already in England by that time, and our hearts were heavy again. The church wrote that "we are like chicks without a mother hen." How many times would this happen? Still, remarkably, they looked upon this as their God-given calling, and at the end of Hasta Ram's imprisonment, they conveyed the event in exceptional terms, saying that Hasta Ram had "completed four months of the Lord's service in prison." Indeed, much in their new lives was being interpreted in the light of Scripture, and the fact that the sacred text was predicting much of what was happening to them greatly enhanced its credibility. Jesus warned the early disciples saying, "Do not think that I came to bring peace on the earth; I did not come to bring peace, but a sword. For I came to set a man against his son, and a daughter against her mother, and a daughter-in-law against her mother-in-law; and a man's enemies will be the members of his own household" (Matthew 10:34–36).

Bahadur, the village *pradhan*, and Jhuparya, one of his council members, were in a rage against the church. But it split their households. Bahadur's wife was a stalwart believer and a wonderful woman, as was his daughter-in-law; and Jhuparya's son, Tejendra, was one of the original seven prisoners and had just been baptized. Everything was in chaos, but their Scriptures made sense of it.

In spite of the church's suffering and vulnerability, the members instituted certain programs that enabled them to participate more fully in the Christian life. In addition to participating in Communion on a regular basis, they also set up what they called a "tithing day," a once-a-month event. This one really surprised me; Khams are incorrigible skinflints. Once, while we still lived in Lower Shera, the rich man of the village, who owned over a thousand sheep and had purportedly stashed away five *dharnis* of gold (about twenty-five pounds, over eleven kilograms), refused to pay the equivalent of five cents for a penicillin shot to cure his pneumonia. Villagers chased government tax collectors out of the village for trying to collect an annual fee of one or two rupees for their farm plots. Now, suddenly, these same villagers were infected with enormous excitement about tithing, and nobody wanted to miss out. If I used carriers from the village on my frequent expeditions into the mountains, I always had to work around tithing day.

In May of 1981, Hasta Ram wrote from the village that followers of the gospel were so numerous that they could no longer fit into the meeting house. On the previous tithing day, he said, they had collected thirty-five

Hasta Ram leads a meeting of believers

pathis of barley (about 285 pounds, or 129 kilos), twenty-one *pathis* of wheat (about 170 pounds, or 77 kilos), and 387 rupees. They also collected firewood, potatoes, and maize, and all these things were distributed to the poor in the church. Everyone knew who they were, and there was nothing secretive about it.

Because of Hasta Ram's early associations with Gyaneshwar Church in Kathmandu, and his attendance there whenever in the city, the congregation in Taka always considered that church as its mother. The Gyaneshwar church was an outgrowth of the churches in Kalimpong and Darjeeling (both in Nepali-speaking areas of India), and many of the attendees were professional people—accountants, professors, secretaries, and government employees. A fair number of them drove motorcycles, and some even wore western suits.

After the church in Taka began its tithing practice, a man was deputized to travel once a year to Gyaneshwar in Kathmandu and quietly drop five hundred or a thousand rupees into the offering bag that was passed around on Sunday mornings. No one outside of the Kham church knew about this, and their deputy, dressed in shabby, homespun clothes, always sat unnoticed in the back of the church.

I always felt that the money was flowing in the wrong direction, but because it was clear that the hearts of the Kham believers were going in the right direction, I said nothing about it. These people would prove to the world, over and over again, that they were not "rice Christians"; they were not following the gospel for financial gain.

In March of 1982, we received a letter in Canada, where we were living at the time, written from the village. On Sunday, the last day of February, "at nine o'clock in the morning, the district and local police along with the village council and village elders came bearing guns, clubs, and sticks; and on our tithing day they surrounded the church, and from it, they looted all our books and twenty boxes of goods. Then they captured all of us—the halt and stumbling, the blind and the lame, the old men and the old women, the boys and the girls; all of us—and are marching us off to Musikot headquarters." The letter had been written by Ram Das; Hasta Ram was with him.

On five or six occasions before this, the Christians had been apprehended and taken to the local police station. They were warned to desist from meeting. But it was difficult finding people to testify against them. By and large, the police were unauthorized to launch cases like this without complaints from the villagers. Sometimes they initiated things themselves and put the villagers up to it, and that was apparently what they were doing this time. It didn't work very well.

The remaining booklets that we had brought in just a year earlier were all confiscated and burned in a big bonfire. Their musical instruments were seized and held as "instruments of crime."

The last day of February was a cold, snowy day. Everything was blanketed in white. Fifty-eight Christians, nearly everybody in church that morning, insisted that if anyone were arrested, they should all be included. The police weren't quite sure what to do, so they marched them out into the village fairgrounds, putting them on public display. They hoped to break their will and get some of them to recant; what in the world were they going to do with fifty-eight people? Villagers came to laugh and jeer at them, but as they were marched away on March 2, they wrote, "We were not harmed. In fact, we are full of joy."

After two freezing nights in the snowy field, no one lost their resolve, and all of them—husbands, wives, children—were marched off to Musikot. Because of the snow and the young, it took them five days to get there. They had to pass through several Kham villages on the way, and people rushed out of their houses to see the spectacle—families marched to prison under police escort. Who had ever heard of such a thing?

"Where are you going?" they were asked in every village.

"We're off to 'stand before governors and kings for Christ's sake, as a testimony to them,'" came the reply. It was a reply that came straight out of Mark chapter 13, from Jesus' words to his disciples about the End Times. Everyone was astounded. Actions that at one time would have been anxiously avoided were now embraced because they were part of the gospel story. These people were participating in the very life of God.

Of the fifty-eight detainees, most were sent back home. They had come carrying their own food, and the government refused to give them anything to sustain them in Musikot. They were on their own. So they had to return home with empty stomachs.

Eight were held in Musikot, and on March 9, they were sentenced to prison. D.B. was able to get the names of the eight from the police wireless, and he sent them to me in Canada. Only two were new. The other six had been to prison once before for their faith. The arrests were still premature, though, and the papers were apparently not in order. The officials knew now that they were being watched from Kathmandu, and this made them a bit more jumpy. The men were released after just one month in prison. The officials still couldn't find anyone in the village to testify against them.

Chapter 30: Relentless Hounding

Joseph in the Old Testament, just because he wished to keep his purity, had to bear the humiliation of sitting in prison under the trumped up charge of adultery. Christians in the Red camp are accused of theft, treason, espionage, currency offences and even of ritual murder. But, please, don't pity them. Don't pity the bride who has gone into the marriage feast leaning on the arm of her bridegroom. The bridegroom loved the cross. She shares the joy of the cross with him. Suffering is involved. But this is no reason to pity her.
—*Richard Wurmbrand,* If Prison Walls Could Speak

I returned to Nepal in September 1982, leaving the family in Canada, and stayed till December. I was hoping to begin work on the revision of the existing Kham New Testament manuscript in Kathmandu, making it more natural and more accurate and bringing it up to a better standard. I had hoped to work with Hasta Ram, Ram Das, and Tejendra, the latter of whom was attending a small Bible school in Kathmandu. (Ironically, Christianity—and even a Bible school—was tolerated in the capital city as a façade of religious freedom presented to the outside world.)

Two days before leaving home, I learned by letter that Hasta Ram and Ram Das had been arrested again sometime in July, along with thirteen other leaders of the Kham church, fifteen in all. One of the men this time was Tipalkya, the hunter; and another was Satal Singh, the man who had gotten into a scuffle in Rolpa about "giving up his language." As in the gospel story, it was the down-and-outers, the poor, and the marginalized who were taking the kingdom of heaven by storm. "From the days of John the Baptist until now the kingdom of heaven suffers violence, and violent men take it by force" (Matt. 11:12). As Thomas Cahill says in his book *How the Irish Saved Civilization*, "the passionate, the outsized, the out-of-control have a better shot at seizing heaven than the contained, the calculating, and those of whom this world approves."

This time the police and the courts had their ducks in a row. Their papers, in addition to arrest warrants, included anti-proselytizing papers signed by the village council. The hand of Bahadur and Jhuparya was all over the latest incident. Whatever were they thinking? Why were they doing this? Were they being coerced by the police? Or was Bahadur stupidly standing behind his adage that "we will always be black because our hearts are black"? If so, I had thought better of him.

Eight of the fifteen were sentenced to one year in prison, the others, six to seven months. The latter were given a more lenient sentencing because their crime was only "defending the other Christians."

The Musikot prison had not been built to accommodate so many people. So twelve of the fifteen were transferred to the high-security provincial prison in Tulsipur, while the remaining three stayed in Musikot. The letters of the twelve men in high-security prison were highly censored, and we learned almost nothing of their conditions or treatment. The three men in the district jail in Musikot, however, were able to smuggle letters to the outside. They never complained of their own treatment, and only once did they make an allusion to the difficulties of their families. Following is an excerpt from a letter they wrote to Tejendra in Bible school on November 1, 1982:

> Even though we, the disciples of our Lord, are chained and confined, it is only our bodies. To our souls they can do nothing. Compared to the suffering our Lord endured for us, our confinement in jail is as nothing. But our wives and children are weeping. Our village neighbors are laughing at them. But we endure because we are confident that our day of laughter is yet to come.

Nancy and I were concerned for the welfare of the families whose husbands and fathers were in prison. It was a considerable burden on the church, not only to care for their families but also to provide things like warm clothing, bedding, and special food items for the men in prison. Brave sympathizers were deputized from the village to transfer goods to the prison and check on their welfare. They would be liable for imprisonment, too, just for sympathizing with the prisoners. Two men, Krishna and Janga, risked their necks repeatedly in this service.

Down in the provincial prison in Tulsipur, where twelve of the men had been transferred, there was considerable freedom of movement and fresh air. The prison sported an open courtyard where the men could mill around and enjoy the sun—a vast improvement over the Musikot jail. Superintendent Sabin, the man I had met earlier, who had grown up in Burma, took a special interest in the Christian prisoners for the same reason that D.B. had: he wanted to know if they were genuine and what motivated them.

He visited them frequently and had every reason to be pleased. Not only were their own lives in order but they had taken under their wing a handful of mentally handicapped prisoners, who were vulnerable to extortion by the selfish machinations of the clever. The believers made sure the mentally handicapped prisoners were not abused; they made sure they received their rightful food rations and pocket change allotments; they kept their books for them. Sabin was impressed and allowed the Christians to keep their little pocket Gospels, much to the chagrin of the prison wardens, as long as they opened them only in their "private Christian wing of the prison."

On Christmas day, the men invited Sabin and his wife to the prison for tea and biscuits in celebration of the birth of Christ. All the foodstuffs had been saved from their rations. When Sabin's wife saw what was happening, her embarrassment was too great, and she couldn't participate.

"How can you possibly hold such men as these in your prison?" she asked her husband openly. "And how can you expect them to entertain you from their prison rations? I'll have nothing to do with this," she said as she turned and left the compound.

"On the day of your release," Sabin instructed the men, "the wardens may give you trouble. If they do, tell them that I want to see you. Inform them that I have arranged a police escort to have you taken to my house. They'll phone me, and I'll verify this." They remembered his words.

D.B. and Sabin had been working together, trying to arrange an early release for some of the prisoners, especially for the seven who had been sentenced to just six months. Their release date would be coming sometime around the end of January 1983, but D.B. and Sabin had applied for a Royal Pardon on King Birendra's birthday at the end of December. This would only gain them a month, but the significant thing would be the enormous statement that such a release would bring. The men would be recognized as model citizens.

King Birendra, always an affable person, granted his pardon, and on December 28, 1982, the men were released and sent home without further ado.

Presumably this left just five prisoners in the Tulsipur prison, but eventually we learned that when the original fifteen went to prison, another seven stood to take their places: conducting church services, caring for the flock, and distributing the tithe. Before long, those seven, too, were arrested, bringing the total number of Christian prisoners to twenty-two.

Of the remaining prisoners in Tulsipur, one was Old Man Dalla, about seventy-five years old at the time. Dalla had never learned to read, not even क, ख, ग (the Devanagari equivalent of ABC). But he had an uncanny ability to listen to someone else read and track along with his lips one syllable behind. It was unnerving for the reader at first, but eventually one got used to it. "We have this one opportunity," he said. "The superintendent has allowed us to keep our booklets; now let's be diligent to read them over and over again." A year later, Dalla could quote most of the gospel story by heart.

When Dalla came out of prison in July of 1983, he went straight home, transferred his houses and farmlands over to his children, and began living with his old wife in a goat-hair tent, herding buffalo. Every summer he lived in the wilderness above Tantung, at about 10,000 feet, and every winter he moved downriver to the confluence of the Sani Bheri, below 5,000 feet, where it never freezes and banana trees grow.

"I have only two concerns in life," he said. "One is to care for my buffalo, and the other is to commune with God. I need to be away from the noise and confusion of the village."

The first time I saw Dalla after he was released from prison was a year and a half later, in December of 1986. The winter before, he had pitched his goat-hair tent outside the low-lying Kham village of Chhamarih, a small village of about twenty houses. Every evening after tethering his buffalo, he and his wife would sit in the flap of their tent, preparing a meal of corn-meal mush. As they sat there, Dalla would begin to sing the gospel in his old, raspy voice. Within a few days, the whole village would assemble outside his tent to listen.

Dalla would sing the gospel in his old, raspy voice

"We want to follow Jesus too. What do we do?" the villagers asked Dalla one day.

"Oh, I don't know anything," Dalla replied. "I'm only an old man. You need to travel up to Taka and meet with the church elders there. They can instruct you more fully."

So the villagers left Dalla to watch over their houses, and all of them—men, women, and children—began the trek to Hasta Ram's village. On the way, they met Christian prisoners being escorted to Musikot by police. "Where are you going?" they asked of each other.

"Oh, we're off to 'stand before governors and kings for Jesus' sake, as a testimony to them,'" the prisoners replied.

"Well, we were hoping to be instructed more fully in the gospel in order to become followers of Jesus ourselves," the newcomers replied.

"Unfortunately, there's nothing we can do right now," the prisoners replied. "As soon as we're released, we'll come to your village to instruct you."

A few months later, the whole village of Chhamarih was baptized. The following winter, the winter I was there, Dalla had pitched his tent outside the large village of Padmi with its two hundred houses. Here too, droves of people assembled every night at the flap of his tent to listen to him sing the gospel ballads.

The Khams have always insisted that they were never Hindus, though the courts tried to cram Hindu identity down their throats every time they were arrested. They pointed to Old Testament laws, many of them uncannily similar to their own; and they pointed to their abhorrence of idols. "We were Christians all along," they argued, "but we lost our way, and now we've come back. Besides, the Christian Scriptures are so at home in Kham that they have to be our own."

The district government responded by building a Hindu temple in the village of Taka, a structure sorely out of place. They used foreign aid money, of course. Not a shred of development money had ever reached the village before, and now this was it. It turned out to be a total waste; everyone refused to attend.

* * *

In July 1983, when the final five of the original twelve men in Tulsipur had completed their sentence and were to be released, they were taken to the prison warden. He had papers prepared saying that they had now expiated their crime of religious conversion and that they were being reinstated as full-fledged Hindus. All he needed was their signature.

"We're still Christians," they replied.

"Well, if you're still Christians, you have to go back into prison for another year," the warden responded.

"Superintendent Sabin wants to see us today," they said. "Call him on the phone, and he'll give instructions."

The warden phoned reluctantly to see what was going on. Sure enough, the Superintendent ordered a police escort to be readied so that the men could be brought to his house.

When the men arrived, Sabin seated every one of them in easy chairs and served them tea and biscuits. When the police saw that the setting was casual, one or two began relaxing, and Sabin barked, "I didn't release you. Remain at attention."

"Permission to speak, Sir!"

"Permission granted."

"Back in their own villages, these men make a mockery of Hinduism. It is said that they even eat beef."

"That's what makes them my friends," Sabin snapped back. "I grew up in Burma, where we always ate beef. It's good. Besides, look at these men. They're strong, they're solid, and they're able to endure. That's because they eat beef. They're not a bunch of rice wimps like you. Now get out of here, all of you. These men are free to go on their own. You will not bother them again."

* * *

The men who had been released from prison on a Royal Pardon didn't fare so well. Back in Musikot, the district police and courts, in their arrogance and hatred, decided to take things into their own hands. Things always went awry as soon as the men were sentenced; that's when the judicial system took over. Better to keep them as police cases for as long as possible; easier to work them over and to give them what they had coming.

For the next couple of years, there was always somebody in prison for his faith. The village police had become like arrogant little kings: they swaggered, they pushed, they raped, they pillaged, and they had the backing of Bahadur and Jhuparya. Their new tactic, forged with the district headquarters, was to give the Christians as much pain as possible without turning them over to the courts. They made it impossible for the Christians to meet anymore. The police had commandeered the meeting house as their new police post. They stopped everybody leaving and entering the village, even slashing sacks of grain in their desperation to find hymnals and Christian Scriptures. Secret meetings in the forest continued, but even these were hard to maintain. The church was beginning to languish.

There were many stories of beatings and torture, but some of the most memorable took place at the police headquarters in Musikot in the fall of 1983. The seven who had been released from Tulsipur under the Royal Pardon were dragged back to Musikot for a final reckoning. They were taken in two lots and on separate occasions. Others were added to their number, too, including Tejendra, Jhuparya's son, who was now living in the village again.

The first group of men included big Karna Bahadur, a man who had been invaluable to me on the Peace Corps expedition. Karna was a strong man with large, bony hands and feet. His face was creased often with a big, wide grin. The police locked him and his buddies into wooden stocks outside the police post, where they were made a public spectacle. Then for twenty days, morning and evening, the soles of their feet were beaten until the thick foot-leather peeled back and their feet were lacerated. The police worked themselves into a rage and became so tired they would have to take turns. One policeman severely damaged the eye of a prisoner, Kami, and another beat Karna Bahadur on the head so severely that his stick broke.

Later, Karna Bahadur would say with a grin on his face, "How stupid could they be? They thought they could beat God out of us with a stick!"

After twenty days, the police gave up. These men couldn't be broken. Nobody would recant. Krishna, a local believer who had been running a small teahouse in the bazaar, took them in and nursed them back to health for a week before sending them off home. It still took them several days to reach home on their mangled feet.

The police devised an even worse tactic for the second lot. This time there were five men, and Tejendra and Jaman Singh were among them. They would tie their feet together in the police post and then drag them by the hair into the street like dogs, locking them into the stocks. They beat them mercilessly, on the soles of the feet, on the legs, and about the body. Then, tying their legs again, they would drag them back and toss them into the corner like ragdolls.

For a week, they were given no food and only a little water. They could endure no more. They were almost too weak to cry out. Pens were forced into their hands, and they were made to sign documents saying that they were renouncing their faith.

"Well done!" the police congratulated the men with mockery. "Tomorrow," they were told, "we're declaring a public holiday. The government offices will be closed, the schools will be closed, and the whole town will be assembling at the Hindu shrine to watch you dance and bow before the Hindu gods. You'd better make a good show of it."

That night the men pleaded with God in their desperate weakness. "We can't go on anymore," they cried. "We're too weak to resist. Please, Lord, rescue us from this terrible shame, and rescue your own name."

The next morning, the whole town assembled. School kids were stationed in front and given the job of beating the drums. A mock stage was prepared by spreading blankets on the paving stones and sprinkling them with flowers. The prisoners were dragged to the square by their hair and dumped in a heap. The crowd laughed and jeered. The drums beat, but the men wouldn't dance.

Police grabbed them and smashed their heads against the bronze and stone idols, becoming one with the idols in their leering imbecility. The paving stones turned red with blood.

Suddenly, out of nowhere, an enormous wind arose, and the new harvest, recently gathered and stacked neatly in front of people's homes, scattered and blew in every direction. The wind spiked, and thatched roofs blew off. The thunder cracked, and the rain began to fall; people ran to save what they could, but for most it was too late.

The five men stood alone. The drummers were gone, the police were gone. They knelt where they were and thanked God for their deliverance. Then, unattended, they slowly made their way back to the police post, where they could at least lie on the straw and rest.

An hour later, the police returned. "Get the hell out of here," one screamed. "Why turn your gods loose on us like that? Go back to your village. We don't want you here anymore."

The men feebly made their way across to Krishna's teahouse. Once again, Krishna fed the men and nursed them back to health before releasing them to return to the village. Their spirits were wounded, though; they felt ashamed that they had been unable to resist the signing of the documents.

Chapter 31: Sustainable Development

[Despite limitations], the ethical imperative of the social gospel, the emphasis on Christian social responsibility, the sharp criticism of any Christian ethics which deals only with "individual morality," the primary concern for the welfare of oppressed classes and races—these remain from the social gospel as an integral part of the Protestant witness...
—Dillenberger and Welch, Protestant Christianity

Nancy and I always wondered how much more we should be doing for the Kham Christians. So far, their only reward for following the gospel had been harassment, imprisonment, and torture. And they had accepted their lot without complaint. Their motivation was the sheer joy of believing in God. What was our responsibility? Should we be doing more? The words of Jesus were haunting: "I was hungry, and you gave me nothing to eat; I was thirsty, and you gave me nothing to drink; I was a stranger, and you did not invite Me in; naked, and you did not clothe Me; sick and in prison, and you did not visit Me" (Matthew 25:42–43).

A major component of the gospel has always been compassion, a holistic concern for the whole man—body, soul, and spirit. But in a country like Nepal, showing compassion through good works always smacked of buying converts. Preaching the gospel was referred to in Nepali as *prachaar*. But *prachaar* was also what people did in political campaigns and propaganda wars. Buying votes was the standard way of doing business. So it was assumed that anywhere there were Christian converts, they too must have been bought.

The whole issue of doing "more" began to come to the forefront in the fall of 1982, before the fifteen men in prison had any visible prospect of being released. I was in Kathmandu, working with Tejendra on revision (this was before his beatings); Tejendra received a letter from the prisoners saying, "our wives and children are weeping." Not knowing what else to do, I sent a letter of appeal through Nancy, in Canada at the time, to our financial supporters for "just a little help to get them through the winter." Their response was overwhelming.

I understood then that my appeal was fraught with the seeds of misunderstanding and ruin. What kind of insanity would it be to dump money into the laps of fifteen families? What about everybody else? Weren't they deserving too? What about the ten or fifteen who would go into prison next year?

After Hasta Ram was released from prison in July of 1983, I notified him that "gifts" had been sent from America to help the families of the prisoners. "What should I do?" I asked him.

"Send it back," Hasta Ram replied vehemently. "Gifts and money will only ruin us. We want nothing to do with them."

Then, I began to hear rumors that even those who had been released from Tulsipur on a Royal Pardon had been re-arrested in Musikot. I hadn't heard the outcome yet. But clearly, imprisonment was going to be an ongoing problem, and short-term solutions weren't going to help.

Some months later, Hasta Ram and I had ample opportunity to discuss our options in greater detail. "What if we could do something that would benefit the entire community, not just the Christians?" we began to ask one another. One idea in particular kept coming to the forefront, and we began looking into it.

Several years earlier, I had become acquainted with some Swiss engineers in Nepal who had developed a portable water turbine that could be assembled in villages with a minimum of know-how. It was locally available at the machine shops of National Structure & Engineering Ltd. right in Kathmandu Valley. We went over to see it.

By good fortune, we were able to meet with Andras Bachmann, one of the developers of the mill, and he kindly took us around the valley to look at various installations. We settled on a model that seemed suitable to our needs, and in May 1984, the machine shop began construction.

The turbine was powered by flowing water, a plentiful resource anywhere in the mountains, and, through a power take-off belt, it could be attached to any number of applications—millstones for grinding grain, presses for extracting oil from seeds, and even small generators for powering saws, planes, and wool-carding machines. The possibilities seemed endless, and the poorest, most common villager would benefit the most. It was the women who got up in the inky black hours before daylight to grind enough grain at their stone hand mills for the daily food supply. Anything to ease their burden would be a big help.

* * *

Building a water turbine in a machine shop in Kathmandu and making sure that it is properly assembled and maintained in a remote village are two different things. Many aid projects in Nepal have floundered and failed because of the immense gap between the two. I have seen brand-new hospital buildings used as herders' sheds, bridges going unused because no one would replace the flooring planks, and hydroelectric generators rusting in their traces. As pointed out by Mr. Bista in his book on development in 1991, the heart of the problem was in Nepal's age-old hierarchical system of privilege and favor.

"A university degree," he says, "is considered a license to reach the top of the social hierarchy, and these people would not wish to lower themselves to the level of *shudra* by soiling their hands; the actual work is done by people who never got any training... the educated are just as loathe to work physically and productively as are the traditionally high-caste people."

But this is where we had the advantage. We were outside the pale of Brahminism. We had men and women who were eager to make things work, and they weren't afraid of sweat, toil, and tears. They had proven that already.

So Hasta Ram and I arranged a meeting with the church elders in the secluded meadow of Pahl, high on the Dhorpatan bench, an eight-day walk from the low-lying *Duns* of Dang Valley. We wanted to broach the topic of the mill and let them know exactly what would be required if we were to have any hope of success. The project would take transparency, it would take commitment, and it would take hard work.

Pahl meadow, surrounded by trees

I was no longer safe in the village; the police were eager to lay hands on me. But in the meadow of Pahl, a full day's walk to the east of Taka and a day's walk north of Nisi, we could meet unmolested. Our camp was high above the main trail, hemmed in on all sides by dense conifer forest, and because of the angle of the terrain, our smoke could not be seen. Herders' sheds dotted the green sward at the center, and only in the summer was the place occupied. Firewood was plentiful, and the sheds were maintained well—ready-made dormitories and meeting halls. This would become a favorite spot for elders' conferences.

Steve had just finished high school in Canada and was free to travel with me on such trips. Accompanying him was one of his high school buddies, who wanted to come along for the trek. Ram Das and Tejendra traveled with us from Kathmandu, and joining us for the last eighty miles were three Kham porters from Dang, all well-established in the faith.

There were six elders from the village; all of them had been selected in advance for their skills and wisdom. Hasta Ram was the chief, and with him came Karna Bahadur, Jaman Singh, and Sonar. All six had been to prison at least once for their faith, and some had been imprisoned three times. Three of the six had been severely beaten, and two of those had succumbed under the torture. I was happy to see that the "weak" were accepted on an equal status with the "strong."

Meeting in the herders' sheds

With our contingent from the south, we were twelve in all.

We spent four glorious days in Pahl. Steve would later say in a letter to home:

> We sat spellbound late into the night as we listened to story after story of their joyful suffering for Christ and the spread of the gospel. We heard of a whole village turning to Christ as they gathered night after night to hear the rasping voice of an illiterate old herdsman singing the Gospel like a ballad. We heard hymns made to the sound of clanking chains as fifty-eight believers were marched off to prison. We heard of hardened enemies, former perse- cutors of the church, reading the Gospel and begging for forgiveness. What other boy has had the privilege of sitting so close to heroes of the faith, men "of whom this world is not worthy"?

Steve writes in his journal

We invited Sonar and Jaman Singh along because they were always tinkering with things. They were always trying new seeds, new plants, and new horticultural methods. They were the first to learn fruit graft- ing. Just a single visit to their houses would impress you with their improvisations. A plow handle wasn't quite good enough for them; they

had to carve a horse's head into it. And where other people were satisfied with pegs and rope loops, they fashioned wooden hoops and rings.
Even their fields were a marvel of canals, sluice boxes, water ladders, and
diversion doors. If anybody could figure out the workings of a water
turbine, it would be these two. When Hasta Ram and I presented our
plans to them, they came alive.

We never let on that we had sufficient funds to construct the mill
outright. It would be better to think of it as a loan and to follow the
time-honored method of raising business capital. When villagers
needed money to launch a new business venture, they borrowed gold
from their friends, deposited the gold as collateral in state-run banks,
and operated off the cash. Usury was high, and many lost their shirts.
Not only did they eventually have to redeem the gold from the banks
with interest, they had to return the gold to its owners with interest,
too. But I was there with real capital to make sure that things didn't go
that far. We would borrow only a token amount of gold and pay it back
quickly.

Generating income from mills was an idea that had been around
the Himalayas for a long, long time. Little wooden paddle wheels
that turned stone querns were all over the countryside. Anyone lucky
enough to have a stream running through his field was able to avoid the
daily backbreaking labor of turning a grinding wheel by hand. If the
stream were big enough, he could grind his neighbors' grain for a fee.

Ours would be an income-generating venture. We should be able to
pay off the loan and return the gold in a couple of years. The men were
well apprised of standard grinding fees in the village—usually different rates for different grains. Payment was in kind. For so many *pathi*
of grain, the miller was entitled to so many *manas* of grain. We would
make sure that we followed the same rates so as not to undermine the
millers already in existence. But we also had the option of pressing oil
and providing other small applications as well. There were no oil seeds
in the higher Kham villages, but lower down, people grew mustard
primarily for its oil. Oil extraction, done in crude wooden mortars, was

exceedingly inefficient, and once we were set up to do it, people walked for days to press their oil in the Taka press.

* * *

The little delegation in Pahl commissioned each of the elders to different tasks that year. They released Hasta Ram to work with me for three months of every year, allowing him to turn the responsibilities of the village churches over to others while he worked on translation. Ram Das and Tejendra were commissioned to work in dialect adaptation and literacy efforts. This was also an area that I was moving into. Sonar and Jaman Singh were commissioned to learn as much as they could about water turbines and mills.

Back in Kathmandu, I went to the machine shop where the water turbine was being constructed and made arrangements for Sonar and Jaman Singh to come into town before the end of the summer. The turbines were built in such a way that they could be dismantled into portable sections and carried out to the villages on the backs of men. But even before the unit would leave Kathmandu, I wanted our two men to practice dismantling and reassembling it so many times that they could do it in their sleep. There would be no opportunity for practice once they were in the mountains.

I also learned that National Structure & Engineering had its own field assembly team. For a fee, they offered a turn-key service, whereby the turbine could be purchased "pre-installed"—no hassle, no fuss. Just pay the money, and all you had to do was flip the switch. It was a great idea, but it defeated the very thing we were hoping to achieve. We needed people on the ground who knew how to install, run, and maintain the machinery. So we made a proposal: "We'll provide free labor for one of your field installations; all you have to do is take our men along." They were delighted and couldn't turn the offer down.

The field team had three turn-key installations to make in faraway Mustang district that fall. "Learn all you can learn," I urged Sonar and Jaman Singh. "You'll be taken advantage of; you'll be exploited. You'll get all the dirty work of digging ditches, lifting boulders, twisting steel, and greasing bearings. But you'll learn how to install a mill."

And learn they did. By the end of the summer, they had installed turbines and hooked up mills in three very different situations. They learned how to improvise, and they learned how to make everything work. Back in Kathmandu, they took ownership of our own turbine and immediately sent to the village for help in transporting it. Church members arrived in large numbers and carried back portable loads on their backs for more than a hundred miles: turbine blades, shafts, penstocks, wheels, pulleys, belts, gears, cogs, concrete, and steel. Within a few short weeks, they had the millhouse constructed, they had the turbine assembled, and they began grinding grain. They had even attached the oil expeller to the power take-off and begun pressing oil.

Getting the oil expeller to the village was no mean feat. It was meant to be installed near a serviceable road, not a hundred miles off-road. It consisted of a huge cast iron crank-case with two worm gears penetrating into its bowels. The only way to make it lighter was to remove the worm gears, but the crank case still weighed close to three hundred pounds (136 kilograms). Little Ujar, no more than five feet tall, but made of bone and gristle, carried it all the way.

The mill was an absolute marvel, and people came from far and wide to see it. A young political activist from outside the area, a member of the Communist party, watched the Christians labor. "You people are like Communists," he exclaimed. "You work together in harmony for the common good."

"We are the *true* communists," Hasta Ram replied. "We do it because it's in our hearts to do so. You do it because Marx demands it."

Everything for the mill is carried out

*Many years later, Hasta Ram and Jaman Singh feed
the still-running mill*

*David helps with the electrical box, installed thanks to the
work of Louie Woodland on location*

Chapter 32: Blacklisted?

By long forbearing is a prince persuaded, and a soft tongue breaketh the bone.
—Proverbs 25:15, KJV

Bahadur and Jhuparya had been harassing the church for years. They were quick to use the *panchayat* stamp for nearly every arrest, every complaint, and every investigation against the Christians. But they weren't gaining anything by it; the Christians refused to capitulate to any demands for protection money. This, apparently, infuriated them even more, and they became irrational in their rage. Bahadur nicknamed the Christians *kharantyas*, a part of the male anatomy, and the unflattering name began to stick as a new epithet of derision.

But the two men were in an awkward position, and they had to play their cards carefully. Bahadur's wife, Dev Maya, had been a believer for years and was considered something of a church matriarch. She continued to serve her husband well, and she pleased him in every respect. She was an efficient manager of the home, and Bahadur couldn't afford to lose her. Besides that, he loved her. *Give her a little time, and maybe she'll get over this fad,* he must have thought.

The church was close to home for Jhuparya, too; Jhuparya was Tejendra's father. But Jhuparya was never an original thinker. As long as I had known him, he had always been nothing more than Bahadur's sidekick. He seemed unconcerned, or perhaps he was too stupid to realize, that his own son might get caught in the web of his machinations. When Tejendra succumbed to the beatings in prison, Jhuparya even seemed to gloat a bit. "Maybe that'll bring him to his senses," he said imperiously.

Tejendra never reviled his father for his actions, and the church never reviled the two *panchayat* leaders. Everyone continued on with an even keel. They took to heart the words of Jesus: "Love your enemies, and pray for those who persecute you" (Matthew 5:44). That is, most people did. Bishnu Gurung began to propagate some disturbing new ideas, making them palatable through the use of parables. "What does a shepherd do when wolves enter the flock?" he used to ask. "Doesn't he destroy them before they destroy the sheep?" But the church continued to collect monthly tithes and, from the proceeds, care for the poor. As an outright repudiation of Bishnu's ideas, they even made sure that the police were comfortable! No one who watched the Christians up close could be unimpressed. And Bahadur and Jhuparya had ringside seats.

During our four-day conference in Pahl, I began hearing for the first time that Bahadur and Jhuparya had been coming to the Christian meetings on a regular basis. This frightened people at first. They supposed that the two had come to spy them out, that they were amassing evidence against them. But over time, the Christians began to realize that their interest was genuine.

"We have come to beg your forgiveness," Bahadur explained to the believers one day as he stood before them. "We have dealt you nothing but suffering and pain," he explained, "and you have repaid us with nothing but kindness. We are ashamed of our actions, and we want to change."

Everyone was stunned.

Then the two men applied to Hasta Ram and the elders for baptism. "We want to cast in our lot with you," they said. "We want to declare our intention to follow the teachings of Christ and of the church."

"How do we know that you're telling the truth?" the elders asked.

"We're not the sort of men who ask for forgiveness," they replied. "But that's what we're doing. We're on our knees, and we're submitting ourselves to you. Do what you like. Only don't reject us."

"Okay," the elders responded. "But we'll need to observe you for a few months. If you demonstrate that you're truly sorry for all your actions and you show an eagerness in following the Gospel, we'll accept you and we'll baptize you."

Bahadur retired from politics that year. "Too much evil," he said. "It's all about plotting against the powerless." His eldest son, Bal Man, a former policeman, was elected *pradhan* in his stead. We did not know how that would turn out. Three months later, Bahadur and Jhuparya were baptized. In the following years, Bahadur learned to read the Scriptures for himself, and the thing that he had earlier declared impossible actually happened. His heart was turned from black to white. He also became a staunch advocate for literacy in Kham.

* * *

I was absent from Nepal for much of the church's formative years, especially from 1983 to 1985, and to their immense credit, they developed their own wise practices and policies. I brought Hasta Ram to the United States for a few months in the winter of 1983–4 so that he could help me finalize the Kham New Testament for publication. After his return, I continued on with keyboarding, formatting, and finally typesetting the final plates.

In August of 1985, Nancy and I returned to Nepal. I traveled ahead of Nancy, enrolling Daniel in high school at Woodstock School in Mussoorie, India. Steve had remained in the States to begin college. I also had the photo-ready plates of the New Testament with me, which I took to Ambassador Press in New Delhi; publication of Scripture was still difficult to arrange in Nepal. When Nancy joined me a couple of weeks later, we moved on up to Nepal, where we began living in a drafty, old Rana palace of the previously ruling dynasty. We dubbed it Ichabod Palace (Ichabod is Hebrew for "the glory hath departed").

The owner of the palace, an "A-Class Rana" who occupied the bottom floor, was an aristocratic throwback to older Rana times. He was preoccupied with guns and hunting, and he adorned his living rooms with the horns and heads of game animals from all over the Terai. He spent countless hours flipping through American sports gear and hunting magazines, dreaming of the latest camouflage jacket or rifle scope. "On your next trip to America, could you bring back one of these compasses that I could embed into the butt end of my rifle?" He was intractable, and I became his number one catalog and trinket supplier.

One thing that unnerved us a bit about Mr. Rana, though, was his position in the government. In fact, the passports of all foreign residents in Nepal had to receive his signature. "I do Interpol checks on them," he told me one day.

I asked D.B. about Mr. Rana, and he referred to him as a "good guy, harmless if he likes you... Besides," he added, "it's better to live in a lion's mane than it is to live at the end of his paws." These assurances helped.

* * *

Early in October, I went to the Central Immigration Office in Kathmandu for our first visa extension. According to standard practice, I left off our passports one day to pick them up the next. When I went in the following day, I was asked to "go upstairs and see the chief."

"Oh no," I thought with a lump in my throat. "Not this again!"

Upstairs, I sat down in a chair opposite the chief, a man by the name of Ganesh (pseudonym) with the rank of Deputy Superintendant of Police (DSP). He wasn't the same fellow I had become acquainted with a few years before. This one had the squinty, devious eyes of a crook, and I didn't like him much. "So why do you want to see me"? I asked.

He eyed me with disdain. "We're giving you just twenty-four hours to leave the country," he answered abruptly. "Your visa cannot be extended."

"Why not?" I argued. "I've only been here for two months this year. Three or more is allowed."

"Your name is on the blacklist," he said decisively. "We expel people on the blacklist."

Things weren't adding up, and I protested once again. "I don't believe I'm on the blacklist. Show me!"

Ganesh hesitated for a moment, and then he opened his desk drawer, pulling out a little copy booklet. He began flipping through the pages, each one emblazoned with the photograph of some unsavory-looking character: drug-runners, kidnappers, racketeers, and who knows what else. They were a rough-looking lot. Then, he came to a page that looked jokingly out of character. It had my photo on one side and Nancy's smiling face on the other.

"Is this you?" he asked.

"Yes."

"Is this your wife?"

"Yes."

"You have twenty-four hours," he said with finality.

"What are the charges?" I asked, still not believing my ears. "I must have been charged with something."

"You're being expelled for crimes committed in Rukum district in 1981," he answered.

"What crimes?"

"I don't have a list of the crimes," he said. "Just crimes."

A bit shaken, I stood to leave. "I'm leaving my passports with you for now," I said. "I'll come pick them up after I talk with some of my friends."

"Who are your friends?" he asked, a bit surprised.

"You'll find out soon enough," I answered, and I left the office.

* * *

"Horrible news," I reported to Nancy back home. "We're stopped in our tracks even before we've started. I'm going over to see D.B. Maybe he can help us."

When D.B. heard the news, he smiled and dismissed it with a wave of his hand. "No problem," he said. "That'll be easy to fix." He immediately went over to the Home Ministry and had a directive issued to Immigration that the visas should be renewed and the passports released. It all seemed rather odd to me, but I'd seen odd things before.

If the problem were related to crimes committed in Rukum district, wouldn't the original directive have come from Home Ministry? How could D.B. overturn it so easily?

On D.B.'s advice, I went back to Immigration to pick up the visas. "It's all fixed up," he said. "All you have to do is collect them."

Back upstairs, I asked DSP Ganesh for our passports. He stalled. I asked again, and he stalled some more. Then, after what seemed an interminable silence, he lost patience and became angry. He slammed the passports onto the table, and taking a red pen, he wrote across the last visa in each passport: "Visa extensions terminated. Never to enter Nepal again."

Wow, what happened? Stunned, I collected the passports and headed home. Later, when I showed D.B., he too was shocked.

Our backs were against the wall now. We couldn't just go to India and apply for a tourist visa back to Nepal. Our passports were all marked up. We had just moved into Rana's house, and we couldn't just leave without explanation. The more we thought about it, the more we realized that we'd have to talk to Mr. Rana about our situation. If we said nothing, we'd have to leave and not come back. And if we did say something, the worst he could do would be to expel us. We were on our way out, anyway. What did we have to lose?

The next evening I went down to see Mr. Rana. I showed him our passports and explained briefly what had happened at Immigration. "Whoa," he said, looking at the red marks with surprise. "What happened here?"

I explained the blacklist and the charges made against me.

"Describe to me what the blacklist looked like."

"Well, it was a little copy booklet full of photographs," I said.

"I don't think that was a blacklist," Mr. Rana said laughing. "You've been caught up in some kind of a scam. Who else is in this thing?"

"Well, D.B. tried to help me out, but that's when everything backfired," I answered.

Rana stroked his chin for a moment and then said, "D.B. may have been the one who set you up in the first place. I suspect that the

Immigration chief went along with his plan because he supposed that he would get half the bribe. When it turned out that there was no bribe, only a favor, he was angered and wrote in your passport. Besides, Immigration never gets lists of crimes. His charge about "crimes in Rukum district" must have been something he got from D.B."

My head was reeling, but suddenly things were beginning to make sense. Now that Mr. Rana was around to help me, it appeared that D.B. was afraid that I would no longer be dependent on him in the same way that I had been before. He needed to stage a dramatic "deliverance" in order to continue making himself indispensable. Unfortunately for him, it backfired. And apparently he knew that I knew. Though we continued to be friends, he became much more aloof and a little embarrassed from that day onward.

Mr. Rana walked me out to his garden and acted toward me like a loving uncle to his favorite nephew. Big, sweet-smelling pine trees were scattered around the yard, and spotted doves made their plaintive calls from the branches above. We sat together on a concrete bench next to the goldfish pond, and he addressed me warmly.

"I know you're not a crook," he said. "I've dealt with crooks all my life, and you're not one of them. But it's going to take me some time to figure this thing out. I'll have to pull the files and see what's there. So when did you say you lived in Rukum district?"

I explained again, making sure he understood the terrible plight of the Christians out there.

"Well, what you need to do now is to go to India for a month or so and let this thing blow over. You'll have to get new passports, of course. Either that, or make the red marks disappear. When you come back, make an overland crossing with a seven-day visa. By that time, I'll have things figured out." An owl screeched from the top of a tree behind us, and another answered from across the grove. Evening was approaching.

By this time, Nancy and I were cautious not to tell "just anyone" everything we were doing. We told people only what they needed to know. But this was, of course, a subjective thing. In times like these, when we were backed into a corner and only one man stood between us and freedom, the choices became much more obvious: we had to come clean. So far, God, in his providence, had always put the right man in our path. First it was D.B., and through him the Inspector General of Police, the Deputy Inspector General, the Superintendent of Police, and the Supreme Court Justice. Now, it was Mr. Rana.

* * *

Nancy and I left for India the next day. We traveled first to New Delhi, where we discovered, to our great joy, that the New Testaments had been completed and were ready for pickup. How beautiful they were! One forgot immediately all the hard work that had gone into producing them. We took a dozen copies with us and had the rest shipped by rail to Raxaul, on the India–Nepal border. For the next month, we stayed at Edgehill, a little guest house on the hillside above Woodstock School in Mussoorie. This was the first time Daniel had been away from home, and we had missed him terribly. It was a delight to see him again, and we planned on having a family Christmas together back in Nepal.

The son of the Canadian ambassador was also staying at Edgehill, and after we become casual friends, I decided to take up the case of my passports with him. My first inclination was to go to New Delhi, lay the case honestly before the Americans, and ask what they would do. He cautioned against that. "If you level with them, I don't think they'll take too kindly to you. It might cause a lot of trouble. I'm not an official with either the Canadians or the Americans, but my personal recommendation is that you lose the passports and start all over again."

I thought about his advice a lot and decided that to "lose" the passports would involve an outright lie. It was also clear to me that the red ink in the passport was not official at all—it was the angered reaction of a corrupt Immigration official who thought he was going to get a bribe. So I did what I thought was the lesser of two evils.

I went to the bazaar and bought some ink remover. With a cotton swab I was able to smudge the writing and almost make it disappear. To my advantage, South Asian visa stamps have lots of ink and smudges in them, and there were smudgy stamps all over the facing pages. So on the pages where faint red still showed, I patted a little water on the facing pages, closed the passports, and pressed them overnight between some heavy books. The next morning, the results were better than anything I could have hoped for. The passports looked like they had been in someone's sweaty back pocket, and the stamps from one page bled slightly onto the page of the next. Nothing overdone. Today, many years later, I myself can't even detect which pages had the red markings.

Nancy and I also met some newlyweds at Edgehill who were traveling in India on a research grant from Stanford University. They became enthralled with our story and wanted to do anything they could to help us. Their next stop was to be Kathmandu, so we burdened them with the first five copies of the newly printed Kham New Testament. They were delighted with the privilege. Nancy and I followed a few days later with another six copies. We crossed the border at Birgunj and got seven days in our passports. They could detect nothing unusual with the passports, and the crossing was uneventful.

Relaxing outside Edgehill Guesthouse

Chapter 33: Fulfillment

The Bible is the means by which Christ is displayed, proclaimed and manifested. Why read scripture? For Calvin, the answer was as clear as it was simple: because by doing so we come "to know Jesus Christ truly, and the infinite riches which are included in him and are offered to us by God the Father."
—*Alister McGrath,* Christianity's Dangerous Idea

...Because [Hebrew and Greek] are not known to all the people of God, who have right unto, and interest in the Scriptures, and are commanded, in the fear of God, to read and search them, therefore they are to be translated into the vulgar language of every nation unto which they come, that, the Word of God dwelling plentifully in all, they may worship Him in an acceptable manner; and, through patience and comfort of the Scriptures, may have hope.
—*The Westminster Confession of Faith, 1.8*

We arrived back in Kathmandu on November 12, 1985, and completely unexpectedly, Hasta Ram arrived from the village with his wife two days later. His wife had never been to the big city, and he had been planning this, he said, for many months.

When he learned from us that we had brought copies of the Kham New Testament with us, his eyes twinkled, and he said, "Aha, now I understand why I had such an urge to come in. And I had supposed that it was to show my wife the sights! How good of God!"

This called for a celebration. Nancy and I wanted desperately to put these books into Hasta Ram's hands, but we needed to do it with as much ceremony as we possibly could. We called Ram Das and Tejendra. "Run into the city," we told them, "and find as many Kham believers from the village as you possibly can. We have a surprise, but we can't tell you yet what it is. Let people know that there will be a feast, too."

We knew a good cook, a fine Christian man by the name of Hari. He had a reputation as one of the best in the city, and his talents were always in demand at the American Embassy. He was currently holding a job with the Director of USAID, and Sunday was his only day off. He was delighted to be a part of our celebration, and we settled on Sunday, November 17, 1985. Only after preparations were well underway did we realize that the date chosen was exactly sixteen years to the day from our first entry into the village of Shera in 1969.

Ram Das and Tejendra managed to scour up ten Kham believers in town: the two of them with their wives, Hasta Ram and his wife, plus another four. So with Nancy and me, we numbered exactly twelve. At about three o'clock that afternoon, we twelve met together in a little upper room in Dhobighat, the place I now used as an office.

Hari had prepared a delectable feast. We had asked him to spare no expense: "Make a feast fit for kings," we told him. He did exactly that. The spices were perfect and made for a subtle blend of taste and aroma that was unequaled. We took our time, and at the end, we all agreed that we had never tasted food this good before.

As we settled back with satisfaction at the end of the meal, Nancy and I turned to the main event of the day. No one, not even Hasta Ram, had seen a copy of the New Testament yet.

"I have with me," I said, "something of immense significance."

Opening a cardboard box, I drew out a dark blue book, almost black, decorated along one edge with a gold design and emblazoned across the cover with gold letters—

ई ध र-ए सा:रो याका-लाव ओपाँ

—"The Words of God's New Covenant." It was silent outside, and a streetlight was beginning to shine through one of the windows. Nancy switched on a small light and lit a few candles.

Before letting them hold copies of the New Testament, I wanted to tell them something of what it took to produce these books. Each book had a thousand pages in it (1,003, to be exact), and based on that round number, calculations were easy to come by. It turned out that for every page in the book, Hasta Ram had walked seven or eight miles, traveling into and out of the village—that's seven or eight *thousand* miles—and I had walked some three miles. For every four pages, I had spent a night in the open, out on the trail, away from home and away from the village. That's 250 days, the better part of a year. (Hasta Ram had spent countless more nights.) For every page, Nancy and I had spent four and a half days in learning the language and producing the first draft—a total of forty-five hundred days, or twelve years. For every page, Hasta Ram and I had spent an additional day—almost three years—in revising the text, making it consistent and accurate. For every page, I had spent another half a day—more than a year in all—in keyboarding the text and getting it ready for publication.

But the most amazing statistic of all was what it had cost the believers themselves. In anticipation of the coming of the book, they had staked their lives on its truths. The people from that one village had spent six and a half man-days in prison for every single page in the book. And in order to emphasize how much that really was, I began turning one page at a time as I counted off the numbers—six and a half days, thirteen days, nineteen and a half days, twenty-six days, and so on. The total comes to sixty-five hundred days or eighteen man-years in prison! Everyone was mesmerized. Nobody batted an eye.

The first copy, I presented to Hasta Ram. But before I gave it to him, I read aloud an inscription that I had written on the inside cover. I had practiced reading it to Nancy several times before, but I had always become so choked up that the only way I could get through it was to stand behind the door, where she could hear me but not see me. Now, I had to read it looking directly at Hasta Ram. But I was ready now. The inscription was written in Kham; this is an English translation:

My Dearly Beloved Friend,

This book I give to you, my dearly beloved friend, from the depths of my heart. Even before we first met, you had already been searching for the words of truth as uttered by the mouth of God. God himself knew your search and sent me to you along with my family. At that time, you were ones lost at the foot of the snows, beyond the notice of your own king, excluded from the citizenship of God, and utterly without hope in the world.

Then, from the day we first met, you and I have traveled together for fifteen years, sharing in sorrows and sharing in joys. In all those years, I have not found another like you, my friend, full of faithfulness and unflinching at difficulty. Sometimes we traveled long, long roads with loads on our backs in the scorching sun. Sometimes we bivouacked deep in the snow, stiff from the cold. But never did I hear you complain.

Still, you and your friends suffered far more than we as a family ever did. You were subjected to beatings. For the sake of our Lord's name, you were despised and bound with chains in the darkness. But in all that, because you could see the footprints of our Savior, you broke out into songs of joy, and you even prayed for those who persecuted you. Because you were confident that your portion in heaven was of greater value than a life of ease, you did not entangle yourselves in the cares of this world.

Therefore, my beloved friends, you who were last have become first. Though the men of this world count you as nothing, you count as the greatest in the kingdom of God. So then, it is to you, the bravest of the brave, the most faithful of the faithful, and the more honorable than the high-born, that I and my family give this book from the depths of our hearts.

I handed the book to Hasta Ram. He accepted it with both hands and clutched it to his chest. His whole body trembled with emotion as the tears flowed down his cheeks. Everyone wept; there was not a dry eye in the room. Then I presented books to the rest of the people there. I had put shorter inscriptions in Ram Das' and Tejendra's Bibles.

After Hasta Ram was able to control his overwhelming emotions, I asked him if there were some word he would like to share with us. After a few moments of deep silence, he spoke as though his whole life had been in preparation for this single moment. He very simply and very profoundly recounted for us the story of Old Man Simeon from Luke chapter 2.

"You will remember," he said, "that Mary and Joseph had taken the baby Jesus into the temple to dedicate him to the Lord. Old Man Simeon was in the temple that day; a man who had received a promise from God that he would not see death before he had seen the salvation of the Lord. Recognizing the baby for who he was, he took him in his hands and lifted his eyes to heaven saying, 'Let now thy servant depart in peace, for mine eyes have seen thy salvation.'

"I am like Old Man Simeon," Hasta Ram went on to say. "I too

Hasta Ram with his New Testament

have waited long for the completion of this book, and today it is fulfilled. I hold in my hands the salvation of God for my people. Whether I live or whether I die makes no difference to me now. My hopes are fulfilled, and my heart is satisfied. Today, God has come not as a Jew but as a Kham!"

What an overwhelming truth: Today, God has come not as a Jew but as a Kham!

Then, Hasta Ram volunteered to pray a prayer of dedication. I pushed the "record" button on my tape recorder and recorded the following:

Thank you, Lord God. At this time, we call on your name and we pray to you—the One and Only, the Living One, the Creator of heaven and earth, the One who created us, the most wonderful Lord. Aye, Lord, we offer you our thanks for bringing us here through all these many days and manifesting your marvelous works to us through the past fourteen or fifteen years. Lord, you are the Lord, the One who speaks in every man's language. And today, Lord, even with us Khams, you have spoken today in Kham.

In order to speak with us Khams, Lord, in order to visit us, you had measured out the time for us even before you created the heavens and the earth. O Lord, for that we offer a thousand thanks. And Lord, in order to accomplish that, in order to visit us, you created David and Nancy, and by dwelling in them, you longed to meet with us. Because of that, Lord, they left their mothers and fathers, and they left their beautiful country for the sake of us Khams, lost at the foot of the snows. And through them, O Lord, you have made yourself today even as a Kham. For that we offer you thanks.

Aye, Lord, the Lord who speaks in every language, today in Kham you have turned toward us, and through this book you are with us. You, our Master and Great Shepherd, for the sake of us Khams, you laid down your life and shed your blood; and for our sakes, you have suffered now for two thousand years. Lord, for this we offer a thousand thanks. So today, Lord, the works you have performed for us are most marvelous. They are immeasurable, and they are impossible to repay. Lord, I can't find words. You speak, Lord.

For these bodies of ours made out of clay, Lord, you provide food for sustenance, clothes for warmth, and houses for shelter. For that too we give thanks. And more than that, Lord, into these bodies of clay you put the Holy Spirit, your own Spirit, to give sustenance to our souls. And today because you have spoken in Kham and have given us this precious seed, we thank you, Lord. For this very reason, Lord, even before you created the heavens and the earth, you had already chosen out and set aside this seed; you had picked out the best grains. Therefore, let not your seed, O Lord, fall by the wayside amongst the Kham people. Let it not fall on stony soil, Lord; let it not fall among thistles, Lord; but falling on good soil, let it bear thirty-, sixty-, and a hundredfold, O Lord.

And also, Lord, the seed which you have already caused to spring from the soil, let it not be knocked down by the winds or swept away by the floods. Aye, Lord, we leave it to you; you know all things. Heaven and earth shall pass away, but that which you have given us today, Lord, this our bread shall never pass away. And you too, Lord, shall never pass away.

Lord, we acknowledge only you. Our desire, Lord, is that in your service, and as ones who are called by your name, that we Khams might somehow be examples to all. This is our request to you. Pour out your Spirit upon us, and make us examples of righteousness, Lord. May your blessing be upon us, that we might live together in love and harmony and that we might be filled with joy, O Lord, never breaking fellowship.

In the good, sweet name of Jesus Christ, our Master and Shepherd, we pray. Amen.

Transition
—*Steve Watters*

I was in Port Angeles, Washington, on November 17, 1985, in my second year at Peninsula College. It wasn't for another two weeks that I received a typewritten letter from Dad chronicling what from the outside seemed to be an inconsequential meeting of twelve men and women in the upper room of Dad's office flat in Kathmandu. Though at the time I was immersed in the world of college, where my past seemed of little relevance, it didn't take very long into reading Dad's letter before the significance of it began to sink in. My eyes welled up with tears, and I began to cry uncontrollably in the privacy of my bedroom.

That Christmas, Dad wrote this inscription in *my* Kham New Testament:

> Dear Steve,
> This book is a reminder to you that the task before you, what-
> ever it may be, is not an impossible one. It is God who works in
> you "both to will and to do of his good pleasure" (Phil. 2:13).
> Dad and Mom

The Kham New Testament has become one of my prize possessions, both as a source of inspiration and as a reference in my own work as a translator. It goes with me on all my trips, always in my carry-on. It goes with me not because there is any magic in it, for it is, after all, just a book. It goes with me because it is a tangible symbol of God's faithfulness, a symbol of the fruit of "a long obedience in the same direction," as Eugene Peterson might say.

Dad was to live another twenty-four years after the dedication of the New Testament. He died on the morning of May 18, 2009, in

Port Angeles, Washington, of a pulmonary embolism, eight days after surgery to have a cancerous bladder removed. He was sixty-five. At the time, he was trying to finish writing *At the Foot of the Snows*.

There is much of the story that he didn't get to tell, or at least, didn't tell as fully as he wanted to. It is clear from the many hints that he put into the text that he wanted to be able to tell the story through to the present. It is a story of crushed dreams, betrayal, kidnapping, and even martyrdom, but clearly a story of joy and triumph as well. Mom, Daniel, and I have struggled with whether or not to fill in the notes and complete the story. In the end, we've decided that most of it is better left unsaid, at least for now.

We would be remiss, however, if we made no mention at all of a few parts of the remaining story. These are written by Daniel and me.

Grandfather
—Daniel Watters

Do you not know that a prince and a great man has fallen this day in Israel?
—King David at the death of Abner, 2 Samuel 3:38, NASB

It is one of the great privileges of my life to have known Hasta Ram, in essence, as my own grandfather. He was always present in some way, holding my hand, cautioning me, encouraging me. Sitting on the mud floor in his home with a plate of spiced mutton, I would stare into the fire as Dad and he would talk about things that I knew must be terribly important. I knew that because they were never in a hurry to say it all; they would let the ideas come slowly, the results of patient thought.

Hasta Ram would live another seventeen years after the dedication of the Kham New Testament in 1985. During those years, Hasta Ram never wavered in his faith but labored tirelessly as the *lomba*, the lead sheep, of the Kham flock.

He understood it to be more than just happenstance that my parents wandered into his remote valley, that God was directing the events of his life to draw him and the Kham people to Christ. In Hasta Ram's own words, "One day, God even came to a place like this and found one such as me, lost in these mountains at the foot of the snows." His faith in God was more to him than just a personal preference or even a reasoned response. For Hasta Ram, his decision to follow Christ was not a casual choice that had no connection to who he was as a Kham; but, having struggled to express every word of the New Testament in his own language, he grasped the deeper reality that placed him in the flow

Daniel and Hasta Ram

of God's salvation history that extended from Jerusalem, into Judea and Samaria, and to the ends of the earth (Acts 1:8). He embraced this as both a great privilege and a great responsibility, and it came to define who he was.

It would take another book to tell the story of the early Kham church, a story that in many ways mirrors the history of the church in the first few decades after Christ: the authority of the Word was confirmed by many miracles, and congregations were birthed in many of the other Kham villages as well. Likewise, the church also struggled with questions of contextualization: what did it mean to be both Kham and Christian? How were they to relate to churches that were springing up in other places in Nepal? How were they to respond to a government that made conversion to Christianity illegal?

Later, when the winds of political change blew through Kham villages with hurricane force, Hasta Ram was resolute in his position that the church was to take no part in the Maoist insurgency that was devastating the country but should remain model citizens of Nepal, exemplifying civil obedience. While he shared in the anger against the injustice that was felt in almost all the rural areas of Nepal, he knew that violence would only feed man's penchant to clutch at supremacy and exploit whoever found themselves on the outside.

This was no small thing for a former Gurkha soldier who at times displayed the temper and passion of the apostle Peter, who himself cut off the ear of Malchus with a sword (John 18:10). Those in the West who met Hasta Ram on his two visits to the U.S. saw him as a gentle man with an endless smile, and that, he was; but in his village he was also fervent about justice and was no pushover for the local mafias. In his stand for Christ, he was resolute and unwavering.

His commitment to Jesus' words "turn the other cheek" (Matthew 5:39) was also no small thing, considering that his own son, Sukha, was executed in 1998 by the police for the entirely false accusation of being involved with the Maoist insurgency that was sweeping the country at the time.

Of course, I remember Sukha well. One day in particular stands out in my mind. I was around seven years old, and Sukha was five or six. My parents had just given Steve and me a package of several toy cars from America, and so, with

Young Sukha

great imagination, Sukha and I spent the afternoon in childhood bliss, rolling the cars around in the dirt in front of our stone house. Upstairs, both our fathers worked away on translation, as they did most days, grappling with nuances of meaning that meant nothing to us. Little did we know that some twenty years later, Sukha and another friend, Gopal, would be slaughtered at point-blank range just yards from where we played. Even their hands and feet would be riddled with bullet holes.

Sukha was his father's son. The meaning of his name, "happiness," aptly described him. He always had a soft heart for the Lord, and he came to understand the persecution his father and others had to endure. He would grow into a young man of solid integrity and conviction, ready to follow in his father's footsteps and endure hardship for his own faith. This made Sukha's execution all the more poignant for Hasta Ram.

In fact, Hasta Ram almost suffered a similar death in 2002, if God had not taken him just a week or two earlier. One morning, Hasta Ram began feeling slightly ill and complained to his wife of a headache and fever. The next day, to everyone's great sorrow, God's faithful servant was ushered into the presence of his Great Shepherd.

While the church from the entire Kham area mourned their spiritual father, police arrived in Taka from the district headquarters to take Hasta Ram and another church leader in for questioning. When they learned that Hasta Ram had just died, they seized another church member in his place, along with the other one they had come for. Then, both of them were marched into the woods near Taka and executed in cold blood.

"Then you will be handed over to be persecuted and put to death, and you will be hated by all nations because of me" (Matthew 24:9).

In my Dad's eulogy of Hasta Ram, he wrote:

Kaka [Hasta Ram] died in his village in Taka-Shera, Nepal, on August 29, 2002. He was seventy-seven years old... Kaka's full name was Hasta Ram Budha Kham Magar, but we knew him affectionately as "Kaka" (Uncle). He grew up a shepherd boy, living in goat-hair tents and caring for his father's sheep in the high, alpine meadows at the foot of the snowy mountains. It was a hard life with few comforts, but through it, he learned strength and endurance along with gentleness and patience.

Kaka was one of the greatest men I have ever known, and I've known plenty—princes, governors, generals, and prime ministers. I was unimpressed by most. But I was impressed by Kaka, right from the start. He was steadfast, faithful, and true. He spent the last thirty years of his life pointing people to Christ, an action that often put him into conflict with a corrupt government. Numerous times, he was arrested and imprisoned, but he thought little of suffering for the name of Christ. He welcomed it. Like the prophets of old, his straight-shooting message and homespun shepherd's garb made a mockery of titles and uniforms. District governors feared him, and when they could, they tried their best to stop him.

For six years Kaka stood alone, the only Christian in his village. At first, no one would respond to his message. When they did, the government moved in to crush it. Seven elders of the newly formed church were arrested and put in prison. But it was there, in prison, that they had personal encounters with God. Writing on scraps of paper, the prisoners penned words of courage and had them relayed to us in Kathmandu. "Even in this dark cell," they wrote, "we experience the glory of God. And because of that," they said, "we look upon this place as the house of God and upon our chains as the ornaments of God."

Kaka spent much of his time working with me, translating the Scriptures into Kham. For years he refused payment. "I don't do this," he told me, "in order to get paid. I do it because I want to do it." Once, when twenty-two men were in prison for six months, I collected money from Christians in America to help in the relief of the families of the prisoners. When Kaka heard of it, he objected. "Send it back," he told me. "Money will only destroy us." Later, after much deliberation, the relief money was used to construct a mill—"something," Kaka said, "that will benefit believers and unbelievers alike."

Today there are hundreds of Kham believers because of Kaka's courage and tenacity. Many have suffered unspeakably, some at the hands of the government and others from a newly founded Maoist insurgency. In November 1998, Kaka's own son was arrested by police, taken down to the river, and shot point-blank twelve times with a high-powered rifle. Kaka's nephew suffered the same fate, as have four other believers. The executioners were given promotions "for their bravery." Kaka's heart was broken. Still, "God has called us as a tribal church to 'fill up the sufferings of Christ,'" Kaka used to say, "and we will be faithful in his call to the end."

A prophet? Certainly so. Like his ancient predecessor, John the Baptist, Kaka lived his life pointing others to Christ. As such, it seems fitting that he should die on the traditional date of John the Baptist's martyrdom, August 29th. "There is not a greater man born of woman," Jesus said of John. Bede the Venerable, one of the first believers in the Anglo-Saxon world, wrote the following, an epitaph fitting not only for John but also for Kaka and all true men and women of faith:

> *To endure temporal agonies for the sake of the truth was not a heavy burden for such men as John; rather it was easily borne and even desirable, for he knew eternal joy would be his reward. Since death was ever at hand, such men considered it a blessing to embrace it and thus gain the reward of eternal life by acknowledging Christ's name. Hence the apostle Paul rightly says: "You have been granted the privilege not only to believe in Christ but also to suffer for his sake." He tells us why it is Christ's gift that his chosen ones should suffer for him: "The sufferings of this present time are not worthy to be compared with the glory that is to be revealed in us."*

A prophet? Certainly so.

Father

—Daniel Watters

From my point of view, he can be called a remarkable man who stands out from those around him by the resourcefulness of his mind, and who knows how to be restrained in the manifestations which proceed from his nature, at the same time conducting himself justly and tolerantly towards the weaknesses of others. Since the first such man I knew—whose influence left its trace on the whole of my life—was my father, I shall begin with him.

—G.I. Gurdjieff, Meetings with Remarkable Men

After the death of someone who means the world to us, there is always the danger of idealizing him, of painting a picture that isn't entirely true. Memory abbreviates and leaves no space for qualifications; love remembers the best and forgets the worst. I have my own memory of the events described in this book, seen from the eyes of a young boy. While they may be idealized or covered over with love, they are, nonetheless, mine.

My earliest memories are of the shamanic visions I had when I was only three, and they form some of the deepest impressions I have of Kham country. I think Dad shared in some of these early impressions; it certainly seems that way when he describes the faint, strange bells of the Kham forest imp and his sympathy for the shaman. To this day, when I'm in some remote village, hidden from the rest of the world under a blanket of cold stars, I still feel the pull of the drum late at night, and it evokes in me some of the strongest feelings I know. It is a feeling of the wild—not in the unfettered, carefree sense of the word but in a raw, powerful, even dangerous sense.

For me, there is no romance in it. I didn't come to that experience through the pages of an anthropology book, but it came to me as it does to every other young shaman initiate: ruthless, terrifying, heartless, and cruel. Later, as a teenager walking along the bank of the rapid river below Taka, I remember describing the experience to Dad as the unforgiving grip of a dark, raging mountain torrent that drags whoever dares to cross the river straight to the underworld. Khams instinctively feel this, too, which is why shamans are so cautious when venturing to set foot in that world through séance. Danger always lurks.

On reflection, I now realize that Dad never tried to explain those experiences to me. There were times when I would ask him something like, "Dad, in my visions, why did I see what shamans are supposed to see according to their mythology, and not some 'Christian' version?" Without brushing me off, he would answer in all seriousness, "I don't know." Later in life, many people would offer me various explanations, but I still prefer Dad's answer.

Dad and his boys

It may be surprising to many people that Dad's greatest struggle was his own doubt. A visit to his study library would confirm this; he read everything because he had questions about everything. Some of my fondest memories are of sitting with him in his library in Port Angeles, the pipe smoke swirling, browsing his books while he read. However, his doubt did not crush him; he held firm to what he *did* know. But it was what he *didn't* know that created in him a great humility and respect for others. He was very non-confrontational, and he understood the Christian life to be about service and sacrifice, lived out in gratitude for God's grace. He was a saint in the proper sense; that is, he loved his Lord imperfectly, knowing that the cross more than covered his failings, and he longed for the Khams to share in that experience.

Steve and I have hiked many miles with Dad, and many of those miles were with Mom as well; we shared many a smoky fire. On those trips, Dad instilled in us far more than just a taste for adventure; he extended to us important lessons in life. In truth, those

David and Steve, recording language data

trips were never easy, and Dad pushed us hard. While he had no patience whatsoever for complaints about the realities of the trail ("My feet hurt too!"), he had endless patience for the people we encountered along the way. He took his place around the Kham hearth as though he had belonged there his whole life. I'm not talking about those trivial things like being able to cross his legs or the ability to swallow hideous food. I mean his ability to see the rough men and women who sat around the fire as real people who carried things around in their hearts just like he did.

When Dad took Steve and me on the trek to climb a remote mountain, we knew right from the beginning that the trip wasn't about the mountain at all. Nearly twelve at the time, I have many memories of that trip, but one of them seems to me to be particularly significant. It had been a long day of hiking, and we had lost the trail several times. Because of that, darkness fell before we could reach our destination—a small village perched high on a ridge. From where we were, though, we spotted the warm light of what we supposed was a shepherd's fire flickering in the distance, and we made our way to his camp.

What we found was an old couple, wrinkled like two leathery characters out of a fairy tale, living in the dirt of a tiny goat shed. Their hair

was wild, they wore rags for clothes, and their knobby knees, exposed
to the warmth of the fire, seemed out of proportion to their bony legs.
Wooden jugs of buttermilk hung from the spindly rafters, along with
the odd bamboo utensil. They immediately made room for us tired travelers and set a pot of potatoes boiling.

I'll never forget how poor they were and yet how willing they were
to share with us everything that they had. But I had opportunity to
observe Dad as well, not just the old couple; he matched their hospitality with his heartfelt gratitude and acceptance. That was the kind of life
lesson we learned on those trips and what made them so much more
than just an adventure.

When I was around eleven years old and we were living in the
Philippines, Dad made a trip back to Nepal for several months. I remember missing him terribly and writing him a letter in which I complained
about how boring school was and how much I missed Nepal. Steve had
similarly written him. To our great excitement, Dad sent Steve and me
an audio tape in response, in which he said:

> One of the things that really thrilled me in the letters that
> I got from you boys is that in reading them, I could detect that
> somehow I've been able to implant at least part of my soul... In
> all the books that we've read together in our lifetime, out in the
> village and so forth, I think that you probably already realize
> that the real reason for those kinds of longings inside of you
> is that you've had little glimpses of heaven here and there, and
> what you're really looking for is God.
>
> ...I don't think I need to remind you boys that [aimless
> searching] is not the trip you want to take or the quest you
> want to go on... [It's no use] to come back home with noth-
> ing more than a good adventure, something like what a trekker
> gets by walking up to Everest base camp or something. That's
> still better than sitting in front of a TV and being like a plastic
> robot, but it still doesn't quite fit the bill... If [our experiences]
> don't lead us to solid conclusions about the laws of God and

bring us into a closer relationship with him, the experiences are really quite useless.

...The voluntary experiences of course are easier to handle than involuntary ones even if they are painful, especially if you know what they're for, like leaving the family like I've done. Because I realize it is for a purpose. And certain involuntary experiences, too, I suppose, especially if they're for a cause like going to prison for your faith, are probably not quite so difficult as some of those other involuntary experiences, like going to school. I understand what that's all about, Daniel. It's those mundane involuntary experiences that have no glory in them, those are the ones that are really hard to master. But, I'll tell you something, if you can master that, and do your best in spite of it all, believe me, you've come a long ways.

...Even though I'm not an old man yet, I have learned one piece of wisdom (and I think your Grandfather Watters will probably tell you the same thing), and that is: if your purpose is to follow after God, you simply just won't go wrong on your quests—and that's whether it be to the outer regions of the Gobi Desert or whether it's to the slums of the inner city. It doesn't really matter. If it is a quest after God, and if it's directed by God, then you're always going to sense a purpose in your life instead of those aimless wanderings like some of these men I've just mentioned... Instead of those aimless wanderings, you'll always see those footsteps [of God] just ahead of you.

These are the big ideas, the big influences, that both Dad and Mom have set upon my life; our own sense of purpose comes from knowing God, and in knowing ourselves, we have ground to respect others. Of course, these big ideas were played out in a thousand ways right up until the day Dad died—a meaningful e-mail, a long drive, a deep discussion, a special gift. I could add a thousand stories to this book. But now, as my own three kids, Benji, Nathan, and Maria, find their own goat-shed moments, eating potatoes in some backwater village, I pray that they will understand the legacy their grandpa and grandma leave them—a legacy whose wealth is in following humbly after God.

Daniel's kids—Benji, Nathan, and Maria—in Mugu, Nepal, on a 200-mile trek

Epilogue
—Steve Watters

But we have this treasure in earthen vessels...
—2 Corinthians 4:7, NIV

About nine months after Dad passed away, I found myself in India on a flight from New Delhi to Siliguri. Once above the dense fog and haze which commonly enshrouds Delhi at that time of year, my plane headed east toward the southern border of Nepal, making its way toward that narrow bit of Indian territory that separates the eastern border of Nepal and the northwestern border of Bangladesh.

It was one of those see-forever kind of days, and it wasn't long before I began to make out the shapes of the Himalayas to our north. Soon they were close enough to recognize. At first it was the peaks that I knew only by name, the peaks that straddle the border between China and India in the upper reaches of the Garhwal. Then we came to the mountainous terrain of far Western Nepal, where I had been on a brief, one-month trek in the late '90s. It was impressive by most standards, but I knew what still lay ahead. My heart quickened as we came closer to the massive flanks of Dhaulagiri and Annapurna and, off to the west, the jumbled mass of black hills that comprise the upper reaches of Kham country. These were the mountains I had once known so well. It had been years since I had traversed them following behind Dad, and in later years, leading out ahead of him. Now, it was as though I were there, traversing them once again, and I could feel the high-altitude sun on the back of my neck, the wind as it blew in my face, the smell of alpine grass, the mesmerizing cadence of the Kham language.

Hunter Tipalkya and Steve

Steve and David on the trail in 1990

Further on, my plane passed by the hills in which I had taken my wife and children trekking, then the hills around Kathmandu where we had gone on day hikes and bike rides, and still further east, I came to where our own story was unfolding. In those few moments, I relived my childhood and adult life, hovering between the surreal of the past and the life of the present.

I missed Dad. I hurt for Mom, who was now without her lifetime companion. I missed my friends in Nepal. I missed my wife, Jean, and our children, Zachary, Kristina, and Jesse, as they settled into what was supposed to be home in the U.S. but was really a huge disruption to home as we knew it. I wanted to rewind time, fly home to Nepal, drive up the alley to our house, and hear the deep bark of our Tibetan mastiff welcoming me home and the slam of the screen door as the kids came running out of the house screaming, "Daddy's home! Daddy's home!"

I was awakened out of my reverie when the man sitting next to me asked me in perfect Indian English if I thought the mountains were

Jean and Steve Watters and their children, Zach, Kristina, and Jesse

beautiful. He explained to me that these were the Himalayas, and that they were the highest mountains in the world.

"It is the abode of the gods itself," he said.

To him, I was just an ignorant American tourist, and he was politely helping to educate me. How could he have known that we were flying over the hills in which I had grown up, and in which I had raised my own family? I didn't bother to correct his perception; it was too complicated to tell him my story.

Dad has told some of that story in *At the Foot of the Snows*. The story as it's written here ends in the mid-1980s, and monumental change has come to the Kham Magar and to Nepal since then. While we are not able to complete Dad's own narrative, it would be misleading to make no mention of a few selective threads. I speak to a few of these here.

David and Nancy, Hasta Ram and his wife, and Steve and Jean's children

In the period since the '80s, Nepal has emerged from the mystique of the only Hindu kingdom in the world to a secular state, stymied in the quagmire of a democratic system yet to deliver on its expectations. In the process, it is said to have lost its innocence, although we who have lived in the hinterlands know that innocence was lost in ages past.

In the spring of 1990, Dad and I returned to Kathmandu from a two-month trip through the northern reaches of the Kham Magar homeland to find that revolution was in the air. On a taxi ride through the streets of Kathmandu, our driver took us the wrong direction down a one-way street. When we protested, he nonchalantly replied, "Haven't you heard? Democracy has come to Nepal. You can do whatever you want now." For ordinary people, it was understood that they would be able to throw off the shackles of the monarchy and do what they wanted, including, apparently, go the wrong way down a one-way street!

A decade or so later, a friend of mine stopped at a large gathering outside someone's house, where a big fight had broken out inside the house compound. The owner had caught some thieves trying to break in, and now he and his neighbors were exacting their own justice. The thieves were being pulverized with bricks, and my friend feared for their lives, even if they were thieves. He asked a policeman standing nearby if he was going to do something to stop them, but the policeman shrugged his shoulders and replied, "This is the way democracy works."

While many Nepalese understood the privileges and responsibilities of a democratic system, such was the sense on the streets of Kathmandu as the country progressed from one misunderstanding of democracy to another, and even more so in parts of the country where there wasn't a pair of eyes to observe what was going on.

Some of the principal players during this time period were the Maoists, who engaged the government from the jungle. Nepal endured a tragic ten-year civil war from the mid 1990s to the mid 2000s, during which time it is said over fourteen thousand people were killed and countless tens of thousands were displaced, losing land and livelihood. The Maoists based much of their training and wartime operations out of Rolpa and Rukum districts, the traditional homeland of the Kham Magar.

The Kham Magar have been deeply affected by this war. It has brought change to their communities at an unprecedented rate and embroiled them in a fight that in some senses was not their own. While the Kham Magar do share some responsibility, much of the blame rests with the others.

Rolpa and Rukum districts were often referred to as "hotbeds of Maoist activity," and the assumption was that any Magar from there was Maoist and, therefore, suspect of subversive activity. My own view, albeit hopelessly sympathetic to the Kham Magar, is that the number of actual Maoist cadres among them was much less than people believed. Having the Maoists run roughshod over villagers, forcing them to join their military campaigns, is quite a different thing from a grassroots movement that seeks to overthrow the tyranny of its oppressors en masse. Clearly, history shows us that there was no such mass movement. In some cases, the Kham became embittered toward their Maoist commanders. When a friend of mine was told to fight in one of their battles, he was offered a gun by his commanding officer, but he refused, saying, "No, I won't take it. If you give me that gun, I'll shoot you. Let me stay behind and take care of the wounded."

Some Kham Magar were taken by the ideology of the Maoists in the hope of what it promised: hope of transparency in the government, hope of being listened to, hope of the same access to power and voice that the Hindu elite and nobility had enjoyed, and perhaps in some cases, hope of bringing about the demise of the elite in vindictive justice. The Maoist leadership cleverly played to the growing sentiment of ethnic identity, promising that they would have political and economic voice through their languages and cultures. It sounded good to ethnicities like the Kham Magar. Now, in the second decade of the twenty-first century, these hopes seem no more real than they were at the turn of the century.

Under the monarchy, there were three things sacrosanct in Nepal: the Crown, the Hindu religion, and the Nepali language. These were attacked head-on by the Maoists. Much of what was reported in the media was the battle over the Crown and the demand that the country become a republic. But the attack on religion and language was often overlooked. In fact, the attack against religion was soft-pedaled. After all, how could the Maoists expect a grassroots uprising from the common man if they attacked what he believed too vehemently?

In regard to language, however, matters were different. While a benign dictionary project in a minority language in the 1980s was suspect, now in post-revolutionary Nepal, it became important to work with language—at least at an academic level—in description and documentation, if not also language revitalization. Much rhetoric was given to incorporating the mother tongue into the educational system and non-formal education projects. This new interest in minority languages continues to this day.

This brings me to another part of the story that needs mentioning, and that is Dad's involvement in the study of linguistics. It is clear from his writing in this book, as well as to those who knew him, that for Dad the study of the Kham language was much more than a perfunctory task to be done as an aid to translation. He was aggrieved by those, especially academics, who assumed he studied language to "foist" his belief system onto the indigenous peoples and stamp out their native religion and culture. In fact, he studied language for language's sake, and he gave much of his time after translating the New Testament to linguistics.

Michael Noonan, a fellow linguist in the study of Nepalese languages, who passed away months before Dad, wrote: "Watters' work is the best grammar yet published of a Nepalese language and one of the best available for any language in the Sino-Tibetan family."

Later, in a review written of *A Grammar of Kham* in the journal *Language*, fellow linguist Garrett wrote, "THIS is how to write a grammar."

Dad's works include many publications on the languages of Nepal, not the least of which is *Notes on Kusunda Grammar*. This work not only rescued Kusunda from becoming an extinct language about which we know nothing, it also established Kusunda as a language isolate.

In addition to his own careful and admirable scholarship, Dad gave much of his time to teaching classes in linguistics and helping young, aspiring translators and linguists like myself. For a number of years in the 2000s, he taught in the Central Department of Linguistics at Tribhuvan University, where he was a valuable mentor to scores of Nepalese students from a diverse array of ethnic and linguistic backgrounds. His contribution will undoubtedly live on in the work of these students for decades to come.

In the weeks before his death, Dad and I were able to spend ten days together. We had numerous conversations about his book. It's a story with a lot riding on it. It brings up complicated issues and comes down on a side that is rarely expedient.

It's complicated because it isn't clear what place minority languages have in Nepal. Does one's involvement in their recognition and development make one a subversive, contributing to the potential splintering of a nation? It's complicated because it isn't clear what place a Christian missionary has in all of this. Does one's involvement in linguistics and translation make one deceitful, as though linguistic research is a ploy to gain access to ethnic peoples to "foist" a Christian belief system on an indigenous tribe? Is Bible translation forcing one's view on another?

Some might say it is. It's complicated because it isn't clear how one is to fight against injustice. Sometimes it would seem we are forced into situations where we have to choose the "lesser of two evils." At what point are we free to disregard man-made laws when they are in contradiction with universal, God-given laws?

We were aware of the risk in telling this story publicly, for the very reason these kinds of questions come up. We agreed that if the story were going to be told, it had to be told honestly, without apology, and without defensiveness, and—for my part, as I write the epilogue—without interpretation.

* * *

In June 2005, our families were invited by the Kham Magar community living in Kathmandu to observe their commemoration of *balku* (the scape-goat ceremony described in chapter 10). Just as in the village, this event was more than a ceremony. It was a community event with a day full of fun for everyone. Dad was invited to be the Chief Guest, and some of the afternoon's activities were centered around honoring him for his contributions to their ethnic nation. It was during this community gathering that he was named their champion.

It was the first time that I had seen some of those from Taka-Shera in several decades. I remembered faces, but I couldn't remember names and connections. Of course, everyone remembered Daniel and me, the little white boys who had stuck out like sore thumbs in the village. We spent the day reminiscing with stories of "Remember the time when…?"

The celebration was held in downtown Kathmandu at Khula Manch, the same field where many of the large political rallies of the past decade had been held. Dad was seated at and spoke from the same podium where the great political leaders of Nepal had sat and spoken. There were plenty of speeches on this day as well, but all of them in Nepali, all parroting what had become popular: fancy rhetoric about language and culture preservation. Few people paid attention, and the

Kham Magar mulled about the field in small groups, strutting their traditional clothing.

But when Dad got up to speak, he addressed them in Kham, and as soon as he did so, the crowd rushed in, packing themselves around the front of the podium. As they ran past Daniel and me, we could hear them say, "It's Grandpa. It's Grandpa. What's he gonna say?"

Dad recounted to them his early experiences among them. People laughed and cried as they heard stories from their past, from a time when things were different. With deep emotion in his voice that only one close to him would recognize, Dad thanked them from the bottom of his heart for their hospitality to our family. He also talked about their language and what a beautiful thing it was, that even though other people had no regard for it, he thought it was worth something—so much so that he had translated the Word of God into it. He said that he did this not to force them to believe—the choice was theirs—but because he could think of no better gift to give them than this. He explained to them that there was nothing that their language could not say. It could express everything that God had to say to them. The crowd sat mesmerized, as did I. Here was Dad, talking in Kham in downtown Kathmandu, from one of the most famous podiums in the country, telling them about why he had translated God's Word into their language. A Kham believer standing next to me said, "Well, now he's said it." It was enough to get him lynched or made a hero.

Such is the risk taken in this book. Now it's been said.

David, at ease with Kham friends

* * *

Words and stories help us remember the past, not the way a photograph helps us remember it, but the way a painting does. Dad has painted a picture of what it was like for us, an American family, to live in a remote village of the Kham Magar and of what they were like, from our perspective, in that period of time. We can't know with certainty what will become of their nation and its language and culture, as massive social, economic, and political change brings upheaval to its people. We can't minimize the effect of climate change and population growth, either, especially on agricultural and animal husbandry practices, and the changes these effects will bring to the Kham Magar's subsistence lifestyle. Much has changed; more will change in the future and, in all likelihood, at an even more accelerated rate than it has in the past.

Dad has also painted a picture of the journey he and Kaka took to translate the New Testament into Kham and the enormity of the work's cost to the few Kham Magar who chose to follow in its path. We are told that "Heaven and earth shall pass away, but my words shall not pass away" (Mark 13:31). God's Word is here to stay with us, perhaps not always in book form, but in the expression of Himself. The greatest expression of Himself came in One who spoke to us in Aramaic. That expression is continued in the story penned here, but this time, He speaks Kham.

In speaking Kham, what were once unfocused gleams of divine truth are now centered on the One who would love the Kham Magar, regardless of who is in power over them. It is this expression of love that endures and this newly focused knowledge that gives the Kham Magar the ability to navigate the vagaries of life in ways not possible before.

It was these things which compelled Mom and Dad to persevere, regardless of what was politically expedient or correct at the time. Yet, in spite of their certainty in the enterprise, they were painfully aware of their own inadequacies, struggling all the while in vessels of earth and clay. The story penned here is also about that struggle, that familiar story of human frailty used in ways not possible were it not for that story of the inexorable march of His purposes.

David and Nancy Watters,
Port Angeles, Washington
(2008)

David, Nancy, and Hasta Ram

David and Nancy

David (1990)

Works by David Watters

BOOKS

2005. Notes on Kusunda grammar (a language isolate of Nepal). Kathmandu: National Foundation for the Development of Indigenous Nationalities.

2004. A dictionary of Kham: Taka dialect (a Tibeto-Burman language of Nepal). Kathmandu: Central Department of Linguistics, Tribhuvan University.

2002. A grammar of Kham. Cambridge: Cambridge University Press [Cambridge Grammatical Descriptions].

1998. The Kham language of West-Central Nepal (Takale Dialect). Ph.D. diss, University of Oregon.

1996. Transitivity and verb alternations in Kham. M.A. Thesis, University of Oregon.

1972. A vocabulary of the Kham language. Kirtipur: Summer Institute of Linguistics, Institute of Nepal and Asian studies, Tribhuvan University.

1971a. Kham phonemic summary. Kirtipur: Summer Institute of Linguistics, Tribhuvan University[Tibeto-Burman Phonemic Summaries X].

1971b. A guide to Kham tone. Kirtipur: Summer Institute of Linguistics, Tribhuvan University[Guide to Tone in Nepal 3].

1973 (with Watters, Nancy). An English-Kham, Kham-English glossary. Kirtipur: Summer Institute of Linguistics, Institute of Nepal and Asian studies, Tribhuvan University.

EDITED BOOKS

1973. (with Hale, Austin). Clause, sentence, and discourse patterns of selected languages of Nepal Vol II.Norman: University of Oklahoma [Summer Institute of Linguistics, Publications in Linguisticsand Related Fields].

ARTICLES IN JOURNALS, CHAPTERS IN EDITED VOLUMES

2009. "!e semantics of clause linkage in Kham". In: Dixon, RMW; and Aikehnvald, Alexandra Y. (eds.), !e Semantics of clause linkage, 96–117. Oxford: Oxford University Press.

2008. "Nominalization in the Kiranti and Central Himalayish languages of Nepal". In: Coupe, Alec R. (ed.) Linguistics of the Tibeto-Burman Area 31[Special Issue on Nominalization]: 21–44.

2008. (with Regmi, Dan Raj). "Direct-inverse in Bhujel". Nepalese Linguistics 23: 429–435.

2006a. "Notes on Kusunda Grammar: A language isolate of Nepal". Himalayan Linguistics 3: 1–182.

2006c. "The conjunct-disjunct distinction in Kaike". Nepalese Linguistics 22: 300–319.

2005a. "Kusunda: a typological isolate in South Asia". In: Yadava, Yogendra P.; Bhattarai, Ram Raj Lohani; Prasain, Balaram; and Parajuli, Krishna (eds.), Contemporary Issues in Nepalese Linguistics, 375–396. Kathmandu: Linguistic Society of Nepal.

2005b. "An overview of Kham-Magar languages and dialects". In: Yadava, Yogendra P.; Bhattarai, Ram Raj Lohani; Prasain, Balaram; and Parajuli, Krishna (eds.), Contemporary Issues in Nepalese Linguistics, 339–374. Kathmandu: Linguistic Society of Nepal.

2005c. (with Rai, Novel Kishore). "Policy, planning and recommendations". In: Yadava, Yogendra P. and Pradeep L. Bajracharya (eds.), The indigenous languages of Nepal: situation, policy planning and coordination, 55–63. Kathmandu: National Foundation for Development of Indigenous Nationalities.

2003. "Kham". In: Thurgood, Graham; and LaPolla, Randy J. (eds.), !e Sino-Tibetan languages, 683–704. London and New York: Routledge.

1999. "The iconicity of direction marking in Kham". Notes on Tibeto-Burman 4: 25–47. Horsleys Green: Summer Institute of Linguistics, South Asia Group.

1995a. "Transitivity types and verb classes in Kham". Notes on Tibeto-Burman 3: 1–49. Horsleys Green: Summer Institute of Linguistics, South Asia Group.

1995b. "An overview of nominalizations and relative clauses in Kham". Notes on Tibeto-Burman 2: 1–53. Horsleys Green: Summer Institute of Linguistics, South Asia Group.

1995c. "Body parts in Kham: A source for spatial dimensions and mental imagery". Unpublished manuscript.

1995d. "Patterns of tone in Kham". Unpublished manuscript.

1994. "Constraints on the ordering of affixes in the Tibeto-Burman verb". Unpublished manuscript.

1993. "Agreement systems and syntactic organization in the Kham verb [Nepal]". Linguistics of the Tibeto-Burman Area 16.2: 89–112.

1985a. "Emergent word tone in Kham: A Tibeto-Burman halfway house". Linguistics of the Tibeto-Burman Area 8.2: 36–54.

1985b. ई ध र-ए सा:रो याका-लाव ओपाँ (God's words of the new covenant; New Testament in Kham). New Delhi: World Home Bible League.

1978. "Speaker-hearer involvement in Kham". In: Grimes, Joseph (ed.), Papers on Discourse, 1–18. Dallas: Summer Institute of Linguistics and University of Texas at Arlington [Summer Institute of Linguistics Publications in Linguistics, Pub. No. 51].

1975. "Siberian shamanistic traditions among the Kham-Magars of Nepal". Contributions to Nepalese Studies 2.1: 123–168. Kathmandu: The Institute of Nepal and Asian Studies.

1973a. "The evolution of a Tibeto-Burman verb morphology". Linguistics of the Tibeto-Burman Area 2.1: 45–80.

1973b. "Clause Patterns in Kham". In: Hale, Austin (ed.), Clause, sentence, and discourse patterns in selected languages of Nepal, Part 1, 39–202. Norman: University of Oklahoma [Summer Institute of Linguistics, Publications in Linguistics and Related Fields].

CONFERENCE, SEMINAR, AND WORKSHOP PRESENTATIONS

2007a. "A and O mirror images in the Tibeto-Burman languages of Nepal". Paper presented at the Research Centre for Linguistic Typology. La Trobe University, Melbourne.

2007b. "Word-class-changing derivations in Kham". Paper presented at the Workshop on Wordclass-changing Derivations in

Typological Perspective. Research Centre for Linguistic Typology,La Trobe University, Melbourne.

2006. "Opposing language types in Tibeto-Burman based on 'What to do with "you"'". Paper presented at the Research Centre for Linguistic Typology. La Trobe University, Melbourne.

2005a. "Direct and indirect speech in Kham". Paper presented at the Workshop on Word-classchanging Derivations in Typological Perspective. Research Centre for Linguistic Typology, La Trobe University, Melbourne.

2005b. (with Govinda Bahadur Tumbahang). "A problem of phonological representation in Chhathare Limbu". Paper presented at the 26th Annual Conference of the Linguistic Society of Nepal. Kathmandu.

2004a. "Interrogative ma- and tense switching in Kham". Paper presented at the 10th Himalayan Languages Symposium. Timphu.

2004b. "Problems in Kusunda phonology". Paper presented at the 25th Annual Conference of the Linguistic Society of Nepal. Kathmandu.

2004c. "Word classes in the languages of Nepal: articles for 'priming the pump'". Workshop presented at the Central Department of Linguistics. Tribhuvan University, Kathmandu, Nepal.

2003. "Some preliminary observations on the relationship between Kham, Magar, (and Chepang)". Paper presented at the 36th International Conference on Sino-Tibetan Languages and Linguistics. La Trobe University, Melbourne.

2001. "Seizing grammatical beachheads: Preemption of agreement paradigms in Kiranti". Paper presented at the Tibeto-Burman Languages and Linguistics Conference. University of California at Santa Barbara, Santa Barbara.

1997a. "An OT interpretation of Kham tone". Paper presented in the Tone Colloquium Series. University of Oregon, Eugene.

1997b. "Transitivity and bitransitive constructions in Tolowa

Athabaskan". Paper presented at the Athabaskan Conference. University of Oregon, Eugene.

1991. "The maintenance of deictic integrity across Kham dialects". Paper presented at the 24th International Conference on Sino-Tibetan Languages and Linguistics. Bangkok.

1988. "Computer aided dialect adaptation: the Kham experiment". Paper presented at the University of North Dakota, Norman.

1985. "Some preliminary observations on the interrelatedness of Kham dialects". Paper presented at the 18th International Conference on Sino-Tibetan Languages and Linguistics. Bangkok.

About the Authors

David E. Watters (1944–2009), with his wife, Nancy, and sons, Steve and Daniel, spent much of his life in the remote Himalayas, working with the Kham Magars of Nepal. A lifelong student, David received his Ph.D. from the University of Oregon in 1998, where he later taught as adjunct faculty. He also taught at Kathmandu's Tribhuvan University, directed SIL International's Oregon school for four years, and served as Associate Editor of *Himalayan Linguistics*. An expert in Tibeto-Burman linguistics, David published many works, including *A Grammar of Kham* (2002), *A Dictionary of Kham* (2004), and *Notes on Kusunda Grammar* (2006).

Stephen Watters (1966–) lives in Woodway, Texas, along with his wife, Jean Watters, and their three children Zachary, Kristina, and Jesse. He holds an M.A. in Linguistics from the University of Texas at Arlington and works in various capacities with SIL International, not the least of which are his roles as linguist and translator.

Daniel Watters (1969–) currently lives in Poulsbo, Washington, along with his three children, Benji, Nathan, and Maria. He holds an M.A. in Applied Linguistics and Exegesis from Trinity Western University, is an active member of SIL International, and co-authored the language textbook *Nepali in Context*, now in its third edition.